A PAULINE THEOLOGY OF CHURCH LEADERSHIP

ANDREW D. CLARKE

BLOOMSBURY

LONDON • NEW DELHI • NEW YORK • SYDNEY

Bloomsbury T&T Clark

An imprint of Bloomsbury Publishing Plc

50 Bedford Square	175 Fifth Avenue
London	New York
WC1B 3DP	NY 10010
UK	USA

www.bloomsbury.com

First published by T&T Clark International 2008
Paperback edition first published 2012

British Library Cataloguing-in-Publication Data
A catalogue record for this book is available from the British Library.

ISBN: HB: 978-0-567-04560-7
PB: 978-0-567-06013-6

Library of Congress Cataloging-in-Publication Data
A catalog record for this book is available from the Library of Congress

Typeset by Data Standards Limited, Frome, Somerset, UK
Printed and bound in Great Britain

Contents

ABBREVIATIONS

AV	Authorized Version
BibInt	*Biblical Interpretation: A Journal of Contemporary Approaches*
BNTC	Black's New Testament Commentaries
BT	*Bible Translator*
BTB	*Biblical Theology Bulletin*
CBQ	*Catholic Biblical Quarterly*
ConBNT	Coniectanea biblica, New Testament
FRLANT	Forschungen zur Religion und Literatur des Alten und Neuen Testaments
ICC	International Critical Commentary
IVP	InterVarsity Press
J Bus Ethics	*Journal of Business Ethics*
JBL	*Journal of Biblical Literature*
JSNT	*Journal for the Study of the New Testament*
JSNTSup	Journal for the Study of the New Testament, Supplement Series
JTS	*Journal of Theological Studies*
NICNT	New International Commentary on the New Testament
NIGTC	New International Greek Testament Commentary
NIV	New International Version
NovTSup	Novum Testamentum Supplements
NRSV	New Revised Standard Version
NTS	*New Testament Studies*
Proc Am Philos Soc	*Proceedings of the American Philosophical Society*
RB	*Revue biblique*
RSV	Revised Standard Version
SBLDS	SBL Dissertation Series
SNTSMS	Society for New Testament Studies Monograph Series
SNTW	Studies in the New Testament and its World
SUNY	State University of New York
TDNT	*Theological Dictionary of the New Testament*
TynBull	*Tyndale Bulletin*
WBC	Word Biblical Commentaries
WUNT	Wissenschaftliche Untersuchungen zum Neuen Testament
ZNW	Zeitschrift für die neutestamentliche Wissenschaft

PREFACE

This book has been a long time in incubation. The intended reason for this has been the requirement first to address the essentially preliminary, historical work, before tackling the theological questions. Significantly, however, many of the provisional conclusions with which I was working in the earlier years of the research have changed markedly before reaching their current form in the following pages. Not only have scholarly methods and approaches about Pauline studies changed markedly during this period – in many cases raising very different questions of the Pauline texts – but my own experiences of church life and leadership have been particularly helpful and significant throughout this time that I have been reflecting on the Pauline texts, and they have caused me to investigate aspects I had not earlier appreciated. The privilege of tackling these issues simultaneously within the academy and the church has been challenging and profoundly formative for me on both counts; each has had an identifiable contribution to the position that I currently hold and is represented in the following pages.

I would especially, therefore, like to thank my staff and student colleagues at the University of Aberdeen for opportunities to explore some very early source material, now unrecognizable in the present product. I am also profoundly grateful to fellow church leaders and members of a number of Christian communities, especially those in Cambridge, Aberdeen and Aberdeenshire, who have graciously tolerated, and created a context for, my incessant questioning of what we do and why we do it. Finally, I should also like to thank my wife for her partnership in church leadership, and my father for his many years of thinking and writing about this subject as a church leader.

Aberdeen
Easter 2007

Chapter One

METHODOLOGICAL QUESTIONS

1. *Introduction*

This project is framed within the genre of a written theology in that it seeks to produce a systematic treatment of an element of Christian teaching. Although there are theologies aplenty, indeed theologies that focus on the subject of ecclesiology, and although there are Pauline theologies aplenty, including some that focus on his ecclesiology, a systematic treatment of his understanding of church leadership is a less well-trodden path, yet one that is sorely needed within contemporary ecclesiastical circles. This book is an attempt, not to solve this lacuna, but to give it due attention. In order to frame such a Pauline theology of church leadership, however, it is as useful at the outset to define not only some of these terms but also some of my chosen parameters, and, in so doing, establish what I do not mean by 'Pauline', 'theology' or 'leadership'.

a. *Leadership*

Towards the end of the twentieth century, the designation 'leadership' became increasingly widespread in many churches as a collective term to describe the combined team of local church office bearers, including the pastors, ministers, elders, deacons, or 'leaders' of other ministries. Significantly, however, the New Testament in general and Paul's letters in particular suggest that such a generic term was not adopted by the earliest churches. A number of general words for 'leader' were certainly available in the Hellenistic Greek of the period and were used in a wide range of contexts.[1] Furthermore, in the Septuagint, two particular terms for leader, ἄρχων and ἡγούμενος, are extremely common,[2] and can be

---

1   General words included ἄρχων, ἡγεμών, στρατηγός and προστάτης, together with their compounds; and were used in military, civic, imperial and other contexts, alongside specific titles for military, civic, priestly or collegial offices.

2   In the Septuagint, the noun ἄρχων occurs 624 times; composite nouns with the prefix ἀρχι-, referring to a leading official in some capacity (e.g. ἀρχιστράτηγος, ἀρχιερεύς, ἀρχηγός), occur 167 times; the present participle ἡγούμενος occurs 129 times; and the noun

found widely across its corpus.[3] Although both of these words also occur in the New Testament, they are not only much less widely spread across the corpus, but they are also much less frequent.[4] Furthermore, where they do occur, they are largely in reference to the Jewish synagogue or nation, the imperial rulers of the day, or demonic powers.[5] The general designation 'leader' is for the most part either not used in reference to the early Christian communities or its nature is explicitly redefined or qualified.[6]

This apparent avoidance of or reluctance to use the commonly available leadership terminology of the day raises a number of significant questions, not least in regard to the appropriateness of 'leadership' as the focal element of a Pauline study. Does Paul's avoidance of such language suggest that the early church was, predominantly, a group of egalitarian communities, which had no use for contemporary, generic titles for leadership? Did Paul object in principle to the appointment of leaders, other than the apostles, within the Christian church? If he did espouse local church leadership, did he, nonetheless, institute or employ an alternative set of terms, titles or characteristics in explicit distinction to the widely used vocabulary of the day? If so, what were those characteristics

---

ἡγεμών occurs 84 times. Frequent phrases include: οἱ ἄρχοντες τῆς συναγωγῆς (Exod. 16.22; 34.31; Num. 31.13; Josh. 9.15; 22.30); οἱ ἄρχοντες [Ισραηλ] (Num. 1.44; 4.34, 46; 7.2; 2 Chron. 12.6); ὁ ἄρχων τῶν υἱῶν [Ιουδα] (Num. 2 passim); οἱ ἄρχοντες πατριῶν (Josh. 14.1; 1 Chron. 7.40; 8.6, 10, 28; 9.9; 15.12; 26.21, 32; Ezra 8.1; 10.16; Neh. 11.13; 12.22); ἄρχοντες οἴκων (Num. 7.2; Josh. 22.14; 1 Chron. 7.2, 7, 9; 9.13); ἄρχοντες τῆς δυνάμεως (2 Kgs 9.5; 25.23, 26; 1 Chron. 25.1; 27.4; Jdt. 14.19; 1 Macc. 5.56); and ἄρχοντες τοῦ λαοῦ (Judg. 10.18; Neh. 10.15; 11.1; Ps. 46.10; Isa. 28.14).

3   These two terms occur in all books, except Ruth, Tobit, 4 Maccabees, Song of Solomon, Joel, Obadiah, Jonah and Haggai.

4   The frequency (measured in terms of the number of occurrences per 1,000 words) of ἄρχων and ἡγούμενος in the New Testament is less than a quarter of that in the Septuagint.

5   Paul uses ἄρχων in Rom. 13.3 of the imperial authorities, and in 1 Cor. 2.6-8 and Eph. 2.2 of spiritual powers. The verb ἄρχω, 'I rule', is used by Paul in Rom. 15.12 when he quotes Isa. 11.10 referring to the root of Jesse who will rule over the Gentiles. Most frequently the word is used in the Gospels and Acts in reference to Jewish national and synagogue rulers. The word ἡγεμών is widely used in the Gospels and Acts as a description of secular authorities, but it does not occur in the Pauline context. Originally a military word, in the Gospels and Acts στρατηγός is used of both Jewish religious and Graeco-Roman civic leaders. Again, however, it does not appear in the Pauline corpus. Similarly, the term ἡγούμενος is not found in the Pauline corpus in reference to leaders; although, the writer to the Hebrews uses ἡγούμενος of local church leaders (Heb. 13.7, 17, 24).

6   The one exception to this may be the verb προΐστημι, which is adopted by Paul on a number of occasions (Rom. 12.8; 1 Thess. 5.12; 1 Tim. 3.4, 5, 12; 5.17; Tit. 3.8, 14), and the associated noun προστάτης, which Paul uses in its feminine form in Rom. 16.2. For the most part, however, these are either in the context of managing the household or are translated in the RSV with the sense of 'help' or 'aid' rather than rule.

and vocabulary, and how did they differ from contemporary, common practice?

Where a Pauline ecclesiology focuses on the apostle's understanding of the 'church' and will necessarily include issues of church order and church structure, the focus of this study is explicitly on the style, ethos, dynamics and practices of leadership, including the relationship between leader and led, and the parameters of what Paul presents as appropriate or inappropriate leadership. It is clear that organizational structures are a relevant aspect of a study on leadership, but they are only an element, and a dominant focus on organizational aspects will leave much still unexplored that is relevant to the topic of leadership, and arguably more fundamental to the outworking of those structures. Accordingly, through the course of the following chapters we shall explore Paul's views about the principles, parameters and practices of appropriate leadership in the early Christian communities; and identify why it may have been that the traditional terms for leadership were apparently avoided.

b. *Theology*
This account is not the historically descriptive task of identifying the actual nature of leadership in each of the early Christian communities; rather it is the theological task of analysing the nature of church leadership, as Paul conceived it and conveyed it in his correspondence. Even a cursory reading of the texts shows that the theory and the practice, although they ought to be closely related, were by no means one and the same. I consider that the historical work of determining what were the practices in the Christian communities is an essential, and prior, task that crucially forms the context for, and informs, the subsequent theological task of reconstructing the theory. However, it is often the case, both in the church and the academy, that the earlier, historical task is often either overlooked or avoided or even confused with the latter, theological task. It will be important throughout this study to build carefully on historical analysis of the nature of the Pauline communities.[7]

It should also be noted that Paul's understanding of leadership was not derived from a theoretical or philosophical exercise conducted in an ivory tower. Rather, it impinged on and emerged from not only his own successes and inevitable failures or regrets as a leader, but also the varied

---

7 The historical foundations for the present work may be found in the analysis of the Pauline communities in their social and cultural contexts that was conducted in two earlier monographs: A. D. Clarke, *Secular and Christian Leadership in Corinth: A Socio-Historical and Exegetical Study of 1 Corinthians 1–6* (Paternoster Biblical Monographs; Milton Keynes: Paternoster, 2006) and A. D. Clarke, *Serve the Community of the Church: Christians as Leaders and Ministers* (First-Century Christians in the Graeco-Roman World; Grand Rapids; Cambridge: Eerdmans, 2000).

and particular situations that he faced. How one might respond to a threat or challenge to one's authority was not a remote possibility to Paul, but an everyday reality. Similarly, Paul's opportunity to reflect on issues of leadership was not a matter of leisure or luxury; rather, in his view, it was a matter of urgency so long as the very integrity of the gospel and the faith of his fellow believers were at stake. For Paul, leadership concerned how to deal with both the powerful and the weak, and how both to nurture and rebuke. In all these regards, the task of defining Paul's theology of leadership cannot be done without specific regard to the varied and particular circumstances with which he was dealing. The task is theological, but both the factors that influenced his thinking and the nature of our extant evidence are rooted in the historical and the social.

c. *Pauline*

If the distinction between 'church leadership' and 'church order', or the difference between the historical and the theological, is not controversial, the same cannot be said for defining and defending what is 'Pauline'. This study amounts to an analysis of perspectives on leadership that may be determined from across the entire, canonical Pauline corpus, including not only the seven traditionally Pauline letters, but also the remaining six, which are widely, but not uniformly, regarded as pseudonymous, namely Ephesians, Colossians, 2 Thessalonians, and the Pastoral Epistles. It is in this canonical sense that I adopt the terms 'Paul' and 'Pauline' throughout the study, although not in order to argue or defend a particular stance in regard to the authorship of these disputed letters.

This is very much a minority position, most especially among studies on New Testament ecclesiology. There are, however, a number of reasons why on the subject of leadership I have chosen to investigate the corpus at its widest extent. Those who have concerned themselves with aspects of Pauline ecclesiology usually, and usefully, do this in relation to what is considered the later, non-Pauline, trajectory represented by the Pastoral Epistles and the household codes of Ephesians and Colossians. Indeed, in ecclesiological studies disproportionately greater focus is often given to these few chapters than to other letters in the New Testament, both Pauline and non-Pauline. In my view, a study of principles of leadership in the Pauline communities that excludes these highly significant letters would thus be regrettable and regarded as deficient.

Furthermore, one of the foundational reasons for arguing in favour of a second or third generation dating of the Pastoral Epistles, and consequently proposing their pseudonymity, are the wide divergences between the ecclesiology of the earlier, and clearly Pauline, letters and these later ones. I am not convinced that this chasm is quite as wide as is often argued, and consider there to be credible grounds for holding there to be sufficient continuity in perspective across the thirteen canonically Pauline letters to warrant a comparative study of them as a discrete group. I shall touch on elements of this continuity through the course of the following chapters, although this will not be presented as adequate grounds in themselves to demonstrate the authorship of the later letters, one way or another.

Finally, to the extent that ecclesiological studies have traditionally focused on church structures, a comparative, diachronic analysis of development that compares and contrasts the earlier and the later is a helpful task. The present study is, however, more interested in the ethos and dynamics of leadership than simply in the organizational structures. Accordingly, it may more readily be able to accommodate the wider corpus and present a synchronic perspective. Indeed, in consequence, it will be able to offer a more broadly based account of leadership, which is less dependent on a particular, or closely defined, structure. That said, this study will be explicit about those particular conclusions that are derived and sustainable only on the basis of the later epistles.

Pauline church leadership is explicitly not limited here to an exploration of the nature of Paul's leading of the churches, that is a consideration exclusively of Paul's qualities of leadership. Rather, the focus is more broadly on Paul's perspectives about church leadership in general, and concerns not only his own leading but also the leadership of other influential figures in the Christian communities.

2. Method

It is important, in the course of investigating Paul's understanding of church leadership, that we are attuned to a number of the particular methodological hurdles that need first to be identified and then surmounted in a theological endeavour such as this, which relies so heavily on the interpretation of social historical data from a context so distant from our own. An integrated element of this study will be a consideration of the many methodological challenges that underlie the identification and exploration of Paul's principles of leadership. These will be introduced here, but further discussed through the course of the ensuing chapters. Our starting point is clearly that Paul has not left a systematic consideration of his understanding of church leadership. If, then, we are to be able to glean such an understanding, it must be reconstructed from this raw source material, addressed as it is to different individuals and communities, concerning disparate and unrelated situations.

a. *The Limitations of the Data*

From the perspective of either a sociologist or a social historian, a major hurdle is that the pool of extant source material is not only extremely small, amounting to just over thirty thousand words, but it is also raw in that comparatively little of it appears to deal in a direct or explicit way with issues of leadership. Secondly, this small pool of source material is prompted by a number of discrete, historical contexts, which are distinguished from each other along cultural, ethnic and social lines, and cannot be considered directly commensurable or equivalent. Thirdly, each of the source letters is presented as deriving essentially from a single hand; that is, notwithstanding a number of references to co-authors, the letters fundamentally reflect one person's reading of a range of social contexts. The researcher does not, therefore, have the luxury of being able to seek clarification about Paul's insights or comments by triangulation or the cross-checking of other witnesses. Fourthly, it is in the nature of this kind of correspondence as a source material that the author is himself remote from the circumstances with which he is engaging. These letters are not personal memoirs in which Paul is reflecting on his own life and thinking; rather they represent his comments on and responses to remote situations with all the limitations that such distance necessitates.

In consequence of all these points, we must identify and seek to accommodate a significant number of variables in the course of evaluating the data and using it as raw material for our reconstruction of Paul's principles of leadership. That is, we need to develop a sensitivity towards our sources that is attuned to variations in colour, texture and hue, and avoids reading the data as if it were monochrome and contextually equivalent.

b. *Distinguishing between Description and Prescription*

A common error in reconstructing Paul's views about leadership is the failure to distinguish between what Paul prescribes and what he describes. Data of both kinds may be useful in our reconstruction of his principles, but each has to be handled differently. Clear instances of prescription may be the instructions to overseers in 1 Tim. 3.1-7 and 8-13, such as 'Now, an overseer must be ...', and 'Deacons likewise must be ...' Passages like this can be incorporated into a set of principles and characteristics of leadership rather more readily than passages that are description, that is, passages that are noting, whether in approval or reproval, the actual behaviour of individuals in a community. A reading that ignores the descriptive runs the risk of overlooking some material that may be most relevant to our reconstruction. Similarly, a reading that identifies the prescriptive, but interprets it as a description of what Pauline churches were like is likely to confuse Pauline theory with historical practice.

c. *The Particularities of the Different Communities*
It is important to be aware that there are distinctions between the different Pauline communities, based variously on the dominant surrounding culture or religious climate. Some communities, for example, emerged and developed in the face of significant religious persecution and were accordingly under pressure to be more syncretistic. In the case of both the Thessalonian and Philippian communities, it is probable that they were resisting pressure to conform to the expectations of the imperial cult, and, if so, this will have affected either their understanding or practice of leadership. The Corinthian community, on the other hand, presented a less conspicuous public profile by virtue of many of their members adopting to a far greater extent the dominant secular values of its competitive surrounding society. Although in writing to each of these communities Paul addressed issues concerned with leadership, his message and emphases may well have differed in order to address and accommodate the peculiar difficulties that each was experiencing. Such distinctions will affect the extent to which it is a straightforward process to transpose material addressed to disparate situations and merge it into a homogenized, single theology.

d. *The Impact of Relationship*
We should also note that Paul's relationship with each of the communities differed in regard to the depth and extent of his prior or existing influence on that community. In a given letter, is Paul writing to a congregation as its founding father, or is his contact with the congregation subsequent to another's founding; alternatively, is he addressing an individual with whom he has travelled and worked closely, and with whom he has discussed such issues at length? Where Paul is addressing aspects of leadership, were they in response to criticisms of his own apostleship, or did they concern issues of exclusively internal conflict? In dealing with specific issues, Paul's rebukes and challenges, his responses and teaching, are likely to have been tailored both in tone and content in relation to his readers. Consequently, we may not always assume that a course of action that is prescribed in order to remedy the situation in one community, or the tone of that prescription, would have been considered by Paul to be appropriate in any and all contexts. Any differences of this kind in Paul's responses may be regarded by some readers as flexibility and particularity in his response to a range of circumstances; others will regard them as inconsistencies either in the overall portrait of Paul as a leader or in his legacy or instructions to other leaders; and, still others will consider that Paul's responses reflect a development in his thought and approach, or evidence of a pseudo-Paul.

e. *The Passing of Time*

One's working assumptions about the span of time between the early Pauline letters and the Pastoral Epistles affect considerably the likelihood or extent of any development in ecclesiology over this period. Similarly, the extent of any perceived development in ecclesiology significantly shapes one's answer to the question of the dating of the Pastoral Epistles. Of course, both of these issues have implications for their authorship. A measure of circularity in this argument is evident, and the Pastoral Epistles have proved to be remarkably malleable on these points. If these letters are compared in turn with the early Paul and the second-century Apostolic Fathers, it may be argued that the style of the correspondence, if not its content and therefore its vocabulary, favours greater proximity to a Pauline figure; whereas many would hold that the ecclesiology seems rather to favour greater proximity to the second-century context. Unfortunately, the differences in genre between a letter to a leader who has been a co-worker and metaphorical son and one to a wider church community severely challenge making like-for-like comparisons – and yet such comparisons have to be attempted.

In this debate, the three core elements of authorship, dating and ecclesiology are closely related, and a starting conviction on any one of these elements can find complementary support from both of the others. My own view takes ecclesiology as a starting-point, and argues that the differences in organization between the Pastoral Epistles and the early Pauline epistles do not require a second or third generation provenance. In consequence, an earlier date is feasible, and Pauline authorship is not ruled out. The wider question about development in ecclesiology, however, is less significant than the question as to whether or not there is evidence of development in 'Pauline' thinking about the nature of church leadership, that is, the ethos and dynamics of leadership.

f. *The Question of Consistency*

Over the course of the following chapters, it will become very apparent that scholarship is starkly divided both in regard to Paul's leadership and his views about leadership. There are many who find in Paul the principal exponent of New Testament ecclesiology and Christian leadership, both in word and deed. There are many others who find Paul's stance and attitude quite intolerant and offensive. Such diversity of opinion should strike us as remarkable given the limited size of the evidence base. While in some cases, the same key texts are being explored but, confusingly, claimed by both camps in support, there are many instances where a selective reading is adopted. In my view, either of these stances, and a wide range of intermediary positions, can indeed be argued from the Pauline evidence; and therein lies a major conundrum. We have noted the extensive range of variables that need to be identified and accommodated in any full treatment. It is in the nature of such a body of source material that we shall see differences that may variously be inconsistencies or sensitivities on Paul's part, or they may be developments or accommodations. He appears to be both strong and forceful, and yet also weak. He defends his own authority and recognizes authority in others, and yet also on occasion he uses egalitarian language and urges mutuality among the members of his communities. In short, some of the qualities associated with Pauline leadership appear to be mutually incompatible and appear to reflect at best a tension.

3. *Hermeneutics*

Attitudes, whether modernist or postmodern, towards authority, power, control and hierarchy in the twenty-first century will inevitably have an influence both upon the interpreter of the Pauline texts, and the subsequent reader of those interpretations. The post-Enlightenment modernist approach reflects a self-confidence and certainty where the potential of the individual, the power of the intellect, and the inevitability of progress are elevated. The possibility of objectivity gives a focus to the confident search for the meaning of a text. The postmodern perspective, in contrast, is often marked by a profound pessimism, and a sense of fragility. Anthony Thiselton writes of this world view: 'Disguise covers everything. Hence a culture of distrust and suspicion emerges'.[8] Accordingly, I shall also explore some of the ways in which these two dominant presuppositions of our day and age tend to influence the process of selecting and prioritizing what are considered relevant sources, and the extent to which we can attain historically credible, theological interpretations of those texts.

The word 'power', potentially a neutral term, can be applied in a range of contexts with either negative or positive connotations. In the context of seeking to purchase a new car, for example, 'power' may well be regarded as a positive term, often associated with speed and acceleration. It could, however, have negative connotations with its implications for fuel consumption, pollution or cost of insurance. Similarly, in the context of individuals and wider society, the word 'power' may be regarded either as a positive influence or a restrictive force. Power is a central preoccupation of postmodernism, where it is overwhelmingly regarded in negative terms as a tool of unsolicited and unwelcome social manipulation; yet, to the

8   A. C. Thiselton, *Interpreting God and the Postmodern Self: On Meaning, Manipulation and Promise* (Scottish Journal of Theology. Current Issues in Theology; Edinburgh: T. & T. Clark, 1995), p. 12.

modernist, the power of the individual appears as a goal and a good. I shall devote a chapter to this issue.

I have already noted the tendency to underestimate the effect of Paul's theology on the social groups to which he was writing, thereby effectively divorcing the social dimension from the theologral and ignoring the former. Such a separation of these dimensions is strongly criticized by postmodernists who tend to view the proposition of truth or knowledge as inseparable from power-interests and social control. In the light of this, Paul's exercising of authority and his appeal to orthodoxy, both in person and in his letters, are often viewed negatively. His theological discourse is an act of social manipulation. A feminist contribution to this debate has adopted a hermeneutic of suspicion to the Pauline texts in order to prompt new questions about Paul's treatment of the weak and marginalized. Appeals to orthodoxy by the apostle are increasingly interpreted as disguised bids to legitimate his personal power over both individuals and whole communities.[9] In the light of such an agenda, the notion of power assumes a strongly negative connotation. It also, however, presents a disarming element of catch 22 in which those interpreters who defend a non-manipulative Paul are only demonstrating that they, like many of his first-century readers, have been duped by his manipulative scheme. This issue will emerge in a number of the following chapters.

It will now be clear that the conclusions of this research, because of its methodological and hermeneutical challenges, are framed as *a* Pauline theology of leadership, rather than *the* Pauline theology of leadership. Whilst I do not hold that the findings over the following pages are necessarily and entirely relativized simply because they are the product of one individual's reading of a text, it is nonetheless clear that the methodological complexities in reconstructing a theological treatment of a series of sociologically remote and diverse situations are significant.[10] Every interpreter is constrained by the limits of the available source material and has to accommodate significant unknowns within that data, unknowns that could have been probed more deeply had such an analysis been conducted of a living individual by a researcher who had access to many of the relevant social contexts. Additionally, every interpreter comes to the text with a set of experiences, perspectives and goals. My own stance has been a core influence in both the selection and reading of texts within these sources. Although an individual, I stand within my own

---

9   Elizabeth Schüssler Fiorenza, Stephen Moore, Elizabeth Castelli and Graham Shaw have been significant contributors to this debate.

10   In this vein, R. Jewett, *Romans: A Commentary* (Hermeneia; Minneapolis: Fortress, 2007), p. 59, is cautionary and urges the interpreter not 'to disregard the circularity inherent in all historical reconstructions, whose weaknesses can be dealt with only by transparency and a willingness to have the results examined by further tests against the rhetorical, historical, and cultural evidence'.

history of scholarly and church communities, each with their own traditions, practices and perspectives, some of which I continue to challenge, and others I hold resiliently. Similarly, the present work will be evaluated both by some who broadly share many of my underlying presuppositions, but also by those who are fundamentally opposed to a large number of them.

4. *Consensus Perspectives on Pauline Leaders*

The question as to whether or not there were local leaders in the early Christian communities is now much less disputed than has been the case in previous decades. At the outset of this study, however, we should note that the rather different question as to whether or not local leadership was one of the features of the earliest Christian communities that was both recognized and endorsed by Paul continues to be marked by debate and difference of opinion. Regardless of the existence of locally influential figures, did Paul favour a construct that was predominantly egalitarian?[11] If there were leading figures, that is those who held local and limited influence, were they, for the most part, not recognized officially by Paul, and consequently we should not expect to see a clear impression of their existence on the extant primary sources? Alternatively, was local church leadership a feature of the early Christian communities that Paul either instigated and authorized, or was it something that he recognized, and adopted, and, in some measure, adapted?

It is clear that the early second-century letters of Ignatius show, not only clear evidence of a developed hierarchy of leading figures in local churches, but also explicit endorsement for their dominant bishop (ἐπίσκοπος, almost always cited in the singular), and group of elders (πρεσβύτεροι always in the plural, and πρεσβυτέριον), and deacons (διάκονοι).[12]

> 'For Jesus Christ, our inseparable life, is the mind of the Father, just as the bishops appointed throughout the world are in the mind of Christ' (*Eph.* 3.2); 'The more anyone observes that the bishop is silent, the more one should fear him. For everyone whom the Master of the house sends to manage his own house we must welcome as we would the one who sent him. It is obvious, therefore, that we must regard the bishop as the Lord himself' (*Eph.* 6.1); 'Let everyone respect the deacons as Jesus

11 This is an issue that I shall explore from a number of perspectives in the course of the following chapters.

12 Ignatius, *Eph.* 1.3; 2.1-2; 3.2; 4.1; 5.1-3; 6.1; 20.2; *Magn.* 2.1; 3.1-2; 4.1; 6.1-2; 7.1; 13.1-2; 15.1; *Trall.* 1.1; 2.1-2; 3.1-2; 7.1-2; 12.2; 13.2; *Rom.* 2.2; *Phld.* 1.1; 3.2; 4.1; 7.1-2; 8.1; 10.2; *Smyrn.* 8.1-2; 9.1; 12.2; *Pol.* 1.1; 5.2; 6.1. Cf. also *1 Clem.* 42.5; 44.5; 47.6; 54.2; 57.1; *2 Clem.* 17.3; Hermas, *Vis.* 8.3; 13.1; 103.2; 104.2; *Did.* 15.1

Christ, just as they should respect the bishop, who is a model of the Father, and the presbyters as God's council and as the band of the Apostles. Without these no group can be called a church' (*Trall.* 3.1); 'Flee from divisions, as the beginning of evils. You must all follow the bishop, as Jesus Christ followed the Father, and follow the presbytery as you would the apostles; respect the deacons as the commandment of God. Let no one do anything that has to do with the church without the bishop. Only that Eucharist which is under the authority of the bishop (or whomever he himself designates) is to be considered valid. Wherever the bishop appears, there let the congregation be; just as wherever Jesus Christ is, there is the catholic church. It is not permissible either to baptize or to hold a love feast without the bishop. But whatever he approves is also pleasing to God, in order that everything you do may be trustworthy and valid' (*Smyrn.* 8.1-2).

In the light of this consistent portrait in the Ignatian letters, an important issue is to determine whether, or at what stage, during the post-resurrection period local leaders were formally appointed or recognized by Paul. While it is clear that Paul was himself active in an authoritative capacity, his letters also highlight that his apostolic authority was often and vigorously opposed. How did Paul regard and react to these competing powers? Was his reaction in effect to reinforce a local egalitarianism or rather to establish either a simple or complex hierarchy within the community that might combat this opposition and strengthen his standing? If we consider that the Pastoral Epistles reflect the second-generation product of the process of institutionalization, was this a process that Paul had earlier and deliberately set in motion or was it the natural adoption by the Christian communities of the characteristics of the stratified society and culture of which they were a part?

Since Paul's extant correspondence is framed, for the most part, as stand-alone, occasional documents as opposed to an integrated and developed series of related letters or a systematic account of a single, recommended church order, it is not immediately clear how answers to these questions might be reached, nor indeed how principles of leadership might be derived from such varied and situation specific source material. Nonetheless, many throughout the history of interpretation of these letters have considered that an accurate reconstruction of Paul's theology of leadership within the early Christian communities is not only possible, but that it provides a valid basis for the constitution of churches in later generations and centuries and quite different contexts. Not surprisingly, a number of starkly differing reconstructions of Paul's leadership principles have been propounded, each of which is defended as reflecting a remarkable continuity between the perceived first-century situation and the pattern adopted by a particular strand of subsequent, even contemporary, church tradition.

In order to establish what were these first-century structures, it is a commonplace that passages that make reference to church order and practice in the book of Acts and the epistles are often juxtaposed and what, in effect, is a composite New Testament model is thereby constructed. This approach has two significant, but questionable, assumptions. First, a consistent, or at least a dominant, blueprint of church order exists within the pages of the New Testament. In other words, the structures of church leadership that existed in Corinth in the mid-first century are assumed to have been largely identical to or in continuity with those that were being implemented in Ephesus, or even Jerusalem, twenty years later or ten years earlier. Secondly, the New Testament churches were themselves both 'orthodox' in their understanding of the nature of the church, and were also faithful in their implementation of these principles. With these assumptions, little distinction is made between how church life was actually ordered, as opposed to how it ought to have been ordered, and what emerges from such a reconstruction is a consistent and universal portrait that can be readily transposed to different contexts in later centuries because it takes little account of development, variation or unorthodoxy within the New Testament period itself. Reading this picture as a theological prescription for later contexts compounds the error of assuming a consistent historical reality.

The Tübingen scholar, F. C. Baur, in nineteenth-century Germany, developed an alternative approach, with a diametrically different starting point. Rather than portraying a monolithic template, it was noted that the New Testament reflects a number of quite disparate, early Christian communities, which in fact changed significantly over the course of the New Testament period; and, rather than being faultless models of church structure, they were tainted by significant division and dissension. The New Testament reflects marked distinctions between the early Jewish and Gentile strands of the church, which mirror the later divisions between the Catholic and Protestant traditions. Towards the close of the apostolic age a single, dominant model began to emerge, which incorporated elements from both the Jewish and Gentile strands, and led to the establishment of the monarchical episcopacy in the early second century.

The early, Jewish strand was centred on Jerusalem and the original apostles, and is particularly apparent in the book of Acts, but is not regarded as being historically reliable.[13] It propounds the early establishment of ecclesiastical officials comprising the twelve apostles, supplemented by seven others who focused on administrative tasks (Acts 6.1-6).

---

13   This view is outlined, and regarded as a Lukan stylization, in J. D. G. Dunn, *Unity and Diversity in the New Testament: An Inquiry into the Character of Earliest Christianity* (London: SCM, 1990), pp. 106–8.

What emerged in these communities over time was an ecclesiology closely based on the Jewish synagogue model of an eldership.[14]

The Gentile strand is reflected in the early Pauline epistles, which were felt to offer a more reliable historical picture. Beyond Jerusalem, these Pauline communities reflected a quite different pattern. Often character-ized as 'charismatic' communities, this meant that authority in the local congregation was vested in no single individual or group of individuals. Rather, there was a mutuality in which all members, gifted by the Spirit, were to exercise ministry in the body of Christ.[15] The model pro-pounded in 1 Corinthians, although almost certainly not reflective of the Corinthian community in reality, with its metaphor of the body, is the chief example of such a model.

The Pastoral Epistles, widely regarded as post-Pauline in date, reflect a notable integration of these two strands, the Jewish and the Gentile, including a marked degree of institutionalization, the formalization of authority in a small group of officials, and an apparent decrease in the importance of corporate mutuality and interdependence.[16]

Foundational to this reconstruction of a straight-line development from the charismatic, egalitarian groups of the early Pauline communities to the more institutionalized churches of the later New Testament period is a distinction between those letters in the Pauline corpus that explicitly refer to ecclesiastical offices in the local community, such as elders, overseer (sometimes translated bishop) and deacons, and those that do not.[17] A glance at this pool of references highlights that there is certainly a very uneven spread of these titles across the correspondence. There is a clear predominance in the later Pauline epistles, and particularly in the Pastoral Epistles to Timothy and Titus. This is reinforced by an absence of such titles in the earliest Pauline epistles, such as Galatians, 1 Thessalonians, and 1 and 2 Corinthians.

When this spread of evidence is extrapolated into the second century, as we have seen from the Ignatian letters, it prompts the predictable conclusion that the reader can discern a process of institutionalization that begins in the latter stages of the New Testament period. On the basis of this evidence it can be concluded that organized leadership was not a feature of the early Pauline communities, but emerged in the later period, and such leaders were identified by the use of specific titles. Working with this reconstruction, we would need to ask whether such a trajectory of development reflects the almost inevitable process of institutionalization, or is something that Paul endorsed, or even set in motion.

---

14   Dunn, *Unity and Diversity in the New Testament*, pp. 108–9.
15   Dunn, *Unity and Diversity in the New Testament*, pp. 109–11.
16   Dunn, *Unity and Diversity in the New Testament*, pp. 114–16.
17   Rom. 16.1; Eph. 3.7; 6.21; Phil. 1.1; Col. 1.7; 4.7; 1 Tim. 3.2, 8, 12; 5.17, 19; Tit. 1.5, 7.

This view that the earliest churches were devoid of established structures of leadership dominated scholarly readings of Pauline ecclesiology from the late nineteenth century through to the late twentieth century.[18] The method that underpinned much of this scholarship was seriously questioned, however, in the later decades of the twentieth century. It was then rightly noted that Paul's letters were responses and instructions to communities where social forces, and not just theological or ideological ones, were at work. To reconstruct historical reality on the basis of Paul's theological constructs alone, or to seek to understand Paul's theological constructs without an awareness of the social forces that prompted those statements in the first place, represents a fallacy of idealism for neither approach takes into account how particular individuals or groups either provoked or may have responded to those ideas.[19] We have seen that where Paul's statements about community organization are mistaken for historical reality, then prescriptions to the early church are misconstrued as descriptions of the early church. Similarly, where Paul's statements about community organization are read without awareness of the situations that prompted them, then a non-contextual reading is likely to ensue. Any such mismatches are clearly exaggerated when Paul's statements are corrective rather than affirmative in nature. Where little or no distinction is made between ecclesiological principle and actual practice, a simplified, and possibly idealized portrait of the early church, and an unreliable picture of Pauline ecclesiology are drawn.

A reaction against the kind of scholarship that overestimates the extent to which ideas either shape or reflect communities has prompted further research into the various historical contexts and social forces. In particular, this has entailed a closer look at the social and cultural aspects of Graeco-Roman, Jewish and Christian groups. The advantage of such methods is that they raise questions not just about theological principles, but also about social interaction, group dynamics and even power politics.[20] A greater interest in the social dimension of these communities has enabled scholars to take into account other evidence within the Pauline letters that presupposes the existence of leaders within these communities, even where Paul makes no reference to their specific titles. As a consequence, a different picture of how the early church looked in particular Greek and Roman cities of the mid-first century has emerged which is markedly different from the previously prevailing

18 See in particular the works of Rudolf Sohm, Hans von Campenhausen, Eduard Schweizer and J. D. G. Dunn.

19 B. Holmberg, *Paul and Power: The Structure of Authority in the Primitive Church as Reflected in the Pauline Epistles* (ConBNT, 11; Lund: Gleerup, 1978), pp. 205–7.

20 A foundational work in this regard is the collection of essays in G. Theissen, *The Social Setting of Pauline Christianity: Essays on Corinth* (SNTW; Edinburgh: T. & T. Clark, 1982).

consensus.[21] The emerging conclusion is that, irrespective of the absence of official titles in the early Pauline epistles, there is clear evidence that there were leaders in each of these communities. Furthermore, on the basis of these readings, it is possible to determine that Paul is critical of many substantive leadership practices, and affirming of others, in a number of these churches. A clearer understanding of the historical context has enabled a more nuanced reading of the theological construct.

There are a number of implications that can be drawn from this as we approach the task of outlining Paul's understanding of church leadership. First, we can indeed incorporate into the broader picture evidence gleaned from even the earliest Pauline letters, since community leadership in some form was an issue of significant importance to the apostle from the outset. Secondly, an awareness of the social context will enable us to identify and explore not simply any principles of church organization, but also any principles of church leadership, that is the dynamics of government and not just the structures of government. We shall also be able to explore to what extent these leadership principles are outlined and applied consistently by Paul across the full extent of his corpus, or are modified for different contexts or altered with the passage of time. Thus, for example, even though the church addressed in 1 Corinthians differed from that addressed in Philippians, in issues addressed, location, time, and possibly also church structure, we may be able to establish whether principles of leadership are presented consistently in each situation. Thirdly, it will be important to include in the broader picture not just Paul's propositional statements about community leadership, but also his critical and corrective reactions to bad practice, together with those passages where he is highlighting the examples of good leadership practice, both his own and that of others. All of this evidence can and should be used, as sources from which to discern his understanding.

5. *The Way Forward*

In the following chapters we shall consider issues of status and power as they relate to the context of church leadership. This will entail a study of some of the ways in which Paul viewed his own role, namely as apostle, father, teacher, servant, co-worker and model. It is clear that some of these categories are mutually incompatible in that they variously presuppose positions of authority, equality and subservience. It will, therefore, be important to see whether or how these categories can be resolved in Paul's own practice and understanding of leadership.

---

21   See Clarke, *Secular and Christian Leadership in Corinth*, with regard to the context of 1 Corinthians; and Clarke, *Serve the Community of the Church*, for a comparison across different congregations.

Additionally, we shall look at Paul's critical and affirming comments about the roles of leaders other than himself, including those with formalized titles such as overseer, elder and deacon. The aim, however, will not be to determine a Pauline blueprint of church order that might be deemed to be universally applicable. Rather, the goal remains the elucidation of what Paul considered to be principles of church leadership. This has been a comparatively neglected element of the wider study of Pauline ecclesiology, but is an issue on which he is especially eloquent.

Chapter Two

HERMENEUTICAL QUESTIONS

1. *Introduction*

In the preceding chapter, the overview of differing perspectives on Pauline ecclesiology revealed a diversity of conclusions about the leadership structures and practices across the Pauline communities, and, in particular, in regard to the nature and extent of any development or differentiation across the cultural and geographical contexts of the different communities. This lack of agreement is not surprising on two counts. First, a key focus of the historical-critical method is to highlight such differences; furthermore, there are significant complexities in selecting and applying a range of methods, models and sources in the task of reconstruction at such a historical distance – a task that is further hindered by the paucity of primary sources that derive directly from the Pauline contexts.[1] Secondly, the many variables that exist in the choice of methods, models and sources are further attenuated by an inevitable tendency to fill those remaining gaps in our data on the basis of our own respective and varied experiences, preferences, or church affiliations. These two hurdles, which I shall here distinguish as the methodological and the hermeneutical, are closely related, but have often become quite separated – leading to a focus either on one or the other, rather than both.

In terms of the first hurdle – the methodological – it is recognized that those conclusions that derive from a flawed method, an incommensurate model or unrepresentative sources cannot provide a reliable platform from which to explore the apostle's conception of appropriate church leadership. Thus, while a reading of the Pauline epistles that is not situational is not likely to be historically plausible, by the same token, a reading that adopts a wrong situational background will also prompt a

---

1 Where New Testament scholars recognize Paul to have provided one of the richest seams of source material from the apostolic period, social historians on the whole would view his correspondence as a particularly narrow seam, providing comparatively little basis from which to derive absolute conclusions about dominant patterns or development.

misreading.[2] It is for this reason that I proposed in the preceding chapter a number of critical questions in regard to methods, models and sources that ought to be addressed in the task of historical reconstruction. These proposals seek to mitigate some of the pitfalls that exist in working at such a cultural distance from the historical context. However, it has to be noted that the careful selection, not only of appropriate primary sources, but also of a complementary research method or model, cannot in itself guarantee an assured set of results. Our remoteness from the original context is further hampered by a second, and related, hurdle – the hermeneutical – which has a significant capacity to influence one's reconstruction of the Pauline communities and Paul's responses to the issues of leadership.

Scholars have long regarded the Enlightenment objective of a pure, scientific neutrality to be a mirage. An interpreter's interests, pre-understanding, presuppositions, even social conditioning, all have the capability, indeed tendency, to influence both the process and results of research. Our methods, models and sources are all variables, and each has the potential to be influenced to varying degrees by the individual perceptions of the exegete. This is the essence of the second hurdle, and it is all the more acutely the case when dealing with texts that not only address community formation in a historical setting, but which also hold varying degrees of programmatic influence in many Christian churches and communities today. Although the potential for these influences is notionally recognized, it has been their latent effect that has been an important feature of much Pauline social studies discussion. Indeed, in this particular field scholars have been criticized for not exhibiting sufficient awareness of this potential for presuppositions to influence their own research processes or conclusions.[3] Over the past thirty years, this field of study has witnessed two significant developments, firstly on issues of method, and more recently in the sphere of hermeneutics. The focus of

2   I am grateful to New Testament colleagues and postgraduate students for an engaging discussion with Professor Jewett in regard to the plausibility of the particular situational reading that he has so thoroughly applied in his Romans commentary. Both the dynamic of 'honour' and Paul's planned mission to Spain 'shape' his reading of the letter in significant ways; cf., for example, the explanation in, R. Jewett, *Romans: A Commentary* (Hermeneia; Minneapolis: Fortress, 2007), p. 59, that his conjectures about the situational context 'are subject to refutation, despite the fact that they are supported by many researchers. In the case of this commentary, however, these conjectures provide the framework for the entire letter'.

3   G. Aichele, *The Postmodern Bible* (New Haven; London: Yale University Press, 1995), p. 14, makes the following statement in regard to biblical scholars as a whole, although it is no less applicable to scholars of Pauline social studies in particular: '[they] have been slow to awaken from the dream in which positivist science occupies a space apart from interests and values, to awaken to the realization that our representations of and discourse about what the text meant and how it means are inseparable from what we want it to mean, from how we will it to mean.'

the present chapter will reflect on the impact of these developments on Pauline social studies. I shall particularly concentrate on the second of these, that is, a consideration of those hermeneutical issues that currently influence debates about Paul and his relationships with his correspondents, with particular attention to their implications for deriving a theology of leadership from the Pauline epistles.

2. *The Focus on Method*

We have seen that during the 1970s and 80s there was a growing sense of the failure of critical scholarship adequately to explore and address the social contexts of earliest Christianity.[4] In some measure this was a consequence of the tendency to focus on the language, literature and religion of earliest Christianity in a way that was too divorced from the social and cultural settings in which those texts first found meaning.[5] However, in the wake of fresh scholarly interest in the application of social scientific tools to the structures and dynamics of the Pauline communities, researchers engaged in a contentious debate over the comparative merits of social theory and social history as research methods.

On one side of this debate, the use of social theory was criticized by those who classed themselves as purer historians. The grounds for this criticism are both that one's choice of theory or sociological model in some measure determines or subtly shapes the results of that research, and that the models that are applied tend to be anachronistic and alien to the first-century ethnic context. On the other hand, those who presented social history as a more value-neutral approach, relying exclusively on the identification and interpretation of comparative, historical sources (justified because they derive from appropriate chronological and ethnic contexts), were also criticized for being naïve to regard themselves as somehow dispassionate, or less personally committed to or influential

---

4   In regard to Pauline church structure, cf. M. Y. MacDonald, *The Pauline Churches: A Socio-Historical Study of Institutionalization in the Pauline and Deutero-Pauline Writings* (SNTSMS, 60; Cambridge: Cambridge University Press, 1988), p. 60, 'The picture of the organization of the Pauline communities as being purely pneumatic, which represents the starting point for much writing on the development of the church, is deficient because it does not fully take into account the relationship between beliefs, social structures and social setting. The leadership structures of Paul's communities are not shaped in a straightforward manner by his theology; the relationship between the structures and the ideas is dialectical. ... A purely charismatic ministry and concept of authority based exclusively on Spirit endowment presents an unrealistic picture of the human society of the Apostle'.

5   P. F. Esler, *New Testament Theology: Communion and Community* (Minneapolis: Fortress, 2005), pp. 33–5, criticizes such a non-historical focus on the New Testament texts.

over their findings.[6] The suggestion that a reliance on the use of historical sources makes the interpreter immune from the insidious influences of ethnocentricity or anachronism is rightly viewed as untenable. One positive attribute of the use of social theory is that at least it is explicit about its chosen interpretative model, whereas the interpretative lenses, underlying research questions or personal values of the social historians are more often kept hidden from view, implying that such influences are negligible. It is clear that the agenda of the social historian, especially when they are hidden from public scrutiny, should be regarded as no less susceptible to ethnocentricity or anachronism since all readings are in some measure politically and socially motivated.[7]

This debate clearly ought to have nurtured the recognition that neither approach can guarantee immunity from those influences that inform the results of one's scholarship.[8] Instead, however, both sides of the debate tended to defend the validity of their own particular approach, in part by downplaying the extent to which present-day perspectives, personal values or cultural assumptions exploit the uncertainties that are inherent in both the primary sources and their chosen method of studying societies at such a historical, cultural and philosophical distance. Instead of recognizing that neither approach can in fact guarantee immunity from the potential of influencing factors, it was frequently the case that proponents of one approach tended to highlight the bias of the other. For some this took the form of a tendency to affirm traditional interpretations, whereas for

6   E. Schüssler Fiorenza, 'Umasking Ideologies in Biblical Interpretation', in W. Yarchin (ed.), *History of Biblical Interpretation: A Reader* (Peabody: Hendrickson, 2004), p. 386, is one of many who have levelled criticism at historical-critical studies precisely because they continue to be subject to 'dogmatic and ecclesiastical controls'; 'The positivist value-neutral stance of historical-critical studies was shaped by the struggle of biblical scholarship to free itself from dogmatic authority and ecclesiastical controls ... The mandate to eliminate value considerations and normative concepts in the immediate encounter with the text is to assume that the resulting historical accounts would be free of ideology and dogmatic imposition'; cf. also, Aichele, *The Postmodern Bible,* p. 2, 'Moreover, historical criticism has implicitly veiled the historical character of biblical scholarship's entanglements with modernity and has therefore left unexamined its own critical and theoretical assumptions as well as the cultural conditions that produced, sustained and validated them'.

7   Cf. D. B. Martin, 'Social-Scientific Criticism', in S. L. McKenzie and S. R. Haynes (eds.), *To Each its Own Meaning: An Introduction to Biblical Criticisms and their Applications* (Louisville: Westminster John Knox Press, rev. and expanded edn, 1999), p. 130; and T. Gorringe, 'Political Readings of Scripture', in J. Barton (ed.), *The Cambridge Companion to Biblical Interpretation* (Cambridge: Cambridge University Press, 1998), pp. 69–70.

8   D. G. Horrell, *The Social Ethos of the Corinthian Correspondence: Interests and Ideology from 1 Corinthians to 1 Clement* (SNTW; Edinburgh: T. & T. Clark, 1996), pp. 9–32, is one who has argued that many of the methodological distinctions between history and sociology are false inasmuch as the use of models, termed research frameworks, is inevitable in both disciplines.

others, producing a novel or innovative interpretation was sufficient challenge in itself to the traditional.[9]

3. *The Focus on Hermeneutics*

Increasingly since the 1990s, however, a greater recognition of the influence of the interpreter has meant that this methodological debate has been supplanted by the more overt exploration and application of new hermeneutical stances in regard to the Pauline texts. There are a number of features that in varying degrees are influencing or characterizing many of the more recent approaches to the Pauline material. Much social historical and sociological research on the epistles is still pursued, but, in addition, and sometimes in combination, there are a burgeoning number of new and very different approaches to the texts, with radically new presuppositions, raising different questions, and reaching non-traditional conclusions.

a. *The Individuality of the Interpreter*
In the current climate, the significance of a particular scholar's interpretative stance in the process of historical reconstruction is not only recognized, but it is often more openly probed, explored and even paraded. It is increasingly common, for example, to find scholars at the outset of their work 'declaring their hand' in regard to their interpretative stance or their intended goals.[10] It is not left to the reader to deduce the peculiar bias or agenda in the interpreter's selection of sources, method, or conclusions. This also avoids the misleading notion that, by remaining silent about their own potentially prejudicial positions, interpreters are implying that the primary evidence speaks for itself, untainted by any subsequent, anachronistic or ethnocentric interference.

---

9   K. J. Vanhoozer, *Is there a Meaning in this Text?: The Bible, the Reader, and the Morality of Literary Knowledge* (Grand Rapids; Leicester: Zondervan; Apollos, 1998), p. 382, criticizes Clines' economic approach whereby an interpretation is justified if it meets the needs of a particular consumer.

10   An especially articulate example can be found in 'Introduction: *For a Biblical (Wo/man) Scholar to Speak in the* Ekklesia', in E. Schüssler Fiorenza, *Rhetoric and Ethic: The Politics of Biblical Studies* (Minneapolis: Fortress, 1999), pp. 1–14; cf. also Esler, *New Testament Theology*, pp. 39–41; and also E. H. Haney, *The Great Commandment: A Theology of Resistance and Transformation* (Cleveland: Pilgrim Press, 1998), p. 6, who has a very full self-description (the final categories of which may be considered less relevant): 'I am white, of northern European ancestry and culture, female, academically trained with a PhD, in a lesbian relationship, a member of a largely white and middle-class Protestant denomination, from a lower-middle-class background, sixty-five years old, representative of the culture's understanding of mental and emotional normalcy, physically able-bodied, and an easterner who deeply loves the ocean.'

Presented as a more honest approach, this greater candidness also reflects a postmodern hesitancy that a historical text is capable of unequivocally revealing a meaning that can be confidently regarded either as the intended meaning or a universalizing meaning. Rather, meaning is individualized because it is coloured by the respective agenda of its later interpreters. That is, what I read from a text is necessarily generated in some measure from my peculiar vantage point – cultural, religious and academic. My learning, my conditioning, my experiences and my imagination all constrain or place boundaries around what will emerge as *my* reading. Consequently, unless the complete set of social and philosophical metanarratives that have helped to construct *my* reading are to be regarded as privileged or prioritized over others, then my conclusions must be regarded as conditional and provisional, rather than definitive and universal.

Those who hold that certainty about the past is doubtful and the influence of the interpreter is pervasive and subject to prejudice, must also regard that neither a definitive, historical reading of Paul's theology of church leadership, nor a universalizing, contemporary reading, can or should be produced.[11] And yet, the search, particularly by the church, for such a contemporary, yet nonetheless historical, theology of church leadership continues. While there is a focus on the individualism or uniqueness of the interpreter's presuppositions, it must be recognized that the vast majority of such research is rightly conducted within a context that is rather more dependent on others, entailing an ongoing theoretical and experiential dialogue in which the past and the present cooperate – a model in which interpretation of the text and evaluation of that interpretation continually engage each other.[12] The task of theology should thus be viewed as a co-operative discourse with other partners, in

---

11 Cf. the perspective reflected by R. J. Evans, *In Defence of History* (London: Granta, 1997), p. 95, 'meaning cannot be found in the past; it is merely put there, each time differently, and with equal validity, by different historians'. A contrary view of J. A. Harrill, *Slaves in the New Testament: Literary, Social, and Moral Dimensions* (Minneapolis: Fortress, 2006), p. 2, urges against despondency: 'The professions of history and of biblical studies have happily moved beyond the objectivism of seeing historical facts naively, as prior to and independent of interpretation. Asserting an interpretative hegemony can no longer be intellectually justified. This should press us into caution, not despair.'

12 Thus, J. D. G. Dunn, *New Testament Theology in Dialogue* (Biblical Foundations in Theology; London: SPCK, 1987), p. 7, 'New Testament theology is a dialogue because any twentieth-century attempt to inquire into first-century writings is bound to be a dialogue, because in engaging the New Testament writings with serious theological concerns we frequently find our questions being clarified and ourselves being put in question, and because the New Testament itself is a product of that dialogue, a dialogue in particular between the first Christians and their Jewish heritage'.

which individual contributors participate in a continuing debate and a corporate hermeneutical venture.[13]

Clearly, each interpreter is attracted to a particular hermeneutical community because of its ideologies. This process, therefore, not only challenges the interpreter in some ways but it also serves to reinforce those ideologies.[14] Just as a theological undertaking of this kind is not exclusively an individual's task, however, neither does it need to be the case that different dialoguing communities work in isolation from each other. Rather, quite diverse scholarly and ecclesiastical communities do indeed influence and dialogue with each other, and many interpreters subscribe to a complex network of communities – represented by affiliations to a diverse mix of institutions, scholarly societies and ecclesiologies. In this way, although I, as an interpreter, may have a complex and unique combination of metanarratives that informs my particular reading of the text, I will share a proportion of these, possibly a significant proportion, with others in a number of different interpreting communities, or, indeed, across a network of such communities. I am then at the same time seeking to influence them and be influenced by them in a dialogical process. Although these communities may exercise an element of interpretative control, they cannot, of course, guarantee against wrong interpretation. Furthermore, those who share a rather different set of hermeneutical assumptions from mine nonetheless exercise an influence over my research and thinking as I seek to understand and engage with them, finding grounds either to accommodate or refute competing stances. In particular, the questions that others ask of the text may well be questions that I would not otherwise have identified, but I can nonetheless reflect on them profitably. A key challenge, however, is for groups with widely differing presuppositions to find sufficient common ground on which to engage usefully in such dialogues. Differing degrees of confidence that texts, whether primary or secondary, are a reliable means of communicating, or differences about the ways in which the primary texts can or should address contemporary contexts, are major challenges to such debate.

However, in recognizing that my particular combination of biographical metanarratives are both complex and unique to me, and that theology is conducted within the context of a wide network of variously sympathetic and antagonistic interpreting communities, I want to suggest

---

13 Cf. the stance presented in J. D. G. Dunn, *The Theology of Paul the Apostle* (Grand Rapids: Eerdmans, 1998), p. xviii.

14 What W. Yarchin (ed.), *History of Biblical Interpretation: A Reader* (Peabody: Hendrickson, 2004), p. xxix, applies to the individual, applies also to the community: 'Meaning in a text certainly qualifies as a socially generated construct, and so, like all social constructs, meanings (i.e., what readers find meaningful) will vary relative to the ideologies or value structures that they support.'

that disclosing a series of personal details or affiliations will be a quite inadequate basis on which others may be able to presume the detail of my hermeneutical stance, although such details may seem initially to be suggestive. A combination of census details and a list of community associations cannot adequately identify my hermeneutical agenda, not least because, in an increasingly pluralistic world, a person's hermeneutical stance is less likely to be identifiable from their colour, gender or age, and an institutional affiliation does not always guarantee whole-hearted identification with that community.[15]

Schüssler Fiorenza rightly urges that those involved in hermeneutics should avoid masking 'their hermeneutical character, advocacy position, and rootedness in historical-religious power-struggles' and focus rather on cultivating 'a critical self-reflexivity on how their socio-political location shapes their research practices and self-understandings'.[16] Clearly, this is not to suggest that increased awareness of the presence of influencing agendas is tantamount to the removal of such presuppositions. This marked shift towards individualism and candidness about one's own hermeneutical stance in regard to the task of historical reconstruction is, nevertheless, only one of a number of characteristics increasingly featured in the current climate in Pauline social studies.

b. *Suspicion is Inevitable*

A second, and related, characteristic of the current climate is a heightened sense of suspicion on the part of the reader towards the assumed agenda of an author – indeed, both the author of the primary source material and the author of the secondary interpretation. This is reflected in Thiselton's comment:

> How different people have interpreted biblical texts may well tell us *even more about them* than about the texts themselves ... We discover what kind of people attempt to use biblical texts for manipulative purposes, whether consciously or unconsciously, and why they do it. Some may do

---

15 R. C. Tannehill, 'Paul as Liberator and Oppressor: How should we Evaluate Diverse Views of First Corinthians?', in C. H. Cosgrove (ed.), *The Meanings We Choose: Hermeneutical Ethics, Indeterminacy and the Conflict of Interpretations* (London: T. & T. Clark, 2004), p. 124, argues that although scholars often do not explicitly reveal their hermeneutical commitments, these may nonetheless be 'hidden in a concluding section called "implications", as if these implications arise out of the conclusions and weren't a motivating force'.

16 E. Schüssler Fiorenza, 'Rhetorical Situation and Historical Reconstruction in 1 Corinthians', in E. Adams and D. G. Horrell (eds.), *Christianity at Corinth: The Quest for the Pauline Church* (Louisville; London: Westminster John Knox Press, 2004), p. 386. She defends, however, that this does not mean adopting an unscientific approach: op. cit., 'Rhetorical Situation and Historical Reconstruction in 1 Corinthians', p. 387.

this sincerely or insincerely, for purposes of self-interest or power, or out of misguided piety or sense of faithfulness.[17]

Accordingly, this hermeneutical climate, which encourages openness about one's presuppositions, also assumes the ubiquity of covert, or even subconscious, agenda, and may foster a climate of suspicion or even distrust. Double meanings abound. Thiselton describes the potential for misunderstandings thus: 'our interpretations of texts and self are hopelessly trapped within the presuppositions, pre-judgements or preju-dices of the traditions to which we belong. ... these factors, more than our own derivative conscious judgements, largely predetermine what we *want* to hear or even are *able* to hear from texts'.[18]

Given that all writers have a personal perspective to accommodate or defend, which may be cultural, religious or philosophical, by the same token all have a political agenda – that is, a reason to produce findings that are intended in some measure to be provocative, to convince others, or to affirm a set of assumptions. As such, the goal of research, not least research into the social context and message of the Pauline communities, is essentially manipulative in that it seeks to evoke persuasion or conviction. The inevitable self-interestedness and self-protectiveness on the part of the reader are linked with a reluctance to concede that any one (or, perhaps, any other) social group holds the key to an authentic, authorized or authoritative claim to truth.[19] Indeed, any such claim to legitimate interpretation is viewed as controlling, and therefore manipu-lative; it constitutes an appeal to a privileged, and therefore oppressive, stance. Such a rejection of authorized interpretations can be seen in deconstruction as a hermeneutical tool, which quite explicitly seeks to challenge others by disturbing the assumed or the familiar[20] – 'a strategy for undoing privileged hierarchies – linguistic and social, philosophical and theological – a way of releasing the "other" from its ideological

---

17   A. C. Thiselton, *Interpreting God and the Postmodern Self: On Meaning, Manipulation and Promise* (Scottish Journal of Theology. Current Issues in Theology; Edinburgh: T. & T. Clark, 1995), p. 65.

18   Thiselton, *Interpreting God and the Postmodern Self*, p. 67.

19   Thiselton, *Interpreting God and the Postmodern Self*, pp. 12–13, 'In matters of race, class, gender and professional guilds, however, the gloves are off. For what counts as true for one group is often disparaged as a manipulative disguise to legitimate power-claims by another group. If different groups choose to adopt different criteria of truth to determine what counts as true, or even what counts as a meaningful truth-claim, rational argument and dialogue become undermined by recurring appeals to what one group counts as axioms, but seem far from axiomatic for another. At this point argument becomes transposed into rhetoric. Rhetoric then comes to rely on force, seduction, or manipulation'.

20   Cf. S. D. Moore, *Poststructural-Ism and the New Testament: Derrida and Foucault at the Foot of the Cross* (Minneapolis: Fortress, 1994), p. 129, explaining Derrida's term 'deconstruction'.

bondage to an interpretive community'.[21] But the apparently more innocent interpreter who wishes simply to convince others of the significance of new evidence is also charged with manipulation.

It is this assumption that another's research conclusions are intended in some sense to challenge my reading of the text, and perhaps also my experience of church, that evokes defensiveness and suspicion in me. The response may be to resist the power-interests of others and thereby protect one's own interests, and to distrust those traditional interpretations that claim to have universal relevance or some other form of supremacy over other interpretations. This is all the more sharply felt where the new evidence or conclusions are presented with a measure of challenge, or universalizing or prescriptive force, whether overt or implied.[22] This may take various forms, including proposing that a particular reading carries an authorized status or by outlining a Pauline community rule as being prescriptive for present-day Christian communities.

Awareness that research findings have a rhetorical force, which encourages a climate of suspicion, is likely to influence both my reading of others, as well as their reaction to my findings. It is to this extent that the logic of the current climate may variously reflect distrust, conflict, and potentially despair.[23] Thus, we see the possibility that:

> the postmodern self lives daily with fragmentation, indeterminacy, and intense distrust of all universal or 'totalizing' discourses. Insecurity, in turn, invites a defensiveness, a letting down of shutters, and an increasing preoccupation with self-protection, self-interest, and desire for power and the recovery of control. *The postmodern self is thus predisposed to assume a stance of readiness for conflict.*[24]

We shall later see instances where suspicion can be applied as a hermeneutical tool, that is, a means of interrogating the text in new, perhaps creative, ways, by assuming an underlying deception in the text and thereby prompting the reader to question assured readings and challenge traditional meanings. A hermeneutic of suspicion is a product of the history of interpretation itself, not least some modernist interpretations. Over the centuries, interpreters have used scripture to legitimate all manner of wrongs, including anti-semitism, exploitation of slavery, the subjugation of women, and colonialism. In consequence, interpreters, and perhaps their source material (for example, Paul) are implicated in what is viewed as a series of interpretative travesties. A hermeneutic of suspicion is then employed as a mechanism by which to liberate a non-oppressive

---

21 Vanhoozer, *Is there a Meaning in this Text?*, p. 382.
22 Aichele, *The Postmodern Bible*, p. 3.
23 Thiselton, *Interpreting God and the Postmodern Self*, p. 117.
24 Thiselton, *Interpreting God and the Postmodern Self*, pp. 130–1.

message from the Pauline texts, despite their history of interpretation, and, some would consider, despite even the texts themselves.

Of course, the subject of ecclesiology offers such a cornucopia of contrasting structures and practices that the opportunities for applying a hermeneutic of suspicion are many. The interpreter may apply suspicion in reading the primary author; in turn, the one who evaluates the interpretation will assume and suspect an agenda on the part of the interpreter. For some, this questioning of the primary texts may be intended as an imaginative and productive approach that is warranted by the history of (mis-)interpretation. Others, however, will view particular instances of it as unnecessarily sceptical, indeed more destructive rather than creative, and will search for supplementary mechanisms of accessing the text.[25]

c. *Method is Marginalized*

A third corollary of some recent approaches is that, in so far as it is conceded that a particular person's interpretation of historical texts is prone in some measure to mirror or be influenced by their own values or the values of the communities to which they are affiliated, then debate about the validity of research methods becomes proportionately marginalized.[26] In other words, if interpretation of a historical context is little more than interpretation of oneself, then the search for ever more reliable historical tools is seen either to be futile or less significant.[27] Accordingly, there is a growing sense of the lack of *relevance* of historical research, and the consequent search for contemporary and individual relevance may be regarded as more important than the search for historical fidelity.[28] It is in this regard that the interpreter may be able to avoid the earlier debates about historical method; instead, a reader-centred approach may offer a liberating alternative that sidesteps the problems posed by the inaccessibility of the historical.

---

25   Thiselton, *Interpreting God and the Postmodern Self*, p. 69, reflecting on Ricoeur, urges that a 'hermeneutic of suspicion' should operate alongside a 'hermeneutic of retrieval', that is, a 'willingness to listen'.

26   On this, I concur with Vanhoozer, *Is there a Meaning in this Text?*, p. 31, that '*we can come to know something other than ourselves when we peer into the mirror of the text*'.

27   Cf. Vanhoozer, *Is there a Meaning in this Text?*, p. 16; the dominant goal becomes determining the interpreter's political agenda rather than the original meaning of the text.

28   D. N. Fewell, 'Reading the Bible Ideologically: Feminist Criticism', in S. L. McKenzie and S. R. Haynes (eds.), *To Each its Own Meaning: An Introduction to Biblical Criticisms and their Applications* (Louisville: Westminster John Knox Press, rev. and expanded edn, 1999), p. 269, 'Like other ideological criticisms ... and unlike traditional forms of analysis, feminist criticism makes no pretense to objectivity; it challenges the notions of universals; it is more interested in relevance than in so-called absolute truth'.

d. *Results are Relativized*

Fourthly, in so far as historical texts lose their element of independence, transcendence or otherness, tainted as they are by being handled by later generations of interpreters, there develops a growing sense not only of the marginalization of method, but also of the relativization of interpretations. If a text is a field of potential meaning, and can simultaneously sustain or even provoke multiple valid interpretations (as well, presumably, as some invalid ones),[29] then it is no longer necessary for one interpretation to be presented or received as a challenge to alternative interpretations. My reading of the Pauline material can be mine, and somebody else's interpretation can be their's. Of course, although this may happen at the level of the individual interpreter, we more often come across it at the level of the community, both academic and ecclesiastical. Although this avoids some of the scholarly discord, it may also have the effect, indeed the goal, of stifling debate or dialogue, rather than engaging with competing perspectives.

e. *Manipulation is both Criticized and Expected*

Fifthly, 'using' the text as a vehicle for reinforcing one's own values and challenging those of others is at one and the same time criticized, yet recognized to be all but inevitable. In a climate of suspicion, one assumes that another's reading will threaten in some way, yet one objects to such a challenge because of its innate stance of intolerance; what is more, the relativization of interpretations obviates the need for engagement. A coherently held position on this is self-evidently paradoxical; indeed, postmodernism advocates and thrives on both its inherent complexity and instability, and does not need to reject the *non sequitur* as necessarily illogical. Thus,

> The most consistently postmodern political critics will eschew claims that their interpretations are true, whereas their opponents' interpretations are 'ideological'; they will acknowledge that there is no universal discourse of truth that could support a distinction between my true interpretation and an opponent's ideological interpretation.[30]

---

29   D. C. Steinmetz, 'The Superiority of Pre-Critical Exegesis', in S. E. Fowl (ed.), *The Theological Interpretation of Scripture: Classic and Contemporary Readings* (Cambridge, Mass.; Oxford: Blackwell, 1997), p. 31, 'Yet the text cannot mean anything a later audience wants it to mean. The language of the Bible opens up a field of possible meanings. Any interpretation which falls within that field is valid exegesis of the text, even though that interpretation was not intended by the author. Any interpretation which falls outside the limits of that field of possible meanings is probably eisegesis and should be rejected as unacceptable ... The notion that scripture has only one meaning is a fantastic idea and is certainly not advocated by the biblical writers themselves'.

30   A. K. M. Adam, *What is Postmodern Biblical Criticism?* (Guides to Biblical Scholarship New Testament Series; Minneapolis: Fortress, 1995), p. 53.

Paradoxically, the consistent postmodern promotes inconsistency, and necessarily compromises and appears to be compromised by the strictures of logical, modernist debate. However, as Aichele argues: 'It is not correct that postmodernism is apolitical and amoral or ethically neutral.'[31] While some argue that there is no limit to the relativity of different interpretative approaches, others will argue that only those views that are perceived to be tolerant are held as tolerable.[32] Carroll envisages, somewhat poetically:

> Some forms of postmodern approach to biblical readings would insist on an egalitarian relationship between competing interpretations whereby everybody's point of view must be respected and acknowledged as equal to everybody else's point of view ... The future will be a paradise of different readings with none privileged and all equally valid: the modernistic lion will lie down with the postmodernist lamb, the Marxist bear will eat straw with the capitalist goat, the pre/postmodernist fundamentalist sheep will safely trade biblical proof-texts with the modernist wolf and the ecclesiastical dove will dwell in peace with the academic serpent. It will be a veritable paradise of (non)aggressive differing-but-equal biblical readings in which every man and every woman will sit under their own vine and fig tree undisturbed by any point of view alien to themselves. The Enlightenment rupture between medievalism and postmodernity will be healed by a return to a future of uncompetitive diverse readings ... A veritable reading utopia will have dawned and the old hierarchies and hegemonies of historical-critical biblical studies will have gone for ever.[33]

f. *Responsibility is Urged*

Consequently, many interpreters now operate within and contribute to a contemporary research context in which, in varying measure, candidness is encouraged, suspicion is inevitable, scientific method may be marginalized, conclusions are relativized, and manipulation is both anticipated and yet criticized. While these factors apply to varying extents in all fields of postmodern scholarship, their implications are particularly keenly felt in the different fields of social studies, and no less Pauline social studies.[34] These are, after all, texts that dealt directly with issues of social

---

31   Aichele, *The Postmodern Bible*, p. 11.

32   Cf. the line adopted by R. Jewett, *Christian Tolerance: Paul's Message to the Modern Church* (Biblical Perspectives on Current Issues; Philadelphia: Westminster Press, 1982), p. 168, as he seeks to demonstrate that the Pauline communities disagreed significantly, and that what is commonly seen as Pauline intolerance is in fact a repudiation of intolerance.

33   R. P. Carroll, 'Poststructuralist Approaches: New Historicism and Postmodernism', in J. Barton (ed.), *The Cambridge Companion to Biblical Interpretation* (Cambridge: Cambridge University Press, 1998), pp. 61–2.

34   Cf. the discussion in P. M. Rosenau, *Post-Modernism and the Social Sciences: Insights, Inroads, and Intrusions* (Princeton: Princeton University Press, 1991); S. Seidman, *The Postmodern Turn: New Perspectives on Social Theory* (Cambridge; New York: Cambridge

transformation in their own historical context, but, for many, they also hold an authoritative and therefore formative influence in religious communities today. The potential for these texts to be used for purposes of manipulation, both in the first century and the succeeding centuries, is, thus, not only exposed but all the more keenly felt. Indeed, I have already reflected that the history of biblical scholarship itself records many instances in which authoritative texts have been used to endorse and justify unspeakable injustices and repression. It is in the light of this that Schüssler Fiorenza has urged a sense of ethical responsibility on the part of the interpreter:

> If scriptural texts have served not only noble causes but also to legitimate war, to nurture anti-Judaism and misogynism, to justify the exploitation of slavery, and to promote colonial dehumanization ... then the responsibility of the biblical scholar cannot be restricted to giving the readers of our time clear access to the original intentions of the biblical writers. It must also include the elucidation of the ethical consequences and political functions of biblical texts in their historical as well as in their contemporary socio-political contexts.[35]

By virtue of the power that the Bible wields, any reading of Scripture is a power reading, and interpreters and their readers are consequently exposed.[36] Schüssler Fiorenza's proposition is clearly that interpreters ought not only to conduct their research with scholarly integrity, but also recognize that it is incumbent upon them to demonstrate ethical responsibility both in determining and presenting their findings. For Schüssler Fiorenza, '*the* litmus test for invoking Scripture as the Word of God must be whether or not biblical texts and traditions seek to end relations of domination and exploitation'.[37] Clearly, this raises different spectres for people depending on their confessional stance. While all would agree that there has been a catalogue of interpreters who have abused the scriptural texts over the centuries, some also hold that the biblical texts themselves, within their own time frame, had a questionable ethical influence. That is, not only have many scriptural interpretations been at fault because they have oppressed, but the primary texts

---

University Press, 1994); and S. Seidman, *Contested Knowledge: Social Theory in the Postmodern Era* (Malden; Oxford: Blackwell, 1998), in regard to the different ways in which postmodernism, in its various forms, has impacted on the social sciences.

35 E. Schüssler Fiorenza, 'The Ethics of Biblical Interpretation: Decentering Biblical Scholarship', *JBL* 107 (1988), p. 15, in her 1987, Society of Biblical Literature, Presidential address. Cf. also R. Lundin, *et al.*, *The Responsibility of Hermeneutics* (Exeter; Grand Rapids: Paternoster; Eerdmans, 1985), pp. ix–x.

36 Aichele, *The Postmodern Bible*, p. 4.

37 E. Schüssler Fiorenza, *Bread Not Stone: The Challenge of Feminist Biblical Interpretation* (Edinburgh: T. & T. Clark, 1990), p. xiii.

themselves are in some instances, and in some measure, implicated in presenting a message that is repressive.

A large proportion of New Testament scholars subscribes to the view that the Pauline epistles hold an authoritative, and consequently normative, status within their ecclesiastical community; yet, even among these, there is by no means unanimity as to what is normative and what is meant by normative. The varying contexts and genres of the Pauline texts are viewed as conveying different qualities of normative status. While there are Pauline injunctions that are held by some to be bound by their original historical and cultural framework, the same injunctions are held by others to be principles that transcend both context and time, and hold a universal or transcendent significance. Issues such as the covering or uncovering of heads, respectively of women and men, are an obvious case in point within certain ecclesiastical circles.[38] Furthermore, one's stance on whether or not a particular Pauline injunction is normative will exercise a subtle influence on how it is to be interpreted. It is both this innate power of the normative to influence the process of interpretation, and the innate power of what is normative to govern a whole community that demand responsibility on the part of the interpreter. Responsible hermeneutics should recognize that it has a public character and influence, and the interpretation of Scripture should, consequently, be pursued within a context in which there is some quality of external accountability. Accordingly, there should be an awareness of what power interests are being served by an individual's interpretation, and what competing interpretations or reading strategies are being marginalized or negated, as well as a readiness to listen and dialogue, and recognize points of ambiguity in the text.[39]

g. *Pauline Integrity*

Within current scholarship, the complexities that arise from an interpreter's individual biases, together with the range of positions held in regard to the normative nature of the Pauline material, are further compounded for some by a simultaneous, and related, questioning of the extent to which the life and writings of the apostle Paul are themselves to be viewed

---

38   In regard to the reasons which may underlie the comparatively neglected Pauline injunction that men should not cover their heads, see D. W. G. Gill, 'The Importance of Roman Portraiture for Head-Coverings in 1 Corinthians 11.2-16', *TynBull* 41 (1990), pp. 245–60.

39   Vanhoozer, *Is there a Meaning in this Text?*, p. 23, further warns that, 'To define meaning too quickly is to launch a preemptive strike on reading strategies that may not be motivated by the same aims or interests'.

as immune from his own partiality and prejudice.[40] That is, if every interpreter is evidently affected by personal agenda, is access to the real Paul, and the situations that he paints, not similarly hindered by inadvertent bias or even dissembling on his part? Does Paul show evidence of, or should the interpreter in any case assume, his susceptibility to partiality, his need to conceal or simply the natural limitations of his perspective?[41]

Where, for more than a century, the primary nature of the first-person record in the Pauline epistles has taken a default primacy over the second-hand and later recorded material presented in Acts, scholars are increasingly questioning whether Paul himself can be viewed as a reliable source of history about the earliest communities, notwithstanding the early date and the eye-witness quality of his epistles. If writers today recognize that they themselves are prone both to external and internal, subtle pressures, the suggestion is posed that Paul was no less immune in the first century from similar vulnerabilities to present his material in the most calculating way.

A confessional stance, which holds the text to have an inspired and transcendent quality as God's communication with humankind, rather than simply Paul's context-bound communication with a specific church or individual, is a matter of widespread and practical disagreement and significantly impinges on the question of both the relevance and intentionality of Paul's injunctions. Different points on this spectrum include the view that Paul was self-evidently biased and unacceptably manipulative, and consequently to be challenged at many points; or that Paul is a faultless ethical and spiritual model, both in what he says and does, and that he presents what is the primary New Testament material from which subsequent generations can develop an ecclesiology; or alternatively a *via media* that Paul presents an account of himself and others that recognizes human fallibility, but he is nonetheless a trustworthy servant of Christ and guide in matters of church structure and governance.

By adopting a critical position vis-à-vis Paul, there is a move to question the assumptions, which have dominated the history of Pauline scholarship, that the apostle's analysis of the situations he is addressing is accurate and that his conclusions are beyond censure. While Paul has largely succeeded in convincing his readers, over the centuries, that 'he is

40 M. Y. MacDonald, 'The Shifting Centre: Ideology and the Interpretation of 1 Corinthians', in E. Adams and D. G. Horrell (eds.), *Christianity at Corinth: The Quest for the Pauline Church* (Louisville; London: Westminster John Knox Press, 2004), p. 282, 'Paul's actual agenda may have been quite different from his stated position'.

41 MacDonald, 'The Shifting Centre', p. 281, notes 'a general inclination to remove Paul from his apostolic "pedestal" and to see him as influenced by a variety of cultural, political, and interpersonal factors'.

right and the "others" are wrong', there are new attempts to read the sources from a perspective other than the Pauline.[42] The history of interpretation has been accused of an unthinking endorsement of Paul over issues about church order, informed by a belief in the canonical status of Paul (and not of the Corinthians).[43]

An example of this criticized tendency to 'side' with Paul over against his opponents might be seen in regard to the majority of interpretations of Paul's own account of his *contretemps* at Antioch with his fellow apostle, Peter.[44] The scholarly tribunal has accepted Paul's account of the event – an account presented to a third party, namely the churches in Galatia. On the basis of this, the tribunal finds in Paul's favour, without the rigour of cross-questioning his account, or the luxury of hearing statements from other witnesses, and, indeed, without even hearing the apostle Peter's own defence. On this reconstruction, Paul's voice is the only one heard, and he is privileged with an apostolic immunity or assumption of innocence that is not accorded to the muted Peter, his fellow apostle. One way or another, apostolic fallibility has to be conceded; and, on the basis of our only extant account, it is conceded on the part of Peter, rather than Paul.

Clearly there is a range of perspectives on the Pauline portrait. Some will argue that Paul is deliberately manipulative here and elsewhere. He had a particular axe to grind in regard to the Galatians, and this agenda will necessarily have coloured how he chose to present both Peter and himself when he recounted to them the Antioch incident.[45] This

---

42   E. Schüssler Fiorenza, 'Rhetorical Situation and Historical Reconstruction in 1 Corinthians', *NTS* 33 (1987), p. 390. See also MacDonald, 'The Shifting Centre', pp. 279–84, who notes that the overriding interest of scholars has been in what Paul thought than in what the Corinthians might have felt; and Tannehill, 'Paul as Liberator and Oppressor', p. 134, who argues that, 'After the provocative work of Schüssler Fiorenza and Wire, we can no longer begin study of the Corinthian correspondence with the assumption that Paul is correct and fair in all his judgments, while those he sought to correct, including the Corinthian women prophets, were necessarily in the wrong'.

43   Cf. Schüssler Fiorenza, 'Rhetorical Situation and Historical Reconstruction in 1 Corinthians', pp. 389–90; also MacDonald, 'The Shifting Centre', pp. 280–1; and J. M. G. Barclay, 'Thessalonica and Corinth: Social Contrasts in Pauline Christianity', in E. Adams and D. G. Horrell (eds.), *Christianity at Corinth: The Quest for the Pauline Church* (Louisville; London: Westminster John Knox Press, 2004), p. 189, 'it is important to be aware how Paul's perspective on the Corinthian church tends to control our description of them'.

44   Cf. Gal. 2.11-21, especially the phrase in Gal. 2.11, 'I opposed him to his face, because he had clearly done wrong/was condemned (κατεγνωσμένος ἦν)'.

45   Tannehill, 'Paul as Liberator and Oppressor', p. 125, writing in regard to the Corinthians, 'We are dependent on Paul's letters for our understanding of the situation in Paul's churches. However, definition of the church's problems requiring intervention is already a part of Paul's rhetoric. Definitions of situations are perspectival, and conflicts arise because perspectives differ. Speakers and writers try to persuade by getting others to see the situation from their perspective'.

correspondence emerged in response to a particular set of circumstances in which much was at stake, and Dunn argues that, 'His letter is probably best read as a vigorous attempt to counter attempts made from Antioch or Jerusalem to undermine his own role and authority as church founder and to assert the authority of Antioch or Jerusalem over the Galatian churches'.[46] If this is so, the threat or tension in regard to Jerusalem may be regarded as having had a major influence on Paul's presentation of the Antioch incident. This is just one instance where the historical predisposition to accept the presented biblical account of events at face value is questioned in Pauline studies. It can be seen that such an approach will open the door to a wide range of creative and controversial readings of the letters.

4. *The Way Forward*

It is clear in the light of these issues that the arena for debating issues about Paul's life, and his teaching about church life, is now much larger, more diverse and more complex than in previous decades. Scholarly and ecclesiastical dialogue partners span a far greater range of hermeneutical and confessional positions in regard to the Pauline epistles. I shall focus on two broad questions that will pave the way for the following chapters. First, do the New Testament texts provide not only sufficient, but also sufficiently historical, and sufficiently reliable, data on which to reconstruct with any confidence Paul's understanding of church leadership; and, secondly, what normative value should be given to any resulting reconstruction of his thought?

One approach has been to assume, with the confidence of the Enlightenment, that careful and informed application of historical-critical tools makes it entirely possible to recover a reliable picture of Pauline ecclesiology. That same Enlightenment perspective, however, may also argue that issues concerning the normative nature of Paul's theology must be avoided by the historical critic because they have the potential to influence or interfere with the essentially prior and ideally isolated task of historical reconstruction.[47] The issues of whether, or to what extent, or in

---

46 J. D. G. Dunn, *The Theology of Paul's Letter to the Galatians* (New Testament Theology; Cambridge: Cambridge University Press, 1993), p. 127.

47 In this regard, W. Wrede and F. C. Baur focused on the historical and expressly avoided assessing or affirming any element of normativity. However, historical criticism now faces censure in failing successfully to bridge the historical divide, either in the sense of demonstrating contemporary, Western relevance or being aware of the extent to which contemporary values or presuppositions hinder a genuine retrieval of those ancient values; cf. Aichele, *The Postmodern Bible*, pp. 1–2. Contrast, H. Boers, *What is New Testament Theology?: The Rise of Criticism and the Problem of a Theology of the New Testament* (Guides

what ways Paul's letters should be viewed as normative are then regarded as belonging to a quite separate scholarly, or perhaps purely ecclesiastical, discipline.

An alternative approach, for which there is also much precedent, is to work from the prior assumption that the biblical text contains what is, in some measure, normative for the Christian church. The recognition that Paul is both the most accessible and most extensive proponent of ecclesiology in the New Testament then suggests that the Pauline corpus is the locus where we may confidently discover what is normative for the church. This approach tends to downplay or even ignore the diversity within the Pauline corpus, and it also tends not to explore or account for the even greater diversity that exists across the less accessible ecclesiological material within other portions of the New Testament. Accordingly, the Pauline epistles emerge as the dominant texts to inform ecclesiology in today's contexts. Each of these approaches is marked by a notable confidence both in the ability of the interpreter and in the capacity of the Pauline text to reveal a clear ecclesiology, and yet neither approach reflects critically on the question as to how the Pauline setting can be normative in today's varied contexts.

In the present climate of New Testament hermeneutics, however, we have seen that the grounds of this confidence are more often questioned. The diversity of competing scholarly positions, indeed even the multiplicity of denominational ecclesiologies, witnesses to a lack of certainty about New Testament and Pauline ecclesiologies. It is clear that definitive or universally satisfying conclusions about whether or not the Pauline corpus is capable of revealing a systematic ecclesiology, and, if so, whether that ecclesiology should be viewed as normative, will not be reached (and some would argue, ought not to be reached). However, awareness and exploration of these divergent hermeneutical issues may nonetheless result in a more nuanced understanding of Pauline ecclesiology and a more considered reflection of its normative force, even though elements of its findings will be rejected, or only partially accepted, or perhaps welcomed in different contemporary circles. Accordingly, these two theoretical issues, the viability of deriving a Pauline theology of church leadership from his letters, and the normative nature of such a theology, ought to be integrated into any responsible exploration of Pauline ecclesiology.

---

to Biblical Scholarship New Testament Series; Philadelphia: Fortress, 1979), p. 85, who regards the history of New Testament theology to be an attempt precisely to answer 'how a collection of documents from the past could be normative for the present'.

a. *Is a Pauline Theology of Church Leadership Recoverable?*

The multivalent question of whether a Pauline theology of church leadership is recoverable captures in some measure these two hermeneutical questions. 'Recoverable' could carry the sense of retrievable from the New Testament text; alternatively, it could mean able to be replicated in our very different contemporary contexts. Indeed, this very ambiguity of meaning in some way parallels the nature of the hermeneutical problem.

Whether or not it is possible to uncover Paul's view of church leadership touches on a number of challenging issues. Clearly, it depends in the first place on Paul having a coherent understanding of church leadership, which is encapsulated in some form within his extant correspondence. It may be that his understanding of leadership developed over time; that he was less dogmatic on some aspects than others; and that there was room for a degree of diversity, which reflected the different contexts or communities with which he was engaging. A reconstructed theology may be able to accommodate each of these variables; indeed, in large measure, scholars who have explored Pauline ecclesiology, resulting, as we have seen, in a range of conclusions, have addressed each of them. The varied and contested nature of these findings, however, is not merely a consequence of the range of working assumptions made in regard to issues of authorship, date, and provenance.

In addition to these historical-critical questions, I have drawn attention to an additional layer of hermeneutical assumptions that influences the interpreter and ought to be the subject of reflection. The problems here concern whether or not the text can reliably reveal Paul's ecclesiology to a remote reader or interpreter who necessarily has a quite different agenda, interpretative context, and set of personal influences. Relevant issues include whether the Pauline text can indeed communicate reliably, despite not simply the linguistic, historical and cultural divides that exist between author and current reader (which historical and sociological methods are seeking to address), but also despite the more subtle, but no less influential, interference introduced by both the author's and the reader's respective political or social agenda. The scope for misunderstanding is clearly present in all communication and accounts for at least some of the diversity in scholarly opinions in regard to the Pauline texts. I shall later explore particular instances of the potential for both the author and the reader to be factors in miscommunication. Nonetheless, I shall maintain that the daily activity of written or spoken verbal communication is not futile, that the potential for a measure of successful communication across the centuries still exists, and that the original meaning of historical texts need not always and entirely be lost, although the respective agenda of both the author and of the reader certainly affect this process of communication.

i. *The Author's Agenda*

It is recognized that if Paul had a coherent view of the nature of Christian leadership in the churches, and if we are to seek to recover this view, we can only turn to his extant correspondence for our core evidence. Yet, we have noted that these letters were written to discrete communities or individuals and were prompted by a range of circumstances peculiar to each context. It is clearly a challenge to construct an ordered and systematic theology on the basis of a collection of documents that is limited in both number and size and also by their occasional nature and singular perspective. On these issues, we face a number of limitations in the very nature of the source material, which do not in themselves reflect aspects of a Pauline agenda.

Furthermore, it is surely significant that the very nature of this source material as correspondence demonstrates that Paul was at the time addressing or responding to situations from which he was himself remote, and people with whom he was not at the time able to communicate face-to-face. In the case of 1 Corinthians, it is clear that Paul's grasp of both the actual and the presenting problems will have been partial, informed as he was by a minority of the Corinthians, who were part of a community that was, in any case, marked by disagreement and dissension.[48] These factors are limitations that were also faced by Paul, although they did not prevent him from at least seeking to tackle the difficulties as he perceived them. If these weaknesses in Paul's sources of information mean that his understanding of the Corinthian context was not as detailed and comprehensive as it might have been had he been present in person, they do not in themselves attenuate the ability of the documents to disclose a theology of leadership. What we read may be considered to be Paul's response and advice to a situation, as he understood it.

There are discrete, but rare, instances of specific issues or questions raised by Paul's correspondents and to which he responded. These include the brief interjections that surface at points in 1 Corinthians where Paul appears to be reproducing specific questions raised by the Corinthians, each of which he prefaces by the formula 'concerning ...' (περὶ δέ).[49] These interjections offer us some limited access to the voice of the Corinthians and their context. However, their questions, concerns and comments are conveyed in the letter only in a form that is both integrated

---

48   The question as to whether there was a single, over-arching problem within the early Corinthian community has attracted a diverse range of responses. In A. D. Clarke, *Secular and Christian Leadership in Corinth: A Socio-Historical and Exegetical Study of 1 Corinthians 1–6* (Paternoster Biblical Monographs; Milton Keynes: Paternoster, 2006), I argue that there is such a singular, underlying problem that accounts for the individual issues raised by Paul.

49   The issues raised in the course of 1 Corinthians include marital relations (7.1), virgins (7.25), food sacrificed to idols (8.1), spiritual gifts (12.1), the collection (16.1), and possibly also the anticipated visit of Apollos (16.12).

with their Pauline response and is presumably highly abbreviated. In these instances, we cannot be certain of the Corinthians' original wording, although it appears that at least some of their questions were conveyed to Paul in writing, and Paul may have precisely reproduced some of that wording.[50] A hermeneutic of suspicion could pose a concerted Pauline agenda to be at work at some of these points when he responds to the reported behaviour of the Corinthians (e.g. 1 Cor. 1.11, 'For it has been reported to me by Chloe's people that there are quarrels among you, my brothers and sisters'; 1 Cor. 5.1, 'It is actually reported that there is sexual immorality among you, and of a kind that is not found even among pagans; for a man is living with his father's wife'; 1 Cor. 6.1, 'When any of you has a grievance against another, do you dare to take it to court before the unrighteous, instead of taking it before the saints?'). It is a reasonable presumption that Paul has had the freedom to select and present the partial information that he has received in such a way as to generate what he deems to be an appropriately reforming response from the Corinthians. We shall later explore the sense in which Paul's documents are clearly rhetorical, and that his intention is evidently and repeatedly and categorically to persuade.[51] We shall also see that he does on occasion reveal an agenda, although the interpreter is left to draw a conclusion as to whether the presenting agenda is no more than a smokescreen for something more insidious, which Paul intended to remain covert.

An additional element of an author's political agenda, and a feature of everyday communication, which may result in a mismatch between what is conveyed through a written text and what are an author's underlying thoughts, include the use of tactful understatement in order to avoid offence or discomfort, where the real force of the underlying thought is not fully communicated; or conversely, the use of deliberate overstatement or hyperbole in order to reinforce what is felt to be an important point that might otherwise be lost. Paul's letters show much evidence of emotional outburst on his part. It seems to me that this kind of com-

---

50   'Now concerning the matters about which *you wrote* (ἐγράψατε)' (1 Cor. 7.1). Note, however, the particular exegetical difficulty here as to whether the succeeding phrase 'it is good for a man not to touch/have physical intimacy with a woman' reproduces the original Corinthian question or alternatively is Paul's opening statement of response.

51   Tannehill, 'Paul as Liberator and Oppressor', p. 125, 'Rhetoric views communication as persuasive action. Paul wants to persuade his audience, that is, to modify its thinking and acting. Our understanding of how Paul is seeking to influence his audience – the communicative force or human impact of Paul's words – depends on our understanding of the situation to which Paul is responding. These matters will, in turn, influence our evaluation of Paul. Was Paul doing the right thing in responding as he did? Although many scholars may want to avoid this question, it is a real and important question for those with ethical commitments. This question is especially forced upon us by recent feminist interpretation'.

munication should be an important element of any consideration of Paul's theology of leadership, and that it should be explored in relation to behavioural patterns on the part of the communicator.

A particular contribution of postmodern studies has been both to raise the profile of the author's agenda and to conclude that it is not possible with certainty to recover the nature of that agenda. We shall see that this does not prevent scholars from attempting to identify authorial intention, not least through a hermeneutic of suspicion. In the course of the following chapters, some of the possibilities and limitations of this kind of endeavour will be explored.

ii. *The Reader's Agenda*

We have seen that just as the author is in a position of power and will exercise influence, so also are all readings political. Readers are far from immune from adopting an agenda; indeed political agenda or personal sensitivities can, and do, blind readers to certain meanings, and predispose them to other readings. In this regard, readers have a tendency to hear either what they want to hear or perhaps what they expect to hear.

It is also clear that subjects such as community leadership and government, church order and structure are going to raise significant reaction in the reader, not least because of their innate tendency to challenge dearly held beliefs and to constrain personal freedoms. The potential for misunderstanding and misinterpretation is clearly considerable – in part through limitations that the reader faces in the nature of the source material; in part through limitations that Paul himself faced through his own remoteness from the situations he was addressing; in part through uncertainties about whether Paul's revealed agenda is shielding a significantly different, suppressed agenda; and, also, in part through our own, sometimes subtle, and sometimes forthright, agenda as readers.

For some, this will unfortunately lead to a counsel of despair, whose only resort is to develop readings that are validated purely by means of their utility or creativity. For others, it will reinforce the ideals of research conducted in dialogue and in a network of communities, where individual and community values can be recognised and probed, and where responsible hermeneutics can be urged – albeit that values and what defines 'responsible' are in themselves not universals.

b. *In what Sense should a Pauline Theology of Leadership be Normative?*

The second question concerns in what sense should a theology of leadership such as this be normative. The pitfalls in tackling this question are both numerous and extensive. Any insinuation that the theology of church leadership that I derive from the Pauline texts equates to Paul's theology of church leadership, rather than my reading would be problematic, and would ignore so many of the hermeneutical hurdles that have been identified. There is also a question as to whether the historical can be normative, in its culture-bound and context-bound state; and, if it can have normative status, what are the mechanisms by which its meaning can be transposed to a range of different contexts? Additionally, is a focused Pauline theology of leadership effectively privileging a Pauline perspective on leadership over that of other New Testament authors, and giving it a special degree of normative status that is not warranted canonically?

A Pauline theology of church leadership that will be viewed by some as, in some measure, normative increases the burden of ethical responsibility on the part of the interpreter, and urges a particular awareness of what power interests may be being served or exercised in pronouncing on ecclesiological issues. Both of these aspects reinforce the importance of a community context for research in which questions are asked and answered in dialogue – although a uniform or universalizing set of conclusions will not be reached.

Chapter Three

THE TITLES OF LEADERS

1. Introduction

We have noted that much study of New Testament ecclesiology has drawn upon the selection and use of particular ecclesiastical titles as an essential foundation from which to investigate church order – notably, the terms overseer/bishop,[1] elder and deacon. Indeed, the presence, or otherwise, of such titles has been seen to provide important clues from which to differentiate between the Jewish, the Pauline, and the post-Pauline ecclesiologies, especially in terms of the relationships between these models of church order and their course of development. The ability to distinguish between 'office' and 'gift' or 'function' has been a significant aspect of this. Do these terms describe an individual's function in the church, for example, their 'serving' (διακονῶν) or 'service' (διακονία);[2] or an established office, for example, that of 'oversight' (ἐπισκοπή); or a group of individuals recognized for their age and wisdom, for example the council of elders (πρεσβυτέριον)?[3]

I have suggested, however, that, for a number of reasons, an emphasis on the presence or absence of these titles has proved to be a flawed approach to recovering these early ecclesiologies. First, it often fails to identify satisfactorily the presence, influence or type of leaders in those communities whose Pauline letters do not mention titles of office.[4]

1　'Overseer' is a literal translation of ἐπίσκοπος, whereas 'bishop' comes from the adopted words in Old English 'biscop', Old High German 'biscof', and Vulgar Latin '(e)biscopus', all of which are ultimately dependent on the Greek; cf. *Oxford English Dictionary Online* (Oxford: Oxford University Press, 2000) ad loc.

2　In Acts 6.1-6, the titles deacon, elder and apostle are not used; but the 'seven' are to focus on 'serving at tables' (διακονεῖν τραπέζαις, Acts 6.2), in order to enable the 'twelve' to concentrate on 'serving the word' (τῇ διακονίᾳ τοῦ λόγου, Acts 6.4). Interestingly, the verb ἐπισκέπτομαι ('look after/oversee/see to'), from the same semantic domain as ἐπισκοπέω, is also used in Acts 6.3, but not the related noun ἐπίσκοπος.

3　Cf. also the paralleled masculine and feminine uses of πρεσβύτερος in 1 Tim. 5.1-2, often translated 'older man' and 'older women', rather than 'elder'.

4　In addition, this approach also has a tendency to downplay the significance of the titles mentioned in the earlier epistles, namely, Phil. 1.1 and Rom. 16.1.

Secondly, this approach gives undue significance to the three titles of overseer, elder and deacon, to the neglect of other terms used elsewhere in the Pauline corpus. Thirdly, these titles, even in their literary contexts, tell us little about the actual function of these posts; consequently, this functional content is often supplied from elsewhere, and is then assumed only and always to be present where these titles occur. Fourthly, this approach is often used in conjunction with an interpretative model of straight-line institutionalizing development that has not sufficiently evaluated that these titles occur very rarely in the corpus, and yet are not restricted to the later letters.[5] Fifthly, insufficient distinction is often made between the letters written to individuals whose concern is local church government and order and those letters that are written to larger communities, where there is less need to mention titled officers or discuss their qualifications. Sixthly, analysis of leadership structures (i.e. church offices) is often pursued independently from critical reflection on the size, structure and congregational context of the historical church communities. We have already discussed a tendency for interpreters' contemporary perceptions inadvertently or deliberately to fill gaps in our historical knowledge. The dominant contemporary model for a local church is one whose principal meeting is as a unified congregation in a single location, and accordingly has a core leadership structure that is centralized and focused in regard to the function and meeting of a single congregation. Where the Pauline communities were predominantly based in homes, rather than a centralized meeting place, their leadership and authority structures must be identified and assessed in regard to a multiplicity of smaller units. In other words, it should be remembered that, in the Pauline letters, the *Pauline* structures of leadership are being outlined for application within *Pauline* communities, with the concomitant requirements demanded by the particular size and household context of their meetings, and the number of such groups within a town.

It is for these reasons that I argue explorations of Pauline ecclesiology are most informative if focused on the much larger corpus of texts that make reference to the presence, function or dysfunction of leaders, than merely on the limited occurrences of key titles in the Pauline letters. Giving undue weight to the significance of these titles, or reconstructing

---

5   The term ἐπίσκοπος occurs only three times in the Pauline corpus (Phil. 1.1; 1 Tim. 3.2; Tit. 1.7); and the term ἐπισκοπή occurs once (1 Tim. 3.1). The term πρεσβύτερος occurs as a title only three times in the Pauline corpus (1 Tim. 5.17, 19; Tit. 1.5); the term πρεσβυτέριον also occurs once (1 Tim. 4.14). (We have noted that in 1 Tim. 5.1-2, the noun πρεσβύτερος occurs twice, in masculine singular and feminine plural forms, referring to older people, who should respectively be treated as a father and as mothers.) The term διάκονος is used throughout the Pauline corpus in many senses, occurring in every letter, apart from the Thessalonian correspondence, 2 Timothy and Titus, but it only refers to a local ecclesiastical office in Rom. 16.1; Phil. 1.1; 1 Tim. 3.

the nature of these posts independently of the particularities of the Pauline ecclesiastical context, will result in a distorted ecclesiology. In this regard, it will be important in due course also to explore the themes of the status and power of Pauline leaders, together with their task and tools of office. This is not to suggest, however, that the choice and use of titles is unimportant; accordingly, the present chapter will identify and investigate the traditional titles of overseer, elder and deacon, together with other related terms. It will, of course, be highly instructive also to identify some of the official titles of leaders within social groupings, both Graeco-Roman and Jewish, that were used extensively in their contemporary society and that are not included in the extant Pauline record.

Before turning to these titles, however, it will be important to return briefly to the issue about the size and nature of the Pauline community groupings, in order that this might provide a context from which to evaluate the references to ecclesiastical titles. The later epistles in the Pauline corpus have been recognized as displaying a significantly patriarchal structure for the local Christian communities based on household structures. Evidence of this is found in the inclusion of the so-called Household Codes (Haustafeln) in a number of these letters.[6] David Horrell has identified greater emphasis on fictive household language in Ephesians, Colossians and the Pastoral Epistles in comparison with the earlier Pauline letters with their alternative focus on ἀδελφός language.[7] A house-church ethos, indeed context, for the later Pauline letters is comparatively clear.

A domestic setting for Pauline communities is evident, however, across a wide range of Pauline communities and throughout the time period spanned by these letters.[8] Although Paul's letters to churches address all the believers in a particular town, he understands that they meet in separate groups. On four occasions Paul describes a particular church as κατ' οἶκον. Gehring argues that in each case the phrase is not drawing attention to the style of the church, that is 'after the fashion of a household' or 'like a household'. Rather the phrase describes its location,

---

6   Cf. Col. 3.19–4.1; Eph. 5.22–6.9; 1 Tim. 2.8-15; 6.1-2; Tit. 2.1-10; 1 Pet. 2.13–3.7.

7   D. G. Horrell, 'From ἀδελφοί to οἶκος θεοῦ: Social Transformation in Pauline Christianity', *JBL* 120 (2001), pp. 293–311; cf. also D. G. Horrell, 'Leadership Patterns and the Development of Ideology in Early Christianity', *Sociology of Religion* 58 (1997), pp. 323–41.

8   Cf. W. A. Meeks, *The First Urban Christians: The Social World of the Apostle Paul* (New Haven; London: Yale University Press, 2003), p. 75, 'the local structure of the early Christian groups was thus linked with what was commonly regarded as the basic unit of society'. The most significant recent study on this is R. W. Gehring, *House Church and Mission: The Importance of Household Structures in Early Christianity* (Peabody: Hendrickson, 2004).

thus the sense is equivalent to ἐν οἴκῳ.[9] Prisca and Aquila are recognized as having a church (assembly) that meets in their home (τὴν κατ' οἶκον αὐτῶν ἐκκλησίαν, Rom. 16.5; 1 Cor. 16.19);[10] Nympha hosts a church in her house (τὴν κατ' οἶκον αὐτῆς ἐκκλησίαν, Col. 4.15); Philemon hosts a church in his house (τῇ κατ' οἶκόν σου ἐκκλησίᾳ, Phlm. 2); and Gaius appears to have been a host both to Paul and to the whole Corinthian community (ὁ ξένος μου καὶ ὅλης τῆς ἐκκλησίας, Rom. 16.23).[11] These few references are not presented in their contexts as anomalous, and may be supplemented by a number of other instances where households are mentioned.[12] Accordingly, the church in a particular location, for example in Rome (Rom. 1.7), actually comprises a number of distinct groups that met in houses rather than together (Rom. 16.5). If we are to assume that this evidence, together with the architectural limitations of domestic settings, significantly limited the size of church meetings, then we ought to presuppose that these early Christian gatherings were normally small, and distributed over a number of domestic settings within a town, as opposed to large, and normally meeting together. This perspective will significantly influence our interpretation of the context in which the early Christian leaders exercised authority and the scope of their responsibility, reflected in the size and number of such groups. This is clearly different from the dominant concept of a large or mid-sized contemporary congregation, the primary focus of whose leaders is on a single congregational meeting, together with the strategy, activities and influence of such a single body of believers (perhaps consisting of a number of smaller groups that are secondary and meet at other times during the week).

9   Gehring, *House Church and Mission*, pp. 155–6.

10   Indeed, R. Jewett, *Romans: A Commentary* (Hermeneia; Minneapolis: Fortress, 2007), pp. 64–9, 958–9, argues for at least five distinct groups in Rome, but only the group that meets at the house of Aquila and Prisca is called a congregation/assembly; this is because they have a house in which to meet, in contrast to the other groups, which met in tenements.

11   G. Theissen, *The Social Setting of Pauline Christianity: Essays on Corinth* (SNTW; Edinburgh: T. & T. Clark, 1982), pp. 83–7, has produced formative work on the identification and role of wealthy householders as leaders of the Corinthian community. The likelihood is that this individual is Gaius Titius Justus (Acts 18.7; 1 Cor. 1.14), whose house adjoined the synagogue. Jewett, *Romans*, pp. 980–1, argues that it is improbable that Gaius' house was used to accommodate the whole congregation of the Corinthian Christians; rather, that he was the one among the Corinthian Christians who offered hospitality to the rest of the church, that is, to Christian travellers who visited Corinth. J. D. G. Dunn, *Romans 9–16* (WBC; Dallas: Word Books, 1988), pp. 910–11, on the other hand, argues that Paul does not use 'church' in this global sense; instead, it is plausible that a large house could accommodate at least 40 people, and that on infrequent occasions more than this number might reasonably, but uncomfortably, have fitted into a large house. Note, however, the phrase 'whole church' in 1 Cor. 14.23 (ἐὰν οὖν συνέλθῃ ἡ ἐκκλησία ὅλη).

12   Rom. 16.10, 11, 14–15; 1 Cor. 1.16; 16.15; Phil. 4.22; 1 Tim. 5.13; 2 Tim. 1.16; 3.6; 4.19.

2. *Titles of Leaders*

The Graeco-Roman world of the first century was a world that shared a preoccupation with the use of honorary and official titles. These existed not only in political contexts, both civic and imperial, but also in priestly contexts, again both civic and imperial. Indeed, the most influential people were those who had accrued to themselves a string of both religious and political titles of office.[13] This is notably evident in the inscriptions from first-century cities and colonies where leading figures were described in terms of their successive offices (*cursus honorum*).[14] Leading figures regarded these formal liturgies highly competitively, and were keen to see them widely publicized, often set in stone. Many of the titles were representative of an honorary status, and were accorded to individuals because of their wealth (and anticipated generosity), rather than their skills in political administration or strategic statesmanship.

It is important to note, however, that it was not just the more rarefied heights of imperial or local civic government that showed a preoccupation with titles of status. It is evident also in the papyrological reports of the first-century voluntary associations (*collegia*) that formal recognition was given to leading figures by means of official titles. Indeed, the practices and titles adopted here were often close reflections of civic and imperial community administration.[15] Interestingly, the contemporary Jewish communities adopted a similar practice, with titles including ἀρχισυνάγωγος, ἄρχων, γερουσιάρχης and προστάτης.[16] In contrast,

---

13   Cf. my discussion in A. D. Clarke, *Secular and Christian Leadership in Corinth: A Socio-Historical and Exegetical Study of 1 Corinthians 1–6* (Paternoster Biblical Monographs; Milton Keynes: Paternoster, 2006), pp. 25–32; and A. D. Clarke, *Serve the Community of the Church: Christians as Leaders and Ministers* (First-Century Christians in the Graeco-Roman World; Grand Rapids; Cambridge: Eerdmans, 2000), pp. 11–58.

14   Civic titles included: *duovir, duovir quinquennalis, decurio, quaestor.*

15   Titles included: *magister, curator, quinquennalis, decurio, quaestor, mater collegii, pater collegii, sacerdos, hiereus* and *archiereus.* Cf. Clarke, *Serve the Community of the Church,* p. 68; J. S. Kloppenborg, 'Collegia and "thiasoi": Issues in Function, Taxonomy, and Membership', in J. S. Kloppenborg and S. G. Wilson (eds.), *Voluntary Associations in the Graeco-Roman World* (London; New York: Routledge, 1996), p. 26; S. Walker-Ramisch, 'Graeco-Roman Voluntary Associations and the Damascus Document: A Sociological Analysis', in J. S. Kloppenborg and S. G. Wilson (eds.), *Voluntary Associations in the Graeco-Roman World* (London; New York: Routledge, 1996), p. 36.

16   Cf. Clarke, *Serve the Community of the Church,* pp. 126–38. L. I. Levine, 'Synagogue Officials: The Evidence from Caesarea and its Implications for Palestine and the Diaspora', in K. G. Holum and A. Raban (eds.), *Caesarea Maritima: A Retrospective After Two Millennia* (Leiden: Brill, 1996), p. 397, goes further, suggesting, 'Since each of the terms that appear in Greek synagogue inscriptions of the Diaspora and Palestine has its parallels in Greek and Roman institutions, it is certain that Jews exposed to the wider Hellenistic scene not only adopted its terminology, but undoubtedly something of its modes of organization and administration as well'.

the rabbinic literature customarily refers to a different set of official titles to those found in the public inscriptions.[17]

It is interesting to note that, although the first-century cultural context in which the Pauline communities emerged was preoccupied with the use and widespread recognition of titles of office, leaders in these communities are contrastingly often not identified by titles in the Pauline epistles. The term most frequently used by Paul to describe specific individuals is 'co-worker' (συνεργός), which occurs twelve times and is widely distributed across the corpus.[18] It clearly reflects no ranking within the church. The next most common ecclesiastical term is prophet, which occurs eight times, predominantly concentrated in two passages dealing specifically with the use of prophecy (1 Corinthians 12 and 14). The title 'teacher' occurs six times, two of which refer to Paul. The term διάκονος is possibly used seven times in relation to serving the church; but only four of these occurrences may carry the sense of an appointed office.[19] With the exception of 'apostle', Paul uses no other title with greater frequency than these.[20] In the light of this, it is clearly important to avoid giving greater significance to titles within Paul's ecclesiology than their usage within the letters might suggest.

Furthermore, given that the surrounding society and community contexts laid so much store by the widespread and public use of titles, it is noteworthy that Paul devotes so little space to addressing either the selection or use of titles of office. Furthermore, there seems to be a fluid use of some of these titles, especially that of διάκονος; and there may be situations in which Paul either does not recognize titles or has no need to include in his letters the titles that may have been adopted in these congregations.

a. *Overseer*

The New Testament titles of elder and deacon have each been the subject of comparatively recent extended research, whereas that of the overseer has received less attention.[21] We have noted that the term ἐπίσκοπος, variously translated 'overseer' or 'bishop', occurs only three times in the Pauline corpus,[22] and the related noun ἐπισκοπή occurs once.[23] Of these,

17   Cf. Levine, 'Synagogue Officials', p. 394.

18   Rom. 16.3, 9, 21; 1 Cor. 3.9; 2 Cor. 1.24; 8.23; Phil. 2.25; 4.3; Col. 4.11; 1 Thess. 3.2; Phlm. 1, 24.

19   Rom. 16.1; Phil. 1.1; 1 Tim. 3.8, 12.

20   This term occurs 16 times in references other than exclusively to Paul.

21   Cf. especially J. N. Collins, *Diakonia: Re-Interpreting the Ancient Sources* (New York; Oxford: Oxford University Press, 1990); and R. A. Campbell, *The Elders: Seniority within Earliest Christianity* (SNTW; Edinburgh: T. & T. Clark, 1994).

22   Phil. 1.1; 1 Tim. 3.2; Tit. 1.7.

23   1 Tim. 3.1; cf. also Acts 1.20 (in a different sense); and *1 Clem.* 44.1, 4.

the reference in Phil. 1.1 to overseers and deacons has posed for many something of a conundrum. Eduard Schweizer makes no detailed attempt to accommodate this verse within his wider schema of Pauline church order. Schmithals and Schenk dismiss the problem by suggesting that the reference is a later gloss,[24] although the tradition does not obviously suggest evidence of an interpolation.[25] Dunn views this apparently anachronistic reference in one of Paul's later extant epistles as the earliest sign of what was later to emerge more fully.[26] The Pastoral Epistles then offer possible signs of a 'growing rapprochement' between the post-New Testament formal structures and Paul's rather more dynamic concept.[27]

These overseers and deacons are to be regarded as a sub-group, but an integral part, of the wider community of saints in Philippi.[28] There is no clear explanation, however, from elsewhere in the epistle as to what was the organizational or structural relationship between the saints who are first addressed in the letter and those who are described next as overseers and deacons, and what were their respective roles. Furthermore, there is nothing within this letter that assists in identifying the particular tasks or responsibilities of the overseers. They are not again referred to by their title within the letter to the Philippians, and no clear function is here ascribed to them.

'Overseer' is nonetheless a common title, found both in Graeco-Roman and Qumran literature,[29] as well as the Septuagint. Significantly, however, the term is not consistently applied to just one type of role or context. The meaning 'supervisor', which is suggested by the unreliable tool of etymology, is supported by a significant number of occurrences in ancient

---

24   W. Schmithals, *Die Gnosis in Korinth: Eine Untersuchung zu den Korintherbriefen* (FRLANT; Göttingen: Vandenhoeck & Ruprecht, 1965), p. 11 n. 5; and W. Schenk, *Die Philipperbriefe des Paulus: Kommentar* (Stuttgart: W. Kohlhammer, 1984), pp. 78–82.

25   The possibility that συνεπισκόποις (i.e. 'fellow overseers') rather than σὺν ἐπισκόποις may have been intended makes little difference to this particular debate; cf. M. Bockmuehl, *A Commentary on the Epistle to the Philippians* (BNTC; London: A. & C. Black, 1997), p. 53.

26   J. D. G. Dunn, *Unity and Diversity in the New Testament: An Inquiry into the Character of Earliest Christianity* (London: SCM Press, 1977), p. 115.

27   Cf. Dunn, *Unity and Diversity in the New Testament*, p. 115.

28   Cf. P. T. O'Brien, *The Epistle to the Philippians: A Commentary on the Greek Text* (NIGTC; Carlisle; Grand Rapids: Paternoster; Eerdmans, 1991), p. 48, who argues that Paul is addressing all those who are saints in Philippi, *including* those who happen also to be overseers and deacons, rather than addressing not only all those who are saints, but *additionally* those who are overseers and deacons, or thirdly, addressing only those saints who are *also* overseers and deacons, or fourthly assuming that all saints are overseers and deacons.

29   The term 'overseer' is associated with the מבקר in Jewish sectarian circles, CD 9.18, 19, 22; cf. especially the notion of the shepherd or spiritual father of a community; CD 13.7-9; 1QS 6.12, 20.

literature, and implies a position of responsibility, but within a wide range of contexts and applications. This connotation of responsible supervision is certainly frequent in the Septuagint.[30] In Num. 4.16, Eleazar the son of Aaron is described as being an ἐπίσκοπος in regard to the oil for the light, the fragrant incense, the continual cereal offering, and the anointing oil, and having oversight (ἐπισκοπή) of the whole of the tabernacle.[31] The sense here is of a position of charge and responsibility. In Num. 31.14, however, it is used in a military context as a generic title, which subsumed those senior officers who were specifically either the commanders of hundreds or, indeed, of thousands (ἐπὶ τοῖς ἐπισκόποις τῆς δυνάμεως χιλιάρχοις καὶ ἑκατοντάρχοις).[32] In Neh. 11.9, Joel son of Zichri is described as an overseer, in contrast to Judah son of Hassenuah who appears to be subordinate, either as second in charge, or as the commander of the second city. This again suggests that ἐπίσκοπος is a position of both seniority and responsibility. In Isa. 60.17 (LXX) God declares δώσω τοὺς ἄρχοντάς σου ἐν εἰρήνῃ καὶ τοὺς ἐπισκόπους σου ἐν δικαιοσύνῃ. Significantly, this reverses the Masoretic text, which, in contrast, has peace as the overseer (using the noun פְּקֻדָּה) and righteousness as the taskmaster (using the verb נָגַשׂ). This suggests a degree of parallelism between ἄρχων and ἐπίσκοπος, both being positions of responsibility and rule. Although there are a wide variety of applications, the term nonetheless carries the consistent picture of one who has specific responsibility and a position of authority, which is exercised either over material things (the temple) or, more commonly, people (a workforce or army).

In Phil. 1.1, however, it has been questioned whether those described as 'overseers' had been regarded as having oversight of the local Christian community in a clearly recognized, or a non-specific or generic sense. The phrase is anarthrous, 'with overseers and deacons', and may not, therefore, refer to a formalized group. Hawthorne takes the καί in σὺν ἐπισκόποις καὶ διακόνοις as epexegetical, and the whole phrase as hendiadys – thus rendering the expression, 'the overseers who serve'.[33] An analogy may be found in the phrase τοὺς δὲ ποιμένας καὶ διδασκάλους (Eph. 4.11) where the second noun is anarthrous and could be translated as 'the pastors who teach'.[34] This is less convincing for Phil. 1.1, however;

---

30 E.g. 2 Kgs 12.12; 2 Chron. 34.12, 17. In the majority of instances, ἐπίσκοπος is a translation of the פָּקִיד word group (cf. also Num. 4.16; 31.14; Judg. 9.28; Neh. 11.9, 14, 22; 2 Kgs 11.15, 18; Isa. 60.17). In Job 20.29, God is the overseer.
31 Cf. 2 Kgs 12.11; Neh. 11.22.
32 Cf. Judg. 9.28; 2 Kgs 11.15; Neh. 11.14.
33 G. F. Hawthorne, *Philippians* (WBC; Waco: Word Books, 1983), p. 7.
34 Cf. O'Brien, *Philippians*, pp. 48–9.

although Bockmuehl suggests that the role of overseer, in so far as it exists at this stage, cannot confidently be distinguished from that of deacon.[35]

We may simply deduce from Phil. 1.1 that there was an identifiable group known both to the writers and recipients of the letter as 'overseers'. Paul provides no details about their role, which has prompted the unnecessary conclusion that there was no formalized role at this stage. Such a deduction plainly cannot be drawn simply from the absence of an allusion to a role, and is a predisposition of those who argue for significant institutionalization during the course of the New Testament period. One common element in non-biblical usage of the term 'overseer' is that responsibilities were specific, whether of people or things. Accordingly, it is possible, but cannot be demonstrated, that the overseers of the Philippian congregation are analogous to the leading figures referred to in 1 Cor. 16.15-18 and 1 Thess. 5.12, or some of the gifted people in Rom. 12.7-8, or indeed the named individuals Timothy and Epaphroditus.[36]

The other two references to an overseer occur in the context of more extended passages and shed rather more light on the qualifications of the overseer. The office of overseer (ἐπισκοπή) is an honourable one, in the sense of noble, rather than merely good (καλὸν ἔργον, 1 Tim. 3.1).[37] The two passages in 1 Timothy 3 and Titus 1 notably include eighteen masculine, singular adjectives that describe the overseer. Twelve of these are essential qualifications: upright/just (δίκαιος), devout/godly (ὅσιος), sober/restrained (νηφάλιος), gentle/gracious (ἐπιεικής), respectable/modest (κόσμιος), sensible/moderate (σώφρων), self-controlled (ἐγκρατής), blameless (ἀνέγκλητος), beyond reproach (ἀνεπίλημπτος), loving what is good (φιλάγαθος), hospitable (φιλόξενος) and able to teach (διδακτικός). The remaining six are disqualifications: arrogant/stubborn (αὐθάδης), quick-tempered (ὀργίλος), greedy for profit (αἰσχροκερδής), [not] covetous (ἀφιλάργυρος), [not] quarrelsome/contentious (ἄμαχος) and a recent convert (νεόφυτος). Interestingly, only two of these adjectives appear in both passages (σώφρων and φιλόξενος). In addition to these repeated adjectives, two nouns appear in both passages as character types that should be avoided: the overly assertive person or bully (πλήκτης) and the heavy drinker (πάροινος). This limited element of overlap suggests that the list was neither formalized nor exhaustive; rather it painted a broad set of appropriate qualities. One further characteristic is that the overseer be well regarded by outsiders (μαρτυρίαν καλὴν ἔχειν ἀπὸ τῶν ἔξωθεν). This

---

35   Bockmuehl, *Philippians*, p. 54.

36   Cf. Bockmuehl, *Philippians*, p. 54.

37   The immortalized act of the unnamed woman, who poured perfume onto the head of Jesus from her broken alabaster jar, is similarly regarded as a καλὸν ἔργον (Mt. 26.10; Mk 14.6).

is not a mere potentiality, as in 'likely to be well regarded', but suggests that the outsiders should already hold positive regard for the prospective overseer.

In all, these character traits say little about the skills required of the overseer, other than the ability to teach (1 Tim. 3.2). This aptitude is dealt with more fully in Tit. 1.9, and includes having a thorough grasp of the message/word with a view to exhorting and refuting people where appropriate. The one remaining skill is described in 1 Tim. 3.4-5 by analogy with the household, and is an argument from the lesser to the greater. The verb προΐστημι is used twice, highlighting the requirement for the overseer to be able to manage his household, demonstrated by his obedient and respectful children, as evidence that he would be able to provide the necessary duty of care and attention to those who are part of the family of God (ἐκκλησίας θεοῦ ἐπιμελήσεται).[38] Paul is envisaging that overseers are likely to be those who are married,[39] and have children, indeed a household.[40] The phrasing is unclear as to whether this statement is intended to sustain the view that those who have no wife, no household, or no children are thereby disqualified, or whether the kind of skills evidenced by the married head of a household are merely a helpful analogy – but it is the skills, not the analogous circumstances, that are essential. The possibility that this is a general, rather than a limiting statement, may be deduced from the supposition that, although the text refers to children (that is a plural noun, τέκνα), the man who has only one child is presumably not excluded;[41] and the overall tone may be taken as positive, focusing on faithfulness, rather than restrictive.[42] It is also

38   Cf. G. W. Knight, *The Pastoral Epistles: A Commentary on the Greek Text* (NIGTC; Carlisle; Grand Rapids: Paternoster; Eerdmans, 1992), p. 161, 'The leadership and caring abilities of the ἐπίσκοπος are evaluated on the basis of his management of his household'.

39   The interpretation of 'a husband of one wife' (μιᾶς γυναικὸς ἄνδρα) is contentious; in particular as to whether it is seeking to disqualify the bachelor, the divorcee, the remarried widower or the polygamous. Additional context is provided in the parallel phrase in 1 Tim. 5.9. Here widows are to be treated in accordance with whether they had previously been 'a wife of one husband' (ἑνὸς ἀνδρὸς γυνή). In other words, the phrase necessarily concerns the widow's previous marital relationship(s). The analogy is then that widowers are presumably not automatically ineligible to be an overseer.

40   This ability in regard to people is consistent with the usage in Acts 20.28 where the Ephesian elders are charged by Paul with the task of being overseers in regard to the church after the fashion of a shepherd for his sheep (προσέχετε ἑαυτοῖς καὶ παντὶ τῷ ποιμνίῳ, ἐν ᾧ ὑμᾶς τὸ πνεῦμα τὸ ἅγιον ἔθετο ἐπισκόπους ποιμαίνειν τὴν ἐκκλησίαν τοῦ θεοῦ). The pastoral motif is also applied in the only other occurrence of the noun ἐπίσκοπος: in 1 Pet. 2.25, the sheep have returned to the one who is both the overseer of their souls and their shepherd (τὸν ποιμένα καὶ ἐπίσκοπον τῶν ψυχῶν ὑμῶν).

41   Note that in 1 Cor. 7.32-35 Paul commends singleness in others, as he is.

42   Cf. I. H. Marshall, *The Pastoral Epistles* (ICC; Edinburgh: T. & T. Clark, 1999), p. 478.

unclear whether 1 Tim. 3.4-5 envisages that overseers should have the ability to manage a community that is comparable in size to a household, or to manage a community after the fashion of managing a household. Nonetheless, if we combine these passages, there are clearly two skill sets required of the overseer: knowing, appropriately applying, and teaching the word of God; and, secondly, being able to lead and care for at least a small community of people. The list of character traits must be seen to qualify the two required skills. In other words, the teaching and the managing are exercised in the manner of the qualities of moderation. There is nothing within these two passages that necessarily suggests these two broadly similar portraits of the overseer are a rather later development of the overseers addressed in Phil. 1.1; and the probability is that the passages in the Pastoral Epistles presuppose a plurality of overseers, as in Phil. 1.1, where each overseer is responsible for his own identifiable community. It is assumed that the use of the singular in 1 Tim. 3.2 and Tit. 1.7 simply highlights that an overseer carries out his task as the singular head of a household, and in relation to a single house-church. It is not evident from 1 Tim. 3.2 and Tit. 1.7 that these cities lacked an overseer, and that Timothy and Titus should now make a new appointment of a single overseer with the qualifications listed, who could superintend the entire Christian community.

b. *Elders*

The term 'elder' is closely related to that of the overseer. They both occur only three times as a title in the Pauline corpus;[43] and they are both widely used in the Septuagint and in other Graeco-Roman sources,[44] although 'elder' is also used very frequently elsewhere in the New Testament. Unlike the term 'overseer', however, 'elder' is not found in the Pauline corpus other than in 1 Timothy and Titus.

Campbell's extensive study of the term draws the conclusion that in ancient Jewish as in Graeco-Roman societies, ' "the elders" is *more a way of speaking about leaders, than an office of leadership itself*'.[45] Campbell regards the Pastoral Epistles to be post-Pauline and resolves the conundrum as to why Paul does not use the term by noting that, '*It is the household structure of the earliest churches which is both the factor that makes the calling of people "the elders" inappropriate in the first generation,*

---

43   1 Tim. 5.17, 19; Tit. 1.5.

44   Cf. Campbell, *The Elders*, pp. 20–96, in which he concludes that 'elder' within ancient Israel and early Judaism was not an office, but an honourable status belonging to the senior heads of families, which attracted an informal authority and a measure of prestige, within what amounts to an aristocracy; and within Graeco-Roman society, the terms οἱ πρεσβύτεροι and οἱ γέροντες denoted a particular class of older person, worthy of respect.

45   Campbell, *The Elders*, p. 140, italics his.

and inevitable in the second'.[46] His point is that an elder is one who is a member of a council of elders. Campbell argues that such people were drawn from those heads of households who were held in most honour within their communities, and reflected an imprecise, but community-wide, recognition. (Thus, arguably, the majority of elders were likely also to have been heads of households, but not all heads of households were necessarily elders.) In consequence, members of a household (or house-church, for that matter) would not identify their head of house, that is their patron, as an elder for this was a collective, not an individual, term. Campbell's deduction about not addressing the head of a single household as an elder may be correct; but, nonetheless, most of our extant Pauline sources are indeed addressed to whole communities comprising multiple house-churches, which, presumably, may have recognized a council of elders, the sum of the heads of house-churches – and yet their titles do not surface in the early letters.[47]

On two occasions, clear connections are made between the ἐπίσκοπος and the πρεσβύτεροι, and this has led to a widely held conclusion that during the New Testament period there was significant overlap, if not identity, between the two. In the Lukan record of the Miletus speech, Paul addresses the Ephesian elders as those who have been appointed by the Holy Spirit to be ἐπίσκοποι (Acts 20.28).[48] In Tit. 1.5-9, Paul directs Titus to appoint elders in various towns; such people are, like the overseers listed in 1 Tim. 3.1-7, to be blameless (ἀνέγκλητος), and to have but one wife; furthermore, children are also mentioned, but on this occasion it is required that they are believers/faithful (πιστά),[49] and that they are neither reckless nor rebellious. Significantly, however, Paul immediately continues his injunction about elders by then stating: 'For an *overseer*, as God's steward, must be blameless (ἀνέγκλητος) . . .' (Tit. 1.7).

In helpful surveys, Campbell and Gehring outline four different solutions to the question about the relationship between the elders and the overseer in the Pastoral Epistles.[50] The first is that these represent two alternate and interchangeable terms for the same office.[51] The second is

---

46 Campbell, *The Elders*, p. 126, italics his.

47 We have seen that Romans and 1 Corinthians in particular refer to multiple domestic units.

48 Although Paul uses the term πρεσβύτερος rarely, Luke's account in Acts records Paul's repeated contact with the Jerusalem 'apostles and elders', as well as the appointment and presence of elders in a number of Pauline churches, cf. especially Acts 14.23; 20.17.

49 The word can mean either, and within the Pastoral Epistles it variously means the one or the other; cf. Knight, *The Pastoral Epistles*, p. 289.

50 Campbell, *The Elders*, pp. 183–93; Gehring, *House Church and Mission*, pp. 269–74.

51 The principal difficulty with this view is that 'overseer' is consistently in the singular in the Pastoral Epistles, and, in Tit. 1.7, 'elders' is plural, immediately followed by 'overseer' in the singular.

that there were only two posts: the overseers and the deacons (as in Phil. 1.1 and 1 Tim. 3.1-12); elders were instead that group of respected older men in the community, as clearly in 1 Tim. 5.1-2, where Timothy is instructed in regard to both the older men and older women.[52] The third view retrojects the Ignatian monepiscopacy into the Pastoral Epistles. In consequence, the juxtaposition of terms reflects a situation in which one overseer presides over multiple elders.[53] The fourth solution is that this context reflects early evidence of an awkward merging of two different ecclesiastical models: the Pauline household pattern of overseer and deacon (Phil. 1.1) and the Jewish-Christian synagogue and community pattern of a council of elders.

Although we have noted that scholars have increasingly begun to recognize that the early Pauline communities did indeed have leaders and a hierarchical organization, there is still a consensus that Pauline church order evolved significantly between these early communities and those represented by the later epistles. A key element of this reconstruction assumes a straight-line development from the earliest communities to the unequivocal evidence that derives from early second-century Ignatian ecclesiology, in which:

> You must all follow the bishop (ἐπίσκοπος), as Jesus Christ followed the Father, and follow the council of elders (πρεσβυτέριον), as you would the apostles; respect the deacons (διάκονοι) as the commandment of God. Nobody must do anything that has to do with the Church without the bishop['s approval]. Only that Eucharist (εὐχαριστία) which is under the authority of the bishop or whomever he himself designates is to be considered valid. Where the bishop is present, there let the congregation (πλῆθος) be, just as where Christ is, there is the universal Church (ἡ καθολικὴ ἐκκλησία). It is not possible without the bishop either to baptize or have a love-feast (ἀγάπη). But, whatever he approves pleases God as well, in order that everything you do may be sure and certain ... It is good to acknowledge God and the bishop.[54]

Although the early Pauline congregations were not as 'primitive' in their church order as previously considered, church order in the second-century communities is clearly far more structured and defined. The combination of assumptions that there was a straight-line institutionalizing develop-

---

52   This view has been propounded by Jeremias. Problems with it are recognized to be the payment of elders in 1 Tim. 5.17, and the designation or appointment (καθίστημι) of elders in Tit. 1.5.

53   Clearly, the plural reference to overseers in Phil. 1.1 reflects an earlier model of church order. Presumably such a singular office in a city would be highly prestigious, and yet the requirements of the postholder are little different to those of the deacon in 1 Tim. 3.8-13. It is difficult to see either in 1 Tim. 3.1-7 or Tit. 1.5-9 that Paul's addressees are to set about appointing someone to so singular and senior a position.

54   Ignatius, *Smyrn.* 8.1–9.1.

ment and the Pastoral Epistles reflect a stage quite different from the early Pauline mission suggests that these letters represent a point somewhere along a likely course of development that eventually led to the Ignatian monepiscopacy. Scholars then differ as to whether they consider the Pastoral Epistles to be closer to the early Pauline context or the Ignatian context.

Campbell's own solution is to argue that the growth of the church through the Pauline and post-Pauline phases was necessarily accompanied by changing connotations for the title overseer.[55] In the early phases, a singular overseer would preside over the church that met in his home. As more house-churches developed in a location, these overseers together comprised an eldership in regard to the wider Christian community – each remaining a singular overseer in regard to his own house-church. In due course, especially in the absence of apostolic oversight, it was necessary for a single overseer to emerge, from among the council of elders, with overall responsibility to direct the affairs of all the house-churches in a town – and the notion of multiple overseers, each over an individual house-church, is presumably dropped. It is this last situation, he argues, that is reflected in the Pastoral and Ignatian Epistles, especially in the appointment of a single overseer from among the elders in Tit. 1.7 and the offering of double honour to certain elders in 1 Tim. 5.17 (which must, therefore, refer to a number of overseers, each with jurisdiction in a different city).

It is clear that the two passages in the Pastoral Epistles that mention the elders do not readily propose an obvious resolution, particularly in the light of the earlier Pauline silence on elders. Not only are these passages short, but also they each contain what appears to be a puzzling transition. In Tit. 1.7, the focus moves abruptly from elder to overseer; it awkwardly repeats in consecutive verses the same qualification 'blameless' (ἀνέγκλητος), applied first to the elder, and secondly to the overseer; it moves from elders in the plural to an overseer in the singular; it uses the somewhat unexpected causal connective γάρ ('for/since/because'); and it uses almost identical phrasing to that describing the overseer (not elder) in 1 Tim. 3.2 (δεῖ γὰρ/οὖν τὸν ἐπίσκοπον ἀνέγκλητον/ἀνεπίλημπτον εἶναι). In an abbreviated form, vv 5–7 might be translated: 'you should ... appoint elders in every town (καταστήσῃς κατὰ πόλιν πρεσβυτέρους), as I directed you: if someone is blameless (ἀνέγκλητος), a husband of one wife, having faithful children ... For the overseer must be blameless (δεῖ γὰρ τὸν ἐπίσκοπον ἀνέγκλητον) ...'

1 Timothy 5 has a very different transitional conundrum. The opening verses instruct Timothy how he should address both an older man (πρεσβύτερος) and older women (πρεσβύτεραι). Instructions about

55 Campbell, *The Elders*, pp. 194–205.

addressing younger men (νεώτεροι) and women (νεώτεραι) are also included. Each should be treated, respectively, as father, mothers, brothers and sisters. The following verses continue to concern some of the older women, notably the widows, some of whom had passed the age of sixty. Depending on whether they fulfil certain criteria, including character qualifications, they should be given due honour (τίμα), and may be eligible for support. Timothy should be careful to distinguish between those widows who act appropriately, and those who do not.

The next section, 1 Tim. 5.17-22, returns again to the elders/older men (πρεσβύτεροι); however, those elders/older men who 'rule well' (καλῶς προεστῶτες) are singled out as deserving double honour (διπλῆς τιμῆς ἀξιούσθωσαν); and, further still, this honour is most especially for those who labour in word and teaching (οἱ κοπιῶντες ἐν λόγῳ καὶ διδασκαλίᾳ). Indeed, Scripture endorses that worthy workers should be supported (1 Tim. 5.18). An elder/older man should not be accused without at least two witnesses. There are, however, those who do persist in sin, and they should be publicly and impartially rebuked (1 Tim. 5.20-21). There are a few parallels between the treatment of the widows and the elders/older men, which are notable.[56] Both may be worthy of honour (τιμή) and support, depending on certain criteria. Not all widows are honourable, and similarly some of the elders/older men may be found to persist in sin. After these parallel verses, preceded by the general instructions in regard to older and younger men and women, Timothy is urged not to be over hasty in the laying on of hands.

As elsewhere, the amount of material with which we have to work makes it difficult to draw confident conclusions. The concept of a council of elders was so widespread in ancient society that there is little need for Paul to be more specific, unless he were wishing to propose a modified understanding of the term. The term πρεσβύτερος occurs sixty-six times in the New Testament, almost always used in the plural as a collegial description, synonymous with the πρεσβυτέριον; but only five times in the singular form. That is not merely to say that a community would always have more than one elder; but, more so, that an elder does not have eldership responsibilities, tasks or duties apart from within the combined meeting or gathering of elders; in this vein, Titus is urged to 'appoint elders in each town (κατὰ πόλιν)' (Tit. 1.5), and not in regard to individual house-churches. The authority of elders is exercised collectively. Accordingly, 'eldership' is not an individual office, but an honoured status, bringing with it membership of an influential and respected body. Such a council of elders would give wise counsel, and each elder would need to display the kind of qualities provided in the short list in Tit. 1.6.

---

56   Similar parallels are noted by Knight, *The Pastoral Epistles*, p. 231; and Marshall, *The Pastoral Epistles*, p. 609.

Throughout the synoptic gospels and Acts, the elders are characterized as a powerful and decisive, even formidable, group. 1 Tim. 5.17-19 insists that elders are honoured appropriately, and are not subject to accusation without at least two witnesses; but if an elder is found to have been at fault, his rebuke should be handled publicly.[57] The Pastoral Epistles add nothing further about how they were or should be perceived.

Among the five occurrences of the word in the singular, it occurs as a comparative adjective describing the 'elder' brother in the parable of the prodigal son (Lk. 15.25); and it occurs as the anonymous and somewhat oblique author of 2 and 3 John. The other two instances of the singular are found in 1 Tim. 5.1, 19. In the first, Timothy is being told how he ought to address an older man (singular). The context suggests it is likely that this is not exclusively a reference to those older men who happen to be elders. The second instance is the situation where an older man, presumably an elder, is being accused of some wrongdoing. This is not a charge against the combined eldership, but against one of its number.

In the Pastoral Epistles, however, we are told nothing of the duties or responsibilities of the council of elders, except that in 1 Tim. 4.14, they had acted together in prophesying and laying hands on Timothy, thereby imparting a gift to him. However, 1 Tim. 5.17 notes that *some* of the elders will also be involved in directing/leading/managing, and where they do this well (καλῶς προεστῶτες), they should be worthy of double honour.[58] This should apply most especially to a further subset of these elders, namely those who additionally labour in the word/message[59] and in teaching (μάλιστα οἱ κοπιῶντες ἐν λόγῳ καὶ διδασκαλίᾳ).[60] This apparent differentiation within the eldership, linked to reward, has proved problematic to interpreters. It is implausible and impractical to suppose that Timothy is being urged to ensure that all elders are rewarded within the community, and that he should ensure that their rewards are strictly in proportion to how well they carry out they responsibilities. A more straightforward interpretation is that not all elders direct/lead/manage a house-church, but those who do so should be rewarded for this

---

57 The implication of this teaching is that either there have been occurrences in which an elder or elders have been acting inappropriately, or there has been a pattern of unwarranted or over hasty accusations.

58 Cf. the similar phrase in Hermas, *Vis.* 2.4.3, 'with the presiding elders of the church (μετὰ τῶν πρεσβυτέρων τῶν προϊσταμένων τῆς ἐκκλησίας)'; and the textual variant at 1 Pet. 5.2, in addressing the elders, 'tend the flock of God among you, exercising oversight (ποιμάνατε τὸ ἐν ὑμῖν ποίμνιον τοῦ θεοῦ [ἐπισκοποῦντες])'.

59 Knight, *The Pastoral Epistles,* pp. 232–3, suggests that this simply means 'in speaking', and parallels 'teaching'.

60 Cf., however, Knight, *The Pastoral Epistles,* p. 232, who argues that μάλιστα means 'that is', rather than 'especially' – in other words the same group of people being further defined.

labour. Consistent with this verse is an understanding of elders as those who act in chorus, making decisions as a combined group, a limited number of whom carry out the additional, specific and individual role of leading; and some of these are also teachers – the two skill sets that we have seen are required of overseers, but are not essential qualifications of elders.[61] It would not be correct, on the basis of this overlap, however, to deduce that the terms 'elders' and 'overseer' are synonymous. Whereas not all elders are required to teach, preach or manage a house-church, these duties are essential for the office of overseer. Those elders who are not overseers act only and in chorus with their fellow elders on the council. In distinction, the *office* of overseer (ἐπισκοπή), with its associated duties and additional qualifications (διδακτικός; ἐκκλησίας θεοῦ ἐπιμελήσεται), was presumably given to specific individuals who would have been drawn from among the group of elders, and who had their own house-church, which they led and taught.[62] This reconstruction, in which those elders who are also overseers are involved in leading, teaching and pastoral care and oversight, is consistent with the disjunction in Tit. 1.7 and the description in 1 Tim. 5.17.

If this Pauline distinction between the collective and general responsibilities of elders and the more individual tasks and more specific duties and responsibilities of the overseer is clear, we are nonetheless left with the question as to whether an overseer in the Pauline conception came to have such a role in regard to the whole Christian community in a town, or just over his own house-church. The answer surely depends on whether teaching, and the care and leading of people was normally done in the context of the house-church, or when significant numbers of house-churches gathered together. Subsequent church history has, of course, predominantly adopted a single unit for the local church, in which almost all teaching and worship take place in a large building, created for the purpose; and where either a single leader or an overseeing group has responsibility for all leading and pastoral care, with no significant division into smaller groups as the primary context for teaching and leadership. Such a church, potentially amounting to many hundreds, clearly requires a quite different strategy and enterprise from one where most teaching, worship and leadership take place in domestic settings. This later historical context has undoubtedly influenced the interpretation of the Pastoral Epistles; however, neither the text nor archaeological evidence of

---

61   The synoptic Gospels and Acts regularly cite elders alongside, but distinct from, the scribes or 'teachers of the law' (γραμματεῖς); Mt. 16.21; 26.57; 27.41; Mk 8.31; 11.27; 14.43, 53; 15.1; Lk. 9.22; 20.1; Acts 4.5; 6.12. Expounding the law was not a core requirement of elders.

62   It may be that this combination of leaders (overseers) and elders has a broad parallel in the regular pairing of 'apostles and elders' in Acts 15.2, 4, 6, 22; 16.4, and perhaps also 'the chief priests (ἀρχιερεῖς) and elders' in the synoptic Gospels and Acts.

domestic houses suggests that teaching or group leading was normally carried out beyond the confines of the household setting. Indeed, Tit. 1.11 draws specific attention to those of the circumcision who are 'upsetting whole households (οἶκοι) by teaching things they ought not to teach', suggesting both the domestic setting for church, and for teaching.[63] Furthermore, there is nothing that convincingly suggests a monepisco-pacy in the Pastoral Epistles, that is a single overseer as head over a subordinate group of elders. The statement in 1 Tim. 3.1 that the episcopacy is a noble task does not require that there be only one overseer; indeed, we would expect rather more instruction for Timothy if this had been the case.

Two texts do highlight duties in regard to the 'church of God', presumably meaning the church of God in a locality: in 1 Tim. 3.5, overseers ought to be those who can 'take care of the church of God (ἐκκλησίας θεοῦ ἐπιμελήσεται)'; and in Acts 20.28, the elders are addressed as those who, by the Holy Spirit, have been 'appointed as overseers to shepherd the church of God (ποιμαίνειν τὴν ἐκκλησίαν τοῦ θεοῦ)' (Acts 20.28). The pastoral context is evident in both, and most clearly in Acts 20.28 (cf. ποίμνιον ... ποιμαίνειν). In this verse it is also evident that they are to 'watch out for ... *all* the flock'. Noting that Paul is addressing a group of elders in Miletus, we cannot be certain whether, unlike the situation outlined in 1 Timothy and Titus, each of the elders was also an overseer (synonymous terms); or alternatively that Paul was momentarily, but not explicitly, addressing only those elders who were also overseers; or that Luke's wording in this section of Acts 'we'-narrative is not intended as a strictly accurate description of Ephesian church order, but is a general and simplified statement. Notwithstanding this uncertainty, the phrases 'shepherd the church of God' and 'care for the church of God' may accommodate either a context where such pastoral care happened at a unified level, or at the level of the house-church unit.

My reading is that the contexts reflected in the Pastoral Epistles and Philippians, and perhaps throughout the Pauline congregations, is one where the domestic unit remained dominant, each with their appointed overseer qualified to teach and refute from the word of God, as well as care for those in their group. Those Pauline contexts where there were a significant number of house-churches may well also have had a council of elders – a group that only acted collegially, and would have comprised the overseers together with an additional number of respected men who were not qualified to teach and did not have their own house-church (and were therefore not overseers), but were nonetheless heads of their family. The duties and responsibilities of the eldership, as distinct from the overseers,

---

63 Cf. also 1 Tim. 5.13; 2 Tim. 3.6.

are not spelled out in the Pastoral Epistles. However, in the Jewish context of the synoptic Gospels and Acts, they were an authoritative group, whose role was predominantly to make decisions and pass judgements from a community-wide perspective. As in so many aspects of Pauline ecclesiology, there are gaps in the overall picture, and we cannot be certain in what ways the contexts, and therefore the instructions, reflected in 1 Timothy, Titus, Philippians and Acts 20 differed from each other.

It can be seen that this picture of the relationship between the overseer and the wider group of elders may reasonably have been a precursor to the monepiscopacy that emerged later.[64] Within the eldership, the overseers may well have been regarded as more influential since they had greater qualifications and specific responsibilities in regard to teaching and the care of a house-church, in addition to their role in the presbytery. In due course, the number of house-churches, and perhaps their size, led to a situation in which a single leading figure had authority over all the groups in a town. Such a person may well have been one of the overseers, since such people were both proficient in the word and in managing a household; and in time this title of bishop was reserved exclusively for that overall leader.

c. Deacons

The second of the two titles in Phil. 1.1 is that of διάκονος, a term that occurs much more frequently in the Pauline corpus than 'overseer' or 'elder';[65] but it is used very rarely in the Septuagint.[66] Paul uses it in a wide variety of ways, and in reference to a significant number of individuals, including: himself (1 Cor. 3.5; 2 Cor. 3.6; 6.4; Eph. 3.7; Col. 1.23, 25), Apollos (1 Cor. 3.5), Timothy (2 Cor. 3.6; 6.4 – implied; 1 Tim. 4.6), Tychicus (Eph. 6.21; Col. 4.7); Epaphras (Col. 1.7), Phoebe (Rom. 16.1), the Philippian deacons (Phil. 1.1), the Ephesian deacons (1 Tim. 3.8-13), the false apostles (2 Cor. 11.15, 23), the Roman authorities (Rom. 13.4), and Christ (Rom. 15.8; Gal. 2.17). They are 'servants' in relation to God (2 Cor. 6.4), Christ (2 Cor. 11.23; Col. 1.7; 1 Tim. 4.6), the church (Col. 1.25), the new covenant (2 Cor. 3.6), righteousness (2 Cor. 11.5), and the gospel (Eph. 3.7; Col. 1.23).

In addition, Paul uses the abstract noun, διακονία, in regard to a wide variety of contexts and range of individuals, including: himself (Rom.

---

64   Cf. the monepiscopacy, together with elders and deacons, in Ignatius, *Magn.* 6.1; *Trall.* 2.2.4; 3.1; *Smyrn.* 12.2; *Poly.* 6.1.

65   The word group including διάκονος, διακονία, and διακονέω occurs in each of the Pauline letters apart from 2 Timothy and the Thessalonian correspondence.

66   The verb διακονέω does not appear in the Septuagint; the noun διακονία appears only in 1 Macc. 11.58; and the noun διάκονος appears in 4 Macc. 9.17; Prov. 10.4; and Est. 1.10; 2.2; 6.3, 5.

11.13; 15.31; 2 Cor. 4.1; 5.18; 6.3; 2 Cor. 11.8; 1 Tim. 1.12), Stephanas and his household (1 Cor. 16.15), Archippus (Col. 4.17), Timothy (2 Tim. 4.5), Mark (2 Tim. 4.11), some of the leading figures in the Roman congregations (Rom. 12.7), some of the Corinthian Christians (1 Cor. 12.5), Christians in general (Eph. 4.12), the ministry of death and condemnation (2 Cor. 3.7, 9), the ministry of the Spirit (2 Cor. 3.8), and relief aid in the form of the collection (2 Cor. 8.4; 9.1, 12–13).

Finally, Paul uses the verb διακονέω in relation to himself (Rom. 15.25; 2 Cor. 3.3; 8.19-20), Onesiphorus (2 Tim. 1.18), Onesimus (Phlm. 13), and the Ephesian deacons (1 Tim. 3.10-13). It is clear from this spread of references that this is a key semantic domain for Paul; indeed, although it is used throughout the New Testament, it occurs significantly more frequently in Paul than elsewhere. Less clear, however, is whether it is possible to determine any unified sense in which he has used these terms. In particular, what is the status of the one who serves; what is the nature of the task of service; and was there significant development in the use of these terms over the period reflected by the New Testament?

As with the terms ἐπίσκοπος, and πρεσβύτερος, the noun διάκονος is the etymological root of an ecclesiastical title used in quite varied ways and in many church denominations today – namely deacon.[67] This denominational investment in what is seen to be a New Testament term has fuelled a number of key issues in twentieth-century scholarly debate concerning the meaning of this word group within the New Testament texts, and how its usage developed during the post-New Testament centuries. In particular, it is questioned whether the ordinary and everyday, Greek usage of the abstract noun διακονία in a domestic, servile context occludes the alternative ministry of an official, and often significant, non-servile intermediary; secondly, whether the actions and attitude of Jesus are perceived by the New Testament writers as the model for Christian διακονία; thirdly, and consequently, whether the word group is imbued already in the New Testament with specific Christian content, and comes to refer more particularly to acts of love, mercy and kindness; and fourthly, at what point the term attracts a specifically ecclesiastical dimension, referring to a church office of some responsibility.

A long-standing consensus has been built upon the 1931 work of the German theologian Wilhelm Brandt.[68] He represented the Christian usage

---

67   The title 'dean' derives instead from δεκανός and the Latin *decanus,* meaning one in charge of ten (δέκα, *decem*).

68   W. Brandt, *Dienst und Dienen im Neuen Testament* (Gütersloh: C. Bertelsmann, 1931). The consensus has more recently been maintained by L. R. Hennessey, 'Diakonia and Diakonoi in the Pre-Nicene Church', in J. P. Williman and T. Halton (eds.), *Diakonia: Studies in Honor of Robert T. Meyer* (Washington: Catholic University of America Press, 1986), pp. 60–86; E. Schüssler Fiorenza, '"Waiting at Table": A Critical Feminist Theological

of διακονία as a 'caring kind of service exemplified in its most sublime form in the actions of Jesus at the supper, where he described himself "as one who serves", and in the self-giving which led to his death'.[69] A more accessible work drawing upon Brandt's conclusions can be found in Hermann Beyer's word study of διακονέω, διακονία and διάκονος.[70] His conclusions are that the dominant New Testament understanding of διακονία maintains its roots in servile or menial contexts, but becomes qualitatively different from that of other Greek usage, and is dependent supremely on the example of Jesus. Thus, service at tables by the Seven in Acts 6.2 is understood to be a demonstration of practical love.[71] He argues that διακονέω 'comes to have the full sense of active Christian love for the neighbour and as such it is a mark of true discipleship'.[72] It is this motivation of love that enables the collection for the Jerusalem congregation to be viewed as fundamentally a service of love, and be expressed in terms of διακονία.[73] While διάκονος sometimes is seen in the New Testament as a reference to a domestic slave,[74] the term is also used in connection with the established ecclesiastical office of deacon. This is evident in Phil. 1.1 and 1 Tim. 3.8, 12, and presumably also in reference to the female διάκονος, Phoebe, in Rom. 16.1.[75]

Diverging from this dominant view is the work of Dieter Georgi in his study of Paul's opponents in 2 Corinthians. Focusing on the term διάκονος Χριστοῦ, he notes that both Paul and the opponents viewed this as a term of respect, rather than of servility. Exploring classical usage, he argues that this word group was also used in the context of sending a message, the work of an envoy.[76] Georgi concludes that the dual meanings of the servant who waits on tables and the envoy who is acting on behalf of a higher authority satisfy most New Testament occurrences of the vocabulary. Indeed, he even concludes that both the overseers and deacons of Phil. 1.1 should be regarded as those who are occupied in missionary proclamation; and that it would be wrong to read back into this early text the sense that transpired in the ecclesiastical settings of the

---

Reflection', in N. Greinacher and N. Mette (eds.), *Diakonia: Church for Others* (Edinburgh: T. & T. Clark, 1988), pp. 84–94; and J. Pinnock, 'The History of the Diaconate', in C. Hall (ed.), *The Deacon's Ministry* (Leominster: Gracewing, 1991), pp. 9–24.

69   J. N. Collins, 'Once More on Ministry: Forcing a Turnover in the Linguistic Field', *One in Christ* 27 (1991), p. 239.

70   H. W. Beyer, 'διακονέω, διακονία, διάκονος', in G. Kittel (ed.), *TDNT* (vol. 2 [D–E]; Grand Rapids; London: Eerdmans, 1964), pp. 81–93.

71   Beyer, 'διακονέω, διακονία, διάκονος', p. 84.

72   Beyer, 'διακονέω, διακονία, διάκονος', p. 85.

73   Beyer, 'διακονέω, διακονία, διάκονος', p. 88.

74   Mt. 22.13; Jn 2.5, 9;

75   Beyer, 'διακονέω, διακονία, διάκονος', pp. 88–93.

76   D. Georgi, *The Opponents of Paul in Second Corinthians* (SNTW; Edinburgh: T. & T. Clark, 1987), pp. 27–8.

Ignatian and Pastoral Epistles where there is a degree of subordination of deacon to overseer or elder.[77]

The most extensive and significant lexical investigation of the διακονία word group is to be found in a monograph by John Collins. He explores the non-Christian Greek literary and some non-literary sources in order to determine whether a servile context for this word group dominated Hellenistic usage. He concluded that a third of all Greek usage of the term διακονία and its cognates is in relation to conveying a message or delivering an errand. This includes being a spokesman or messenger of god.[78] A further application concerns the carrying out of deeds, rather than the conveying of words. These are fewer in number, but again do include specific actions carried out at the behest of a god.[79] Such tasks are neither menial nor servile, but the key idea is consistently that of a 'go-between' or representative. In Plato's *Republic*, διάκονος describes the merchant or trader who renders service to the state as an exporter and importer of goods from other cities. As such, he is an essential 'go-between' and performs a commercial, rather than servile role; and, in terms of social status, is, therefore, part of the commercial, rather than servile, class.[80]

These contexts in which διακονία language is used of a go-between, whether of messages, goods or deeds, do not resolve the meaning of such language when found in relation to clearly domestic and servile contexts. Therefore, Collins devotes significant space to examples that reflect such contexts. The subjects are often slaves, and the tasks often concern household chores, including waiting at tables. He argues, however, that dominant even within these contexts is 'activity of an in-between kind'.[81] The idea of menial service is neither essential nor dominant. He concludes that,

> the words show no signs of having developed in meaning over the course of changing literary eras, the sense 'to serve at table' cannot be called 'the basic meaning' ... and the more comprehensive idea of 'serving' is vague and inadequate. If the words denote actions or positions of 'inferior value,' there is at the same time often the connotation of something special, even dignified, about the circumstance.[82]

---

77   Georgi, *The Opponents of Paul in Second Corinthians*, pp. 29–31. This is an instance where the prior assumption of a process of significant institutionalization between the early Pauline letters and the Pastoral Epistles determines that Phil. 1.1 must either be anachronistic or carry an alternative interpretation to its usage 1 Timothy.

78   Collins, *Diakonia*, pp. 96–132.

79   Collins, *Diakonia*, pp. 133–49.

80   Plato, *Republic* 370–1, cited in Collins, *Diakonia*, pp. 78–9.

81   Collins, *Diakonia*, p. 335.

82   Collins, *Diakonia*, p. 194; cf. also ibid., pp. 93–5.

Collins concludes from his survey that, although the word group most commonly occurs within a servile context, the terms carry no *necessary* sense of lowliness, servitude or inferior status.[83] Indeed, people of all classes occupy such roles, and while they are subordinate to those they serve, there is no necessary derogatory note attached to their service or status. It is this element that, Collins considers, undermines the dominant consensus in regard to New Testament usage of the terms.[84] Instead, he argues that early Christian usage was broadly consistent with non-Christian usage. In other words, the root sense remained one of agency or representation. It is the nature of the task that is the dominant idea, rather than its servile status. Accordingly, individuals of high status regularly perform work that is described as διακονία, and, in the main, these refer to messages from heaven, messages between churches, and commissions within a church, and therefore presuppose a mandated authority. It is in this vein that he understands the phrase διακονία τοῦ λόγου in Acts 6.4. The Son of Man saying in Mk 10.45, 'the Son of Man came not to be served but to serve [διακονηθῆναι ἀλλὰ διακονῆσαι], and to give his life as a ransom for many', should be understood in the context of the soteriological focus of the last clause in the statement, 'give his life as a ransom for many', which significantly qualifies the nature of the service as a divine commission. Paul's self-description as a διάκονος of Christ (2 Cor. 11.23) does not mean that he carried out menial work at the behest of Christ, but that his authority derives from his position as an agent of Christ. In this way, a διάκονος at the same time holds a position of subordination to the one whom he serves, and yet, as a representative of the one he serves, he carries the responsibility and authority that derives from the one he serves.[85] Similarly the collection for the Jerusalem Christians was a commission, and the dominant concept underlying the designation 'deacon' is not serving at tables but attendance on a person; and that person is the bishop, not the congregation. As such the deacon is subordinate to the overseer and attends him.[86] These conclusions, if correct, presage a major overturning of the consensus generated by Brandt and Beyer. At the heart is a sense that the early Christian church did adopt and make significant use of the διακονία word group; but, in the process, they did little to imbue it with new meaning. Thus, although διακονία and its cognates are used comparatively rarely over a thousand

---

83   Collins, *Diakonia*, p. 75; 'service at table is the most common single reference' accounting for 'about a quarter of all instances' and a further quarter might broadly be considered menial domestic contexts.

84   Collins, *Diakonia*, p. 335.

85   Cf. Campbell, *The Elders*, p. 134.

86   Collins, *Diakonia*, p. 337.

years of Greek literature, their use is remarkably consistent, and is generally adopted within the New Testament.[87]

The model of Jesus is often taken to be a lynchpin for arguments as to whether or not Paul used the διακονία word group with peculiarly Christian content, and by extension whether there is additionally an ecclesiastical office in mind. There are three over-riding elements to the argument for a dominical source to Christian usage: the Isaianic servant songs,[88] and the only two synoptic statements that use the verb διακονέω in relation to Jesus. The parallel passages of Mk 10.45 and Lk. 22.27 apply the verb to Jesus, in different contexts – one more obviously of waiting at table: 'For who is greater, the one who is at the table or the one who serves (διακονῶν)? Is it not the one at the table? But I am among you as one who serves (ὁ διακονῶν)'. Unlike in the ransom statement of Mk 10.45, the soteriological element is absent in this instance, and instead the focus is servile, and is to be emulated by his followers. In the surrounding contexts of both of these sayings there are dominical instructions to the disciples to act as servants.[89] It is clearly significant, however, that in both of these settings, it is a dispute among the disciples as to which of them should be regarded as the greater that prompts Jesus' contrasting model of himself as a servant. Similarly, in both contexts there is a contrast between Jesus and the Gentile rulers, the former characterized as a servant, and the latter as authoritarian leaders.[90] The underlying thrust of the dominical message is clearly addressing the inappropriate assumption of high status. Collins, however, adopts the unsatisfactory conclusion that the original context of the saying underlying these two verses is sufficiently clouded to preclude reaching a clear conclusion as to the sense of διακονία in these synoptic parallels. Instead, he focuses more on the meaning in non-biblical sources. He notes that scholars differ widely on their understanding of the nature of the Son of Man's service as described in this verse; with such lack of agreement, he then concludes that there are little confident grounds for assuming that the modern ecclesiological and

87 Collins, *Diakonia*, p. 74.

88 Although, note that the Septuagint of the servant songs predominantly uses the παῖς word group, and secondarily the δοῦλος word group; not the διάκονος word group.

89 Although Collins argues that the uncertainty about the original setting of these sayings weakens their influence as a basis for later meaning, it seems to me on the contrary that the consistently servile element reinforces the meaning of the concept. Cf. Collins, *Diakonia*, pp. 61–2.

90 Cf. Collins, *Diakonia*, pp. 46–62, particularly with regard to Mk 10.42-45 and Lk. 22.25-27. P. Ellingworth, 'Translating the Language of Leadership', *BT* 49 (1998), p. 130, points out that in Lk. 22.26 Jesus is recorded as advocating precisely that quality of servanthood that is contrasted with that of civil, military and religious leaders, thus, ὁ ἡγούμενος [γινέσθω] ὡς ὁ διακονῶν; whereas in Mt. 2.6 Jesus is described, in civil leadership terms, as a ἡγούμενος, albeit one who will 'shepherd (ποιμανεῖ; RSV, "govern") the people of Israel'.

technical uses of διακονία find precedent in the much more general use of the concept recorded in Mark. Furthermore, Collins argues that the use of simile in Lk. 22.26-17 – Jesus is among them *as* one who serves, the greatest amongst them should be *as* the youngest, and the one who rules *as* the one who serves – weakens the connotation of 'service' in this verse.[91] He argues, unconvincingly, that 'the simile refers only to events there at table; the image of waiter would be an unnatural figure by which to allude beyond the supper to situations like Jesus' care for the disciples or for the sick'.[92] In regard to the phrase 'If any one would be first, he must be last of all *and servant of all* (πάντων διάκονος)' in Mk 9.33-35, Collins notes again that 'the teaching has an uncertain home in the tradition',[93] and, 'No special significance, consequently, attaches to the occurrences of the term διάκονος in these sayings, and there is no call to explain its presence by way of a connection with its currency in the language of church order or in any other part of a presumed Christian lexicon'.[94] Notwithstanding these arguments, Collins does concede that διακονία words 'In the gospels ... mainly designate menial attendance of one kind or another'.[95]

This extended foray into the synoptic accounts has been important in order to evaluate to what extent Collins' attempts to detach from the διακονία word group the idea of service have been convincing. In these particular instances, I remain unpersuaded by his arguments, and consider, instead, that the notion of service was in any case an integral element of the dominical message and was, at times, conveyed by means of this word group. This is not to say, of course, that Georgi and Collins have been wrong to identify the aspects of spokesman and emissary in this word group. Rather, the divorcing of all aspects of menial service is clearly forced.

We have already noted both the wide range of individuals who are

---

91   Collins, *Diakonia*, p. 246, 'we are thereby alerted to the fact that the point of the teaching is not going to be found in its literal reading'.

92   Collins, *Diakonia*, p. 247.

93   Collins, *Diakonia*, p. 247. Cf. ibid., pp. 330–1, where he notes that Mk 9.35 includes 'slave of all', but does not suggest that this allows for any more widespread an application.

94   Collins, *Diakonia*, p. 248.

95   Collins, *Diakonia*, p. 245. We see, for example, that the clearly menial word 'slave' (δοῦλος) is sometimes linked with the verb 'to serve' (διακονέω) in the context of serving at tables. Collins points out that it is the Hellenistic evangelist who brings out this connection. In Lk. 17.7-10, for example, a parable is recorded that cites a slave (δοῦλος) who waits at table (διακονέω) for his master, and who expects no more than to fulfil this duty as an 'unworthy slave'. The distinction in status and expectations between the master and the slave is emphasized. Similarly, in Lk. 12.37 a parable is recorded where the slaves (δοῦλοι) of a master are commended for being ready for their master's return. The master rewards them by seating them at the table and waiting on (διακονέω) them himself. The notion of spokesman is not intended. Rather the reversal of status is here significant.

identified by Paul as διάκονοι, and the variety of tasks described as διακονία. It is immediately clear that the narrow ecclesiastical office of 'deacon' will account for very few of the occurrences of these words.[96] Furthermore, the notion of serving is a clear element of Pauline leadership, and his choice of words is not limited to this particular word group.[97] Nonetheless, those interpreters who assume διακονία always carries menial or servile connotations are incorrect. In similar fashion, a servile element is also not an essential ingredient, of course, of the English words, 'servant', 'service' or 'serve'.[98] Rather, the διακονία word group carries a range of meanings, including, on occasion, the sense of an authorized 'go-between', as identified by Collins. As with a few of the synoptic texts, however, we have seen that it would be wrong to divorce the notion of low status and menial tasks from all of these references. I have argued elsewhere that Collins' interpretation of 1 Cor. 3.5 in which Paul and Apollos are divine spokesmen, mediating the word, again misinterprets the wider context.[99] Paul and Apollos, the διάκονοι, are not presented here as honoured intermediaries of God. The metaphor of menial work is significant. These apostles are workers with God (θεοῦ ... συνεργοί), but have quite different tasks from him, and their status is expressly 'nothing' (1 Cor. 3.7), which is reinforced within a passage that criticises the Corinthians for acting according to secular values and boasting about status (1 Cor. 3.1-4, 18-23); and is succeeded in the following chapter by further analogies of the apostles as servants and stewards (ὑπηρέται Χριστοῦ καὶ οἰκονόμοι, 1 Cor. 4.1). Similarly, in both 2 Cor. 6.4 and 11.23 Paul's self-description as θεοῦ διάκονοι is juxtaposed with a catalogue of sufferings that highlights his lack of status, rather than his honour.[100] There are, consequently, instances in which the status of divine intermediaries of the word is not the main idea conveyed by these terms.

The noun διάκονος occurs only five times in the synoptic Gospels; on four occasions, as we have seen, on the lips of Jesus.[101] It occurs in one

---

96   Of the twenty-one instances of διάκονος in the Pauline corpus, the NRSV translates only four of these as 'deacon/s': Rom. 16.1; Phil. 1.1; 1 Tim. 3.8, 12.

97   This will be explored further in the next chapter.

98   Similarly, the sense that 'minister' has a menial or subordinate connotation is obsolete; cf. *Oxford English Dictionary Online* (Oxford: Oxford University Press, 2000) ad loc.

99   Clarke, *Serve the Community of the Church*, pp. 241–2; cf. Collins, *Diakonia*, p. 195.

100   Cf. Clarke, *Serve the Community of the Church*, pp. 242–3. Note that Epaphras and Tychicus are described in terms that juxtapose the serving and the servile word groups (Ἐπαφρᾶ τοῦ ἀγαπητοῦ συνδούλου ἡμῶν, ὅς ἐστιν πιστὸς ὑπὲρ ὑμῶν διάκονος τοῦ Χριστοῦ, Col. 1.7; Τύχικος ὁ ἀγαπητὸς ἀδελφὸς καὶ πιστὸς διάκονος καὶ σύνδουλος ἐν κυρίῳ, Col. 4.7).

101   Mt. 20.26; 23.11; Mk 9.35; 10.43.

Johannine pericope in reference to domestic servants.[102] Additionally, in Jn 12.26, the one who serves Jesus is described as his διάκονος. Apart from these eight references, all of the remaining twenty-one New Testament occurrences of the noun are Pauline. Almost all of these references are not to a local ecclesiastical office, however; rather, they include διάκονος of: God,[103] the Lord,[104] Christ,[105] the church at large,[106] a new covenant,[107] the gospel,[108] or Satan.[109] Although within the New Testament this is a predominantly Pauline term, only three passages identify someone as a διάκονος of a local church. These few references are distributed as widely as Romans, Philippians and 1 Timothy.[110]

We have determined that the passage in Phil. 1.1 reveals no further content about the role or nature of being a deacon, other than as a role alongside the overseers. Rom. 16.1 introduces Phoebe as a deacon of the church in Cenchreae,[111] a seaport to the south-east of Corinth. It has been deduced that she was a wealthy lady within her church, evidenced by her apparent status as a generous benefactor (προστάτις, Rom. 16.2),[112] and this verse additionally highlights Paul's endorsement of women as

---

102   Jn 2.5, 9. Cf. also Mt. 22.13.

103   Rom. 13.4; 2 Cor. 6.4.

104   1 Cor. 3.5; Eph. 6.21; Col. 4.7.

105   2 Cor. 11.23; Col. 1.7; 1 Tim. 4.6.

106   Col. 1.25.

107   2 Cor. 3.6.

108   Eph. 3.7; Col. 1.23.

109   2 Cor. 11.15.

110   Rom. 16.1 (Cenchreae); Phil. 1.1 (Philippi); 1 Tim. 3.8-13 (Ephesus).

111   Dunn, *Romans 9–16*, pp. 886–7, argues that it is the presence of the participle (οὖσαν ... διάκονον) that suggests a designated role in the church; although he suggests that this is one of hospitality. Dunn's view of significant development between the early Pauline contexts and the Pastoral Epistles means that he has to conclude, with many others, that: 'it would be premature to speak of an established office of diaconate, as though a role of responsibility and authority with properly appointed succession, had already been agreed upon in the Pauline churches ... the same is true of Phil 1.1, where responsibilities are not even hinted at; but in 1 Tim 3.8-13 the reality of church office has taken clear form'. C. E. B. Cranfield, *A Critical and Exegetical Commentary on the Epistle to the Romans* (ICC; Edinburgh: T. & T. Clark, 1979), p. 781, is convinced that there is parity between the title here and that in Phil. 1.1 and 1 Tim. 3.8, 12. Although he finds no evidence of the function of the deacon in any of these passages, he surmises that the role is not one of leadership: 'there is nothing in any of these passages in any way inconsonant with the inherent probability that a specialized use of διάκονος in NT times will have corresponded to the clearly attested specialized use of διακονεῖν and διακονία with reference to the practical service of the needy.'

112   This term, here in its feminine form, is variously taken to be either a wealthy benefactor or merely a helper. In the Septuagint, its masculine form, προστάτης, is used to identify a ruler or other officer (1 Chron. 27.31; 29.6; 2 Chron. 8.10; 24.11; 1 Esd. 2.8; 2 Macc. 3.4). Cf. my wider discussion of Phoebe as patron in A. D. Clarke, 'Jew and Greek, Slave and Free, Male and Female: Paul's Theology of Ethnic, Social and Gender

deacons.[113] The passage that offers the most information about the deacons is 1 Tim. 3.8-13, immediately following the description of the overseer. In so far as neither Rom. 16.1, nor Phil. 1.1 provides content to our understanding of the nature of the deacons, many interpreters, again influenced by the overwhelming consensus of a straight-line development of Pauline ministry from the early letters to the Pastoral epistles, assume that Phoebe and the Philippian deacons had qualitatively different roles from that presupposed in 1 Tim. 3.8-13.[114] This is clearly an argument that none of these passages can sustain or refute.

As with the overseers and elders in the Pastoral Epistles, Timothy is instructed in regard to the disposition of the διάκονοι. They are to be of good character (σεμνός), holding to the mysteries of faith with a good conscience,[115] not hypocritical or given to pretence (δίλογος), and not shamefully greedy for material profit (αἰσχροκερδής). Furthermore, they must be tested before being permitted to serve as deacons. As with the overseer, the deacons are expected to be blameless (ἀνέγκλητος), not persistently given to drinking wine (οἴνῳ πολλῷ προσέχοντας), able to manage their household and children well (καλῶς προϊστάμενοι),[116] and be the husband of one wife. In addition, the 'deacon's wife' must also be of good character (σεμνή), not a gossip (διάβολος, deriving from διαβάλλω, 'slander/gossip'), entirely trustworthy/faithful (πιστῆς ἐν πᾶσιν), and like the overseer, she must be sober/restrained (νηφάλια). It is disputed, and far from clear, whether the introduction of the wives/ women at this point is a reference to female deacons, or to the spouses of

---

Inclusiveness in Romans 16', in P. Oakes (ed.), *Rome in the Bible and the Early Church* (Carlisle; Grand Rapids: Paternoster; Baker, 2002), pp. 115–18; also Jewett, *Romans*, pp. 946–7; and Dunn, *Romans 9–16*, pp. 888–9.

113 Jewett, *Romans*, p. 944, considers that Phoebe may even have been the leader of the congregation in Cenchreae, although this cannot be substantiated. In support of this he adduces Rom. 11.13; 12.7 and 13.4, but a connection between Phoebe and the nature of διακονία in these other verses is not clear. Similarly, E. Schüssler Fiorenza, *In Memory of Her: A Feminist Theological Reconstruction of Christian Origins* (London: SCM Press, 1983), p. 171, supposes that Phoebe is involved in missionary work and preaching, but the text does not sustain such details.

114 O'Brien, *Philippians*, p. 48, and others, maintain that both titles in Phil. 1.1 refer to established offices at the time of Paul's writing to the Philippians.

115 Marshall, *The Pastoral Epistles*, pp. 485–7, translates this as 'the deep truths', and suggests that this is analogous to the ability to teach required of the overseer. I agree with Marshall that it is not necessary to suppose that the primary role of the deacon was in carrying out practical tasks; I argue for greater overlap than many between the roles of the overseer and the deacons by virtue of their proven ability to lead a household; however, a requirement to teach is not clearly present.

116 Cf. 1 Tim. 3.3, in reference to the overseer.

deacons, or whether this list of qualifications suggests that a husband and wife may well work together in a team ministry.[117]

Timothy needs to be told nothing in regard to the role of deacons. By analogy with the description of the overseer, however, it may be that the references to the family and household suggest that their function is within the domestic context of the house-church. In this way, both the overseer and the deacons have a duty to lead (προϊστάμενοι) within the house-church. On this reconstruction, the role of the deacon is neither menial nor servile, and it concerns the leadership of people, rather than the administration of things. We have noted that Phoebe was probably being commended for her generosity as a patroness, in which case we may reasonably assume that she had and managed her own household (Rom. 16.1-2). Our reconstruction of the office of overseer, however, recognized both a leadership and teaching role in regard to an individual house-church, together with a function within the council of elders. In contrast, the deacons are mentioned in the plural, and it is therefore not clear they have a singular role in regard to a house-church, neither do they have a teaching responsibility, and nor are they associated with the council of elders. From this, it may reasonably be deduced that the overseer had greater responsibilities than the deacon, but that there is a measure of overlap in their spheres of duty.[118] Such a reconstruction is not inconsistent with the pairing and ordering of the two titles in Phil. 1.1.

The requirements of both the overseer and deacons in regard to a wife and a household context may suggest that, in both cases, the husband and wife together would share responsibilities in regard to the house-church, just as both would have had significant roles in regard to their own household. We have already noted the pairing of Aquila and Prisca/Priscilla who are understood from Acts 18.2 to be a married couple; and also the recognition of Phoebe as a deacon of the church at Cenchreae. These two observations suggest both the possibility of married couples sharing a role in regard to a house-church and of a woman acting,

---

117 Knight, *The Pastoral Epistle*, pp. 171–2, makes a plausible case that this list of qualities favours a team ministry shared between husband and wife, especially given the household context. Marshall, *The Pastoral Epistles*, pp. 492–5, argues on the contrary that female deacons is implied by the comparative ὡσαύτως, thus, female deacons, in the same way as male deacons. He notes the absence of an evaluation of the wife of an overseer.

118 An interesting distinction between two qualitatively different roles is seen in the following quotation from a quite different context (cited in Collins, *Diakonia*, p. 149): Iamblichus, *De Myst.* 1.20: 'That which is divine is of a ruling nature, and presides over the different orders of being [ἡγεμονικὸν καὶ προιστάμενον]; but that which is daemoniacal is of a ministrand nature [διακονικόν], and receives whatever the gods may announce, promptly employing manual operation, as it were in things which the gods intellectually perceive, wish and command.' In 1 Tim. 3.12, however, deacons are required to be able to demonstrate being προϊστάμενοι. As a head of a household, a servile connotation is, therefore, out of place.

apparently alone, as a deacon. These instances, together with the apparently unsystematic and overlapping list of character qualifications for the overseer, elders, deacons and deacons' wives may suggest that the instructions about the overseer and deacons in regard to their households are not tightly framed, and may not preclude heads of household who were unmarried, or were female, or had no children.

3. *A Collective Title*

At this point we should note one skill that has been identified in regard to the overseer, deacons, and a number of elders – namely, that of leading or managing (προΐστημι) a household; in regard to the overseer: τοῦ ἰδίου οἴκου καλῶς προϊστάμενον, and τοῦ ἰδίου οἴκου προστῆναι (1 Tim. 3.4); in regard to the deacons: τέκνων καλῶς προϊστάμενοι καὶ τῶν ἰδίων οἴκων (1 Tim. 3.12); and in regard to some of the elders: οἱ καλῶς προεστῶτες πρεσβύτεροι (1 Tim. 5.17). It is surely significant that this verb is also used in regard to a gifted individual in Rom. 12.8 (ὁ προϊστάμενος ἐν σπουδῇ)[119] and the entire group of leaders in 1 Thess. 5.12 (εἰδέναι τοὺς κοπιῶντας ἐν ὑμῖν καὶ προϊσταμένους ὑμῶν ἐν κυρίῳ καὶ νουθετοῦντας ὑμᾶς).[120]

The reference in Rom. 12.8 occurs as part of a list of variously gifted individuals, including the prophet, the teacher, and the exhorter/preacher. The reference in 1 Thess. 5.12 is our earliest Pauline reference to leaders,[121] and describes their tasks as 'labouring' (κοπιάω)[122] among the brothers and 'admonishing/exhorting' (νουθετέω) them in the Lord. The first of these terms is used in 1 Tim. 5.17 in connection with those elders

---

119   Cranfield, *Romans*, pp. 625–6, cites Rufinus's version of Origen, *qui praeest ecclesiae*, suggesting a leader; although, he finally adopts a line later taken up by Dunn, *Romans 9–16*, p. 731, who, favours the sense of 'give aid' rather than 'lead' on the grounds that it ranks too far down the list of gifts to be a reference to a leader, and that it occurs between two 'forms of aid giving'.

120   F. F. Bruce, *1 and 2 Thessalonians* (WBC; Waco: Word Books, 1982), p. 118, notes that these three present participles are governed by one article, and therefore they reflect a single group of people; however, occurring second in the list, προϊσταμένους is not to be taken as an official designation or title, but a description; cf. similarly C. A. Wanamaker, *The Epistles to the Thessalonians: A Commentary on the Greek Text* (NIGTC; Grand Rapids; Exeter: Eerdmans; Paternoster Press, 1990), pp. 192–4, who argues that there were no official leadership roles appointed by Paul at this stage, but that leading figures had emerged. In this instance, he draws a parallel first with the cognate word προστάτις applied in regard to Phoebe in Rom. 16.2, and suggests that a similar idea of patronage is intended; and secondly with Stephanas in 1 Cor. 16.16-18, who appears to have been a patron figure in Achaia.

121   Cf. also the similar idea conveyed in regard to οἱ ἡγούμενοι in Heb. 13.7, 17, 24.

122   Cf. also in 1 Thess. 1.3.

who 'labour in the word',[123] and it also describes the work of the leaders in the household of Stephanas (1 Cor. 16.16), and three women mentioned in Rom. 16.6, 12 (Mary, Tryphaena and Tryphosa). Paul additionally uses it repeatedly of his own ministry (Gal. 4.11; Phil. 2.16; Col. 1.29; 1 Tim. 4.10). Not only does Paul 'admonish/exhort' (1 Cor. 4.14; Col. 1.28), but he also urges the readers of a number of his letters to 'admonish/exhort' where appropriate (Rom. 15.14; Col. 3.16; 1 Thess. 5.14; 2 Thess. 3.15) – although it may well be that these general exhortations to admonish would only be carried out by those recognized as leaders within a congregation. The verb suggests challenging the spiritual, moral or ethical conduct of fellow believers.

The verb προΐστημι used in 1 Tim. 3.4, 12; 5.17 clearly has the sense of an elevated position ('set over/at the head of'), and has associated connotations of protecting, guarding, helping or caring.[124] In these three instances, together with 1 Thess. 5.12, and presumably also Rom. 12.8, the role is significant in regard to a defined group of people.[125] If, as is likely, the word carries a similar sense in all five passages, then the analogy of being the head of a household significantly qualifies the nature of that leading, and ought to influence one's interpretation; in other words, it is not being applied to the leading of a large group, with its associations of significant honour.[126] In a number of these contexts it is associated with teaching or exhorting (1 Thess. 5.12; 1 Tim. 3.4; 5.17), and it is also juxtaposed with teaching in Rom. 12.8. A number of these contexts also share the notion of the honour and respect associated with the role. In 1 Thess. 5.12 this is conveyed by the verb 'to recognise' (οἶδα);[127] in 1 Tim. 3.4, the children of the overseer are to be marked by their respect

---

123   Cf. Wanamaker, *The Epistles to the Thessalonians*, p. 192, who argues that it is normally associated with spreading the gospel.

124   Knight, *The Pastoral Epistles*, p. 161 associates in 1 Tim. 3.4-5 the verbs προΐστημι and ἐπιμελέομαι, thereby stressing the caring and pastoral qualities of προϊστάμενος, rather than the leading. Gehring, *House Church and Mission*, pp. 198–9, associates the 'caretaker' and the 'ruler' aspects of this term, considering them not mutually exclusive in the Graeco-Roman world. The patron figure had a duty of care. He considers the same set of notions of helping and directing are conveyed by the juxtaposed pair of terms ἀντιλήμψεις and κυβερνήσεις in 1 Cor. 12.28; and the notion of protection conveyed by the patronal word προστάτις in Rom. 16.2.

125   Bockmuehl, *Philippians*, pp. 53–4, associates the task of oversight with both the προϊστάμενος of Rom. 12.8 and the προϊστάμενοι of 1 Thess. 5.12.

126   English translations adopt a range of words, not all of which are immediately obvious from the household context: 'rule' (1 Tim. 3.4-5, 12, KJV; 1 Tim. 5.17, RSV/NRSV/AV; Rom. 12.8, AV); 'direct' (1 Tim. 5.17, NIV); 'manage' (1 Tim. 3.4-5, 12, NIV/RSV/NRSV); 'govern' (Rom. 12.8, NIV); 'lead' (Rom. 12.8, NRSV); 'give aid' (Rom. 12.8, RSV); 'be over someone' (1 Thess. 5.12, NIV/RSV/AV); and 'have charge' (1 Thess. 5.12, NRSV).

127   Wanamaker, *The Epistles to the Thessalonians*, p. 192, suggests 'acknowledge'.

(σεμνότης);[128] in 1 Tim. 5.17, those elders who lead their households well are to be worth of double honour (τιμή); in 1 Cor. 16.18, the household of Stephanas is to be recognized (ἐπιγινώσκω); in Rom. 16.2, Phoebe is to be treated worthily;[129] and we have noted that the overseer in 1 Tim. 3.7 is even to have earned the respect of outsiders.

What now emerges as significant, however, is that teaching, labouring, respect, and being a competent head of a household are common themes across a number of these references, although not all aspects are present in every instance. Furthermore, these leaders who, in large measure share similar duties and qualities, are identified in a number of different Pauline epistles, ranging from the earliest (1 Thessalonians) to the latest (the Pastoral Epistles). This combination of texts suggests the significant possibility that there was remarkable consistency across the Pauline congregations during the New Testament period. As noted above, this is not to suggest that there is little institutionalisation in the later contexts, but simply that the later contexts are not as markedly different from the earlier ones as the majority of scholars have held; and certainly that the differences between the later and the earlier letters are not sufficiently clear to demand that the same terms in both should be understood differently.[130] The fact that one or more of the titles overseer, elder and deacon occur in Romans, Philippians, 1 Timothy and Titus, but not in 1 Thessalonians, 1 Corinthians or elsewhere is not necessarily significant. Whether or not people with such titles existed in these other communities cannot be determined on the basis of the absence of such titles in a particular letter. There may have been differences between these churches in terms of the name and number of titled roles that each required; but, nonetheless, such titled roles existed in communities represented by a significant number of the letters, and deriving from a significantly wide time period, and addressed to quite different geographical areas.

Significantly, the verb προΐστημι links both the earliest and the latest of the Pauline letters as a descriptive term that identifies the leaders. In 1 Thess. 5.12 the present participle οἱ προϊστάμενοι is a generic descriptor that seems to incorporate all those who lead in the church. In much the same way the present participle οἱ ἡγούμενοι is consistently used in Hebrews as a collective term always to describe their leaders.[131] In 1 Tim. 3.4, 12; 5.17 the term is separately used to describe the skills of the overseer, the deacons and, I have argued, those elders who additionally

128 Knight, *The Pastoral Epistles*, p. 162, however, allows the possibility that both the children and the father should demonstrate this quality.

129 Jewett, *Romans*, p. 945, associates this with the Latin *dignitas*, that is 'honors suitable to her position as a congregational leader'.

130 Cf. especially the tendency to understand the titles in Phil. 1.1 and Rom. 16.1 differently from the same titles in 1 Timothy and Titus.

131 Heb. 13.7, 17, 24.

have a leading role in a household. In neither 1 Thessalonians, Hebrews nor Romans are the leaders identified specifically as overseers, elders or deacons, although we have seen that Rom. 12.7 does highlight one person who is involved in διακονία, and the church in Rome is introduced to one from Cenchreae who is a διάκονος of that church.[132] I have argued that in Acts 20.17-35 and 1 Tim. 5.17-25 'elders' is a term that includes the overseers, a term used in connection with those who oversee a particular house-church, but it is not synonymous with overseers.

Although in Phil. 1.1 Paul uses the distinct titles of overseers and deacons, it is my contention that the term οἱ προϊστάμενοι would have been an alternative, inclusive term that all the believers in Philippi would have understood; and similarly the readers of both 1 Timothy and Titus would have understood this term, without confusion. By extension, although this is more suppositional, I would argue that Paul might well have used one of the alternative, but more convoluted, phrases, 'overseers and deacons', 'elders and deacons' or 'elders, overseers and deacons' in 1 Thess. 5.12.[133] We do not, of course, know which of these three offices existed in Thessalonica, if any. It may plausibly be argued that the church in Crete, to which the letter to Titus refers, was at such an early stage that it had no deacons. It is also possible that the church in Philippi had no need for a council of elders. Consequently, it seems to me not only that different churches had different combinations of these three offices, depending principally on the size and number of their house-churches; secondly, that all the leaders in a given location, irrespective of their titles, could reasonably be recognized by a collective term – which might be translated 'leaders'; and thirdly that the clear existence of overseers and deacons in Philippi in perhaps the late 50s CE (depending on the location of the imprisonment), and of deacons at the time of writing Romans in the mid-50s CE, does not preclude that the church in Thessalonica had their own overseers, and perhaps also elders and deacons, who were together identified by a collective term in the earliest of our New Testament documents.

---

132   Jewett, *Romans*, p. 748, suggests that it is too early for the term in Rom. 12.7 to be a reference to an ecclesiastical office, and yet in Rom. 16.1 he allows this in the case of Phoebe from Cenchreae; Dunn, *Romans 9–16*, p. 729, plausibly notes that the focus in Rom. 12.7 is on the particular ministry (διακονία), rather than on the person (ὁ διακονῶν); and Cranfield, *Romans*, p. 622, argues that it denotes 'a range of activities similar to that which came to be the province of the deacon' – although, in regard to Phoebe, he, like Jewett, is convinced that such an office already existed.

133   Gehring, *House Church and Mission*, p. 198, adopts the hypothesis that 'initially a person's status as office holder did not appear worth mentioning and that over time the office holders naturally emerged out of the house church setting'.

4. *Missing Titles*

Although we have noted that each of the three titles of overseer, elder and deacon occurs only rarely in the Pauline corpus and that there are instances where Paul does not, or cannot, use official titles for leaders, it is also significant that a number of other available and contemporary titles are apparently not adopted within the Pauline communities. In particular, ἄρχων which occurs in Rom. 13.3, 1 Cor. 2.6, 8 and Eph. 2.2, is reserved for reference to the imperial rulers, the rulers of this age, and the ruler of the power of the air. In the synoptic records and Acts, it is used most frequently by Luke, and it reflects contemporary usage as a title for the ruler of a synagogue;[134] a ruler of the Pharisees;[135] the Jewish rulers;[136] the demonic ruler;[137] the 'rulers of the Gentiles';[138] a Gentile ruler;[139] the magistrate;[140] and generic ruling.[141] An associated word is ἀρχηγός, which occurs very widely in the Septuagint especially of a significant leader of a very large group of people, but in the New Testament it is used exclusively of the exalted Christ, and does not occur in the Pauline corpus.[142] These related terms have a number of connotations, many of which could well have been viewed by Paul as inappropriate for the church, and especially in a domestic setting. The notion of 'ruling' is strong, and is often applied in a sovereign or imperial context.

The present participle ἡγούμενος, which is often regarded as having similarities with προϊστάμενος, occurs extensively in the New Testament, including in reference to Jesus,[143] and Christian leaders; we have already noted its use in regard to the Christian leaders identified in Hebrews 13.[144] It is also used as a description of Paul,[145] but is not used by him to describe Christian leaders.[146] In the Septuagint, however, the term is associated with more despotic rulers or national rulers, with connotations of ruling and commanding[147] – contexts that are rather different from the smaller, domestic setting of the Pauline house-churches, and, accordingly,

---

134 Mt. 9.18, 23; Lk. 8.41.
135 Lk. 14.1; Jn 3.1.
136 Lk. 23.13, 35; 24.20; Jn 7.26, 48; 12.42; Acts 3.17; 4.5, 8; 13.27; 14.5; 23.5.
137 Mt. 9.34; 12.24; Mk 3.22; Lk. 11.15; Jn 12.31; 14.30; 16.11.
138 Mt. 20.25.
139 Lk. 18.18; Acts 4.26.
140 Lk. 12.58; Acts 16.19.
141 Acts 7.27, 35.
142 Acts 3.15; 5.31; Heb. 2.10; 12.2.
143 Mt. 2.6.
144 Acts 15.22; Heb. 13.7, 17, 24.
145 Acts 14.12.
146 Cf., in a different sense, its use in Phil. 2.3.
147 Cf., for example, Gen. 49.10; Deut. 1.13; 5.23; Josh. 13.21; Judg. 9.51; 11.6, 11; 1 Sam. 15.17; 22.2; 25.30; 2 Sam. 2.5; 3.38; 4.2; 5.2.

may not have been considered appropriate by Paul. Perhaps significantly, the role of the ἡγούμενος is expressly qualified by Jesus in Lk. 22.26 – 'the greater should become lesser, and the one who leads (ὁ ἡγούμενος) should become as the one who serves (ὁ διακονῶν)' – and, if Paul is aware of this dominical tradition, he may explicitly have wanted to avoid adopting this term in the Christian communities.

5. *Conclusion*

This analysis of leadership titles in the Pauline corpus has concluded that the small house-church and household setting are essential pre-requisites for understanding the roles and provenance of these leaders. That is, the Pauline letters are seeking to apply a Pauline conception of leadership structures to Pauline church communities, whose principal congregational units in a town were multiple and accommodated in domestic settings.[148]

I have argued that a deacon, or deacons, where they existed,[149] co-operated with an overseer in a house-church setting; but that the overseer had more significant responsibilities, by virtue of carrying the additional task of teaching. The duties of the deacon are less specifically delineated, except that they involved leadership of people, and we note that Phoebe was of considerable help to Paul and others.[150] The popular association with the temporary difficulties associated with the Jerusalem church in Acts 6.1-6 is an unhelpful background that has led many to hold that the duties of deacons were practical or administrative.[151] There is nothing in the Pauline corpus to suggest this; on the contrary, being an accomplished head of a household, an ability also required of the overseer, suggests people skills.

An overseer would have been recognized as a member of the council of elders, where such a council existed. A small community of believers,

---

148 It is questionable whether this Pauline structure can be readily transposed to churches where the primary congregational unit is large, the setting is non-domestic, and where the strategy, enterprise and principal activities of the church have a different focus and are of a different order of magnitude. Such a conception of church and setting for the congregation would surely require in its leaders a skill set that extends beyond that of both managing one's children and household and teaching within a small group setting, as presupposed for the overseer and deacons in the Pastoral Epistles. However, even the smaller congregation, perhaps meeting in a home, cannot and ought not replicate the Graeco-Roman household setting (cf. the wider observations in Gehring, *House Church and Mission*, pp. 300–11).

149 We have seen that Paul's letter to Titus makes reference to overseer and elders, but not deacons.

150 Rom. 16.1-2.

151 The title 'deacon' does not occur in Acts 6. Furthermore, the word 'service' is something that characterizes the responsibilities of both the Seven and the apostles.

where there was only one house-church, would not have had a single elder, since elders were always part of a council alongside fellow elders. I have argued that this council is likely to have been more than the sum of the overseers, and will have included other respected men who were heads of their own households, but who did not themselves have oversight of their own house-church and were not qualified to teach. The responsibilities of the eldership are unclear, but were community-wide, that is with regard to all of the house-churches, rather than an individual house-church. Elders did not have individual duties, but acted as a council. Within the council of elders, those who were also overseers were considered worthy of greater honour, and are likely to have been regarded as more senior – and, in the post-New Testament period, this paved the way for a single overseer to emerge as head of a community.

It is commonly argued that leadership of New Testament communities is plural; and yet I have argued from 1 Tim. 3.2 and Tit. 1.7 that the overseer is a singular role in regard to a house-church. In some instances, he would have been accompanied by a deacon or deacons, although no deacon is mentioned in the letter to Titus.[152] I have also argued that an eldership may well have emerged where there were a number of overseers and other heads of household. The context can be envisaged for a limited period, therefore, where an overseer, or a few overseers, in a locality are effectively working alone. While not impossible, this would not be the norm in a context where the house-churches in a town are increasing in size and number; and even in the case outlined in Tit. 1.5, Titus is already being encouraged to appoint a plurality of elders in every town.

This reconstruction accommodates data from Phil. 1.1, Rom. 16.1-2, 1 Tim. 3.1-13, 5.17-22, Tit. 1.5-9 and Acts 20.28. In addition, I have noted the use of similar language, although without using these titles, in 1 Thess. 5.12, 1 Cor. 16.16-18 and Rom. 12.8. In all, this suggests a pattern of notable consistency that might have applied widely across the Pauline communities, and does not require that the later letters reflect a process that is significantly more institutionalized than the situations that obtained in the earlier Pauline communities.

Furthermore, this account is consistent with a portrait of the Pauline communities, both early and later, that were clearly hierarchical, where

---

152 I have argued that it is generally not significant that many letters do not mention titles of leaders. However, it is unexpected that the title 'deacon' does not occur in the letter to Titus. Knight, *The Pastoral Epistles*, p. 175, and Marshall, *The Pastoral Epistles*, p. 488, argue that this is because this situation is so very new (Tit. 1.5), and a requirement for deacons had not emerged. While Knight argues that the deacons' role was one of service (contra Collins), I hold that a menial connotation is not necessary, and that there was rather more overlap between the overseer and the deacon. If I am right, this provides a stronger explanation for the absence of deacons in a very new, and therefore small, church – the work of the overseer does not need to be supplemented by a deacon.

the primary role of leaders was to lead, albeit that all the marks of the character of such people should be those of moderation, and not authoritarian or bullying (πλήκτης).[153] In this regard, it is noteworthy that a number of the contemporary titles for leaders, which had connotations of ruling, are absent from Paul's understanding of church order. Although Pauline leaders were to be honoured, it is also evident that their titles were not honorary, as in many of their contemporary social groups. Rather, their roles were associated with toil and labour.

In general, it is accepted that the amount of available data with which to reconstruct the roles of the overseer and elders is very limited, the range of contexts in which we find the term 'elder' is especially narrow, and the data in regard to the duties of deacons is especially restricted. However, this particular approach, which has drawn on common vocabulary across a wide selection of Pauline letters, including some of the evidence of those leaders who are not identified by their titles, has provided more confident grounds from which to find similarities and draw parallels, and, on this basis, construct an understanding of Pauline church order. This material must, however, be read alongside the evidence that amplifies this ecclesiology by describing the status, task and tools of leadership.

---

153   Cf. similarly the character traits listed of Timothy: 1 Tim. 4.13-16.

Chapter Four

THE STATUS OF LEADERS

1. *Introduction*

In any community, both the self-perception of leaders as to their status and the perception of others of the status of their leaders impinge significantly on the task, the ethos, the manner of that leadership, and inevitably on the relationship between leader and led. Accordingly, this exploration is not simply an investigation of status from a structural, organizational, or church order perspective. It concerns the effects and implications of grades of status. The goal in this chapter is not to identify and explore the historical realities of the status of leaders, although Paul's reactions to such situations will be informative in regard to his theology of leadership. Rather I shall focus on what Paul conceived to be an appropriate understanding of the status of leaders relative to each other and relative to those who were not leaders. In significant measure, this will deal with the status of Paul, and how he handled that status. However, it will be important not to equate our exploration of Pauline leadership simply to Paul's leadership.

The issue of the standing of Christian leaders relative to others in the church tends to be explored, both in the church and the academy, in three distinct arenas, each of which is exploring a different model of status, with only a measure of overlap and interchange between them. In this chapter we shall compare these three models. The first arena is focused on the portrait of leaders as those whose status was pre-eminent; that is, the suggestion that Paul considered leaders, by definition, should hold an authoritative position and commensurate status within an ordered hierarchy. The second is focused on the contrasting ideal of an egalitarian community. Such a model may, nonetheless, include a few who are recognized as having a measure of privileged status, but the more dominant ethos propounded by Paul is otherwise one of egalitarianism – whether or not this was achieved in reality. The third explores the metaphor of the leader as servant, in which leaders should adopt a position within what might be regarded as a simple hierarchy, but at the bottom, rather than the top, and at least implying a status that is inferior in so far as it focuses on the servile.

It seems to me that there are a number of reasons for the lack of an umbrella debate that successfully tackles all three of these models of leadership status within the church. First, each of these arenas has its own very polarized debate between proponents and detractors, each with highly developed and deeply entrenched ideological positions, variously parading and ignoring key texts. Secondly, the search for historical reconstruction and the search for theological ideal are quite different, yet they are clearly related, often overlapping, and frequently confused with each other. Thirdly, although each of these models is said to be legitimated both by biblical precedent and injunction (that is, the historical and the theological), they are so fundamentally contrasting as to be clearly incompatible, at least not without significant modification or compromise. I shall outline and compare each of these models of status in turn, identifying the extent to which each is promoted in the Pauline corpus.

2. Hierarchical Leadership

We have noted that interpreters' contemporary experiences of leadership will in some measure affect not only the questions that they ask of the New Testament texts, but also their selection of which texts are deemed to be relevant in answering those questions, and, of course, their conclusions.[1] Accordingly, we would expect that the debate about this first model of the status of leaders might be influenced, whether patently or latently, by the ways in which hierarchical leadership is exercised, experienced, encouraged or contested within contemporary churches. It is interesting that, although the early etymology of hier-archy concerns government by holy beings, for example an angelic group, and later meanings referred to a priestly ranking or series of orders (ἱερός + -αρχης, cf. the inverted ἀρχιερεύς), contemporary usage focuses rather on a ranking of persons or things with no necessary reference to what is holy.

---

1   This is not to deny that commentators can be both aware of a number of these subtle influences, but also, in some measure, able to reach conclusions that are not congenial to their natural disposition. J. H. Elliott, 'The Jesus Movement was not Egalitarian but Family-Oriented', *BibInt* 11 (2003), p. 205, expresses something of this in the closing paragraph of his article: 'On a personal note, I must confess that I have not enjoyed mounting this critique. With every fibre of my egalitarian being I wish it were demonstrable that the Jesus movement had been egalitarian, at least at some point in its early history. This surely would make it easier for today's advocates of equality, among whom I count myself, to appeal to our past as a source of inspiration and moral guidance for the present. But, as the historical and ideological critic in all of us insists, wishing and politically correct ideology cannot make it so'.

One, now obsolete, meaning of 'hierarchy' is 'rule/dominion'.[2] This may be a returning element in contemporary usage, where the word, when applied to rankings of individuals rather than things, often conveys negative connotations of subordination and, therefore, domination.[3]

If Paul did indeed endorse hierarchy within his communities, key questions concern whether the particular construct of hierarchy that he was endorsing was typical of a first-century social context; whether such a hierarchy should be complex, including a number of ranks or grades; and whether or not, over time, Paul developed his views about a hierarchy of leaders within Christian communities. Scholars currently adopt a range of positions on these points, each defended as being historically credible, and each attracting wide support. At one pole of the spectrum is the portrait of a singular, authority figure, who reinforces a simple hierarchy, and who is normally remote from the local congregation over which he is in authority. It is clear that Paul considered, on the basis of his calling as a minister of the gospel, that he held a position of high status amongst fellow believers, even among those whom he did not know personally or had never met.[4] He considered that his status was conjoined with that of the gospel that he proclaimed, and could not be separated from that gospel,[5] and it was also inextricably linked with the revelation of Jesus Christ that he had received.[6] In this vein, he was able to write confidently and authoritatively to a number of Christian communities, as the opening words of so many of his extant letters demonstrate. This certainly presents a picture of a hierarchy in which Paul occupies the senior position; indeed, in comparison, other rankings pale as insignificant, if they are present at all. Clearly, this portrait of hierarchy may simultaneously accommodate what may otherwise be an egalitarian structure within each local community. Inevitably, the scope and nature of the Pauline evidence that we possess privileges a construction of church history that gives the apostle Paul a status that is both dominant and abiding. The mere survival of this collection of letters speaks of that high status, and consequently of a hierarchy that, at the least, included Paul's assured view of himself as an apostle, recognized in some measure by Jerusalem as well as by many other Christian communities.

It is also the case, however, that Paul occasionally writes in a more

---

2   Cf. 'hierarch' and 'hierarchy' in the *Oxford English Dictionary Online* (Oxford: Oxford University Press, 2000).

3   Cf. the negative connotations also of the concept of power in chapter 5.

4   This may be the case in regard to the Roman congregation (cf. Rom. 1.1); although it is clear from Romans 16 that, if this closing chapter is indeed an integral part of the letter and was originally addressed to the Romans, that there were a number of Roman Christians whom Paul had met other than in Rome, and whom he knew quite intimately.

5   Cf. Gal. 1.8.

6   Cf. Gal. 1.11-12.

defensive tone. There were a number of dissenters who questioned and challenged his authority, both within and on the periphery of the Pauline congregations. In this respect, the evidence reveals a hierarchy in which Paul's position was contested. We are not concerned here with the fact or nature of such opposition, but rather with how his response to that opposition reflects his view of his own status in relation to theirs, and whether there are other factors in his presentation that also reflect aspects of his self-perception. It does seem consistently to be the case that Paul unequivocally defends his standing in relation to the gospel,[7] and, on a number of occasions, he also asserts a unique standing in relation to particular communities, notwithstanding pockets of opposition.[8] In addition, and surely significantly, Paul also draws attention, often *en passant,* to the relationship that he has across a number of congregations – a co-ordinating relationship between communities, as opposed to a singular relationship with individual communities.[9] In these regards, Paul projects his position, and consequent status.

In addition to this, however, he also endorses others who equally have a trans-local reputation and standing. In particular, Paul is keen to present other leading figures as having their own domains (Gal. 2.9: 'when James and Cephas and John, who were acknowledged pillars, recognized the grace that had been given to me, they gave to Barnabas and me the right hand of fellowship, agreeing that we should go to the Gentiles and they to the circumcised'), and that he had no intention of building on another's foundation.[10] Notwithstanding his hesitation to build on others' founda-tions, Paul appears to have been content that others would build on the foundation that he had laid; thus, he considers that, although he laid the foundation for the Corinthian church, another is free to build on it.[11] Similarly, in discussing the personality politics that were focused around apostolic figures in Corinth, Paul does not seek to put a fence around his own position and role, but encourages none of the apostles, least of all him, to be hoisted by the Corinthians onto an exclusive pedestal.[12] In these three aspects, Paul does present at the very least a simple hierarchy. He writes as one who is often assured of his position; where challenged, he

---

7 Cf. Gal. 1.9; 2 Cor. 11.4.

8 Cf. 1 Cor. 4.15; 5.3; 1 Thess. 2.7. Note here the mixed metaphor of νήπιοι juxtaposed with τροφός; for a defence of this textual reading and the necessary interpretative punctuation, cf. J. A. D. Weima, '"But we Became Infants among You": The Case for νήπιοι in 1 Thess 2.7', *NTS* 46 (2000), pp. 547–64.

9 Cf. Rom. 16.4, 16; 1 Cor. 4.17; 7.17; 11.16; 14.34; 16.1, 19; 2 Cor. 8.1, 18, 23–24; 11.8, 28; 12.13; Phil. 4.15; Col. 4.16; 2 Thess. 1.4.

10 Rom. 15.20.

11 1 Cor. 3.10.

12 1 Cor. 1.10-17; 3.5-15.

regularly defends his status, conjoined as it is with the gospel of Christ and his commission; but he also holds that this is not a unique status.

The view of a more complex hierarchy asserts that the Pauline communities were not only subject to the apostle Paul, but also that Paul recognized a local ranking of leaders, at least sometimes referred to as overseers or elders, and deacons. Where such a hierarchy did exist, it would be unsurprising if we were to find that a number of these leaders had been domineering. Indeed, the evidence does suggest that there were certainly those in some of the Pauline communities who were bullying, but it must unfortunately be deemed inconclusive, although not irrelevant, whether these individuals were part of a legitimated hierarchy of local leaders.[13] Our concern here, however, is not with how the hierarchy was presented; but, where Paul endorsed a hierarchy of local leaders, how complex was that hierarchy, and what kind of status did he consider should be accorded to such leaders?

Beyond the portrayal of Paul's own status, we have already drawn attention to the long-held and influential view that the early years of the Pauline mission reveal remarkably little evidence of either the presence or appointment of leaders who had a recognized status, that church government was rather more fluid,[14] that the early letters reveal very little awareness of, or interest in, local leadership, and, furthermore, there is little recognition of a differentiation in status between local leaders and other members of the communities. Accordingly, the casual reader has often overlooked references to leaders, or texts that appear to presuppose the presence or influence of leaders. This presentation is neither necessarily at odds with the portrait of an authoritarian apostle who disregards the notion of privileged status in others, nor of the apostle who decries the preferential, pedestal status accorded by the Corinthians. It simply accedes that *if* there were a hierarchy of local leaders in the early years of the Pauline mission that differentiated other than simply between Paul and the rest, then his letters do not give it significant exposure. On the basis of this, it has been argued that Paul is ambivalent about the existence of local leaders, and therefore we should expect to find little in his early letters that concerns his view of their status relative either to him or to their congregations.

We have now seen, however, that commentators have increasingly become attuned to seeing within the Pauline letters an alternative portrait of communities that not only had leaders, but were also urged to recognize a cascading authority. Indeed, in the previous chapter we saw that on a

---

13   Paul certainly speaks disparagingly of those who were leading astray the communities of the Corinthians, Galatians, and Philippians, as well as the communities that are presupposed in the Pastoral Epistles.

14   See the discussion in Chapter 1.

limited number of occasions he specifically endorses the presence and role of local leaders, and urges that their status be recognized and respected. Among these are Stephanas, Fortunatus and Achaicus, whom Paul legitimates with these words:

> I urge you, brothers and sisters, you know that the household of Stephanas were the first converts in Achaia, and they have devoted themselves to the service (εἰς διακονίαν) of the saints; I urge you to submit (ὑποτάσσησθε) yourselves to such people, and everyone who works and toils (συνεργοῦντι καὶ κοπιῶντι) [in this way]. I rejoice at the coming of Stephanas and Fortunatus and Achaicus, because they have made up for your absence; for they refreshed my spirit as well as yours. So recognize (ἐπιγινώσκετε) such people. (1 Cor. 16.15-18)

Likewise, we have noted those in Thessalonica, in support of whom Paul writes: 'But we appeal to you, brothers and sisters, to recognize (εἰδέναι) those who labour (κοπιῶντας) among you, and lead/guide (προϊσταμένους) you in the Lord and admonish (νουθετοῦντας) you; esteem (ἡγεῖσθαι) them very highly in love because of their work (ἔργον)' (1 Thess. 5.12-13); and in writing to Rome, we have seen that Paul again recognizes the person who is described as ὁ προϊστάμενος (Rom. 12.8), and urges such a person, or people, to carry out their work with zeal (ἐν σπουδῇ). In writing to the Corinthians, Paul notes that in the church there were those who had gifts of κυβέρνησις (1 Cor. 12.28), a term often used of a leading sea-farer or a navigator on-board ship.[15] These people in Corinth are placed by Paul within an ordered hierarchy that includes a plurality of apostles, together with prophets, teachers and workers of miracles: 'first ... second ... third ... then ...'. It is probable that a number of the individuals identified in Romans 16 may also have been leaders, respectively of at least five different Christian groups in Rome.[16] On a number of occasions, Paul endorses and reinforces the status of specifically named co-workers, who represent Paul to and among the various Christian congregations, and to whom Paul accords the status of his representatives as they visit congregations. These include Timothy (cf. 1 Cor. 4.17; 16.10; 1 Thess. 3.2); Epaphroditus (Phil. 2.25; 4.18); and Epaphras (Col. 1.7; 4.12; Phlm. 23).

In addition to these references, which show clear Pauline endorsement of a local hierarchy of leaders, we have also seen Paul's use of specific titles of office, especially elders, overseers and deacons in 1 Timothy and Titus. These rare instances of titles show Paul's unopposed recognition of the existence of local hierarchy. Church history, together with contemporary

---

15 Cf. the κυβερνήτης in Acts 27.11; Rev. 18.17.
16 R. Jewett, *Romans: A Commentary* (Hermeneia; Minneapolis: Fortress, 2007), p. 61.

ecclesiastical contexts, predispose us to assume that there were differentiations in status, and not just role, between the various titled offices.

It is clear that these references, both generic and particular, titled and untitled, predicate not simply the presence of leaders within the Christian communities, but that their status is endorsed and reinforced by the apostle. Paul was certainly aware of the predominance of hierarchies within non-Christian social groupings; and, had he explicitly rejected such hierarchies, we might expect to have seen explicit reference to a contrasting picture of the existence of local hierarchies that is consistently presented elsewhere in the New Testament,[17] and is not evidently rejected by Paul. Structured communities were, after all, a well-established pattern in the synagogues and the voluntary associations of the day.[18]

Such Pauline support does not, of course, imply that an appointment process had formally legitimated the position and status of all such leaders. Indeed, the references in Romans 12; 1 Thessalonians 5; 1 Corinthians 12 and 16 seem to suggest that Paul's bolstering of the status of these leaders is not on the basis of their formalised appointment on a prior occasion, or their title, or their financially privileged status. Rather, his endorsement of these individuals is addressed to the community as a whole, and is on the basis of the task that these people had been fulfilling. There is an encouragement that these leaders carry out their duties diligently, and that the rest of the community is urged to respect, indeed to recognize (ἐπιγινώσκετε), such people. Thus we see the apostle recognizing the qualities of certain individuals and urging that they be accorded appropriate status.

Significant by its absence, however, is clear evidence in the early Pauline letters of a process of identifying potential leaders or an established practice of making such appointments.[19] In particular, it is unclear whether all such individuals already had significant social status, independent of their endorsement by the apostle. It can readily be argued in regard to Gaius, Stephanas, Phoebe, Aquila and Prisca that they had the social benefits of wealth or property.[20] Were such people educated and articulate, and would they have been regarded as having comparatively

---

17   Cf. Acts 14.23; 15; 16.4; 20.17-38; 1 Pet. 5.1-5; Heb. 13.7, 17, 24; Jas 5.14; and 2 Jn 1; 3 Jn 1.

18   Cf. the discussion in A. D. Clarke, *Serve the Community of the Church: Christians as Leaders and Ministers* (First-Century Christians in the Graeco-Roman World; Grand Rapids; Cambridge: Eerdmans, 2000), pp. 59–77, 103–41.

19   Cf., for example, Acts 14.23.

20   Cf. the discussion in A. D. Clarke, '"Refresh the Hearts of the Saints": A Unique Pauline Context?', *TynBull* 47 (1996), pp. 277–300; and idem, 'Jew and Greek, Slave and Free, Male and Female: Paul's Theology of Ethnic, Social and Gender Inclusiveness in Romans 16', in P. Oakes (ed.), *Rome in the Bible and the Early Church* (Carlisle; Grand Rapids: Paternoster; Baker, 2002), pp. 103–25.

higher status irrespective of their endorsement by Paul? Is it that Paul singled out these, not merely because they had independent social standing, but because, in addition to this social privilege, they had further qualities that merited respect within the churches, and he urged that this combination be recognized? It does need to be noted that, merely as household patron figures, these individuals are not to be compared with the leaders of large groups or communities. Various estimations as to the size of these groups have been made, and are dependent on whether or not we are to assume a large, private dwelling or a more humble apartment or *insula*. Estimates range from as few as ten to as many as forty.[21] At either extreme, however, the numbers are not large, and the natural status of such patron figures ought to be considered accordingly. Interestingly, among the leaders in the Roman congregations, Jewett argues that there were a number who were not patrons, and therefore lacked the significant property of Aquila and Prisca. Rather, they lived in the much poorer tenement buildings that scattered the Trastevere region of the city. Among such 'leaders', Jewett argues that none 'appears to have a position of prominence over the others',[22] and that 'the pattern of leadership appears to be egalitarian in tenement churches'.[23] By this, he means that the congregational structure in a tenement church lacked a patron.[24] However, 'egalitarian leadership' sounds like an oxymoron, and it may be less confusing to speak of leadership that did not reflect differences in status that were as stark as in the case of the patrons, whose social status may have enhanced their position. There is clearer evidence to suggest that Fortunatus and Achaicus, mentioned in 1 Cor. 16.17, were probably part of the wider household of Stephanas, the patron, but that these were slaves or freedmen who were being acknowledged alongside their patron, Stephanas, as equally deserving of honour and respect as leaders.[25]

Those wealthier individuals who had higher social status, but whose behaviour was not, in Paul's view, compatible with a leading role in one of the churches, conversely received only reprimand from Paul, and remain anonymous.[26] Alastair Campbell certainly argues, in regard to Acts 14.23, that the 'appointing' of elders by Barnabas and Saul was a process not of selecting leaders from the whole pool of believers in a locality, but of recognizing and blessing those whose social status in the Christian

---

21 Jewett, *Romans*, p. 64.

22 Where Jewett, *Romans*, p. 65, goes on to say that this is a sign of egalitarianism, it seems to me, on the contrary, that this exemplifies a simple, rather than complex, hierarchy.

23 Jewett, *Romans*, pp. 65–6.

24 Jewett, *Romans*, p. 69, describes 'a social system alongside house churches that enabled congregational groups to function without patrons'.

25 Cf. the argument in Clarke, ' "Refresh the hearts of the saints" ', pp. 277–300.

26 Cf., for example, the argument that the misbehaviour at the Lord's Supper is prompted by the wealthy who were not regarding their poorer counterparts (1 Cor. 11.21-22).

community was already recognized.[27] Whether or not Campbell is correct in his reading of Acts 14.23, it seems to me that this may explain why some individuals had social status and were publicly endorsed as leaders by Paul, and yet there is no reference to a formal appointing procedure. They were 'naturally' in positions of influence. In contrast, there were those who may similarly have had social status, may equally have not been appointed by the apostle, but, in addition, they also lacked Pauline approbation.

In later decades, best exemplified by the Pastoral Epistles, many have argued that leadership is rather more formalized, with a more complex hierarchy that includes deacons who appear to be subordinate to a group of elders or overseers. The majority of scholars regard such a ranking of grades to be a late innovation in the Pauline communities, although we have seen that this argument does have to be predicated *e silentio*. A graded hierarchy is presented in the Pastoral Epistles neither as a novelty nor a recent advance. We have already noted that the titles of overseer and deacon were included, *en passant* and unremarkably, in the opening of Paul's letter to the Philippians, and not again referenced as such – although some of the individuals who occupied those positions may well be alluded to, obliquely or otherwise, without their titles, later in the letter. Furthermore, the title of elder was remarkably widespread across the New Testament record, including, as we have seen, in the synoptic Gospels, Acts, James, 1 Peter, 2 and 3 John and Revelation, and was ubiquitous across a number of first-century societal contexts.[28]

For our purposes, however, we should note that there is in the later Pauline corpus the clear sense not only of a recognized status for local leaders, but also of a more complex hierarchy. I have argued that not only is there a distinction between the overseer and the deacon, but also between the overseer and the elder.[29] The Pastoral Epistles recognize the status of the leaders, and evidently urge that the behaviour and character of elders, overseers and deacons should be commensurate with that preferred status (1 Tim. 3.2-13; Tit. 1.5-9). In particular, such leaders should have a good reputation (μαρτυρία καλή, 1 Tim. 3.7) among outsiders.

---

27   R. A. Campbell, *The Elders: Seniority within Earliest Christianity* (SNTW; Edinburgh: T. & T. Clark, 1994), pp. 166–71.

28   Cf. the detailed account given in Campbell, *The Elders*, pp. 20–96.

29   Cf. the discussion in the preceding chapter in regard to 1 Tim. 5.17, in which those elders who 'rule' (προεστῶτες) and teach are overseers. Similarly, if an accusation is to be brought against an elder, there are strict criteria that should be applied (1 Tim 5.19), which do not need to be applied in the case of non-elders. This is discussed at length in the dissertation, W. Kowalski, 'The Reward, Discipline, and Installation of Church Leaders: An Examination of 1 Timothy 5.17-22' (unpublished PhD dissertation, University of Gloucestershire, 2005).

Also significant to this portrait of hierarchy are the number of instances where Paul urges that believers both obey and submit to their leaders. Believers are called to obey, not simply Christ, but also Paul (cf. Phil. 2.12). Paul gives commands, including the instructions to both the Galatian and Corinthian churches regarding the collection in 1 Cor. 16.1. Timothy is also urged to command those in his church not to teach falsely (1 Tim. 1.3). The obedience of the Corinthians is something that should accompany their confession of Christ (2 Cor. 9.13); but Paul also 'tests' them to see whether they are obedient (2 Cor. 2.9), and urges that 'we will be ready to punish every act of disobedience, once your obedience is complete' (2 Cor. 10.6). We might expect Paul to urge submission to the governing bodies (Rom. 13.1, 5; Tit. 3.1); but he also urges submission to certain individuals who are characterised by their labour for the saints (1 Cor. 16.16), as well as to those who are 'over you' in the Lord (οἱ προϊστάμενοι, 1 Thess. 5.12) and are to be respected.

Given the dominant cultural context of deeply embedded stratification in Graeco-Roman civic society, as well as the voluntary associations, the Jewish synagogue communities and the Mediterranean family,[30] it would perhaps be unsurprising if there were a predisposition for believers to adopt a broadly similar approach to the social structuring of their Christian communities. It seems to me, therefore that, although the debate as to whether or not the early Pauline communities had a complex hierarchy or ranking of local leaders has to be pursued in the absence of overwhelming textual evidence, we should accord greater weight than is often acceded to the non-titled references to leaders in the Pauline communities; to the apparently non-innovative use of titles both in the comparatively early Phil. 1.1 and the rather later Pastoral Epistles; to the widespread use of titles such as elder and overseer, not just in the rest of the New Testament, but also in the surrounding contemporary society; and also to the dominant ethos of social stratification in Graeco-Roman society. The impact of this evidence clearly demonstrates not only the presence of local leaders in the Christian communities, but it also hints at the existence, at least in some communities, of a more complex hierarchy of ranks. The apostle Paul is presented as endorsing such hierarchies, in large measure by urging the believers in the communities to recognize the status of such leaders, and urging Timothy in particular that the behaviour of leaders be commensurate with their status. In this regard, there is recognition of hierarchy, but an encouragement that the ethos not be domineering.[31]

30   Cf. my argument in Clarke, *Serve the Community of the Church*.

31   Such a perspective is paralleled in the 'not lording it over' (κατακυριεύω) passages in Mt. 20.25 and Mk 10.42 (cf. also the use of κατεξουσιάζω ad loc.) and 1 Pet. 5.3 – as well as widely, and sometimes more positively, in the Septuagint.

3. *Egalitarianism*

The evidence for Paul's endorsement of a hierarchy of leaders with elevated status, which included him and local leaders, is wide-ranging and compelling. However, in the second arena, the contemporary appeal of an egalitarian society over hierarchical leadership is obvious, and an influential number of studies has argued the attractive thesis that egalitarianism was not only an innovative and fundamental aspect of Jesus' mission, but that it was also a key characteristic of the earliest Christian communities. Not all protagonists for a New Testament egalitarianism regard it as having been a historical reality; rather that it was held as an ideal or an eschatological concept – indeed, one that has unfortunately been replicated rarely, if ever, since.[32] Even if not achieved in the New Testament period, evidence that egalitarianism within the local churches was a Pauline goal or ideal would form a strategic aspect within an account of his theology of leadership, and would have widespread ramifications for other aspects of that theology.

Schüssler Fiorenza's reconstruction of Christian origins, entitled *In Memory of Her,* is an extensive and detailed treatment, which has been deservedly influential in the field, not simply for its reconstruction, but also for its discussion of method and hermeneutical principles.[33] In it she adopts the phrase a 'discipleship of equals' to describe the group that was called by Jesus.[34] Male and female followers of Jesus sought to fulfil Jesus' mission and were incorporated into a band that was characterised by the lack of any baggage of hierarchy or differentiated status. The 'remembered record' of Jesus' ministry is regarded as having challenged aspects of patriarchal domination, and at no point does this record impose or endorse the submission of women.[35] Many have noted that patterns of social equality are identifiable also in the immediately post-Pentecost church in Jerusalem, evidenced by Luke's portrait of 'all things in common' in the cameos of community life in Acts 2.42-47 and 4.32-37,[36] and by the outpouring of the Spirit with its concomitant sense of an

---

32 Cf. the fundamental inequalities evidenced in the problems addressed in 1 Corinthians, as noted by Elliott, 'The Jesus Movement was not Egalitarian but Family-oriented', p. 193.

33 E. Schüssler Fiorenza, *In Memory of Her: A Feminist Theological Reconstruction of Christian Origins* (London: SCM Press, 1983).

34 Schüssler Fiorenza, *In Memory of Her,* pp. 140–50; cf. also idem, *Discipleship of Equals: A Critical Feminist Ekklesia-Logy of Liberation* (London: SCM Press, 1993).

35 Schüssler Fiorenza, *In Memory of Her,* pp. 52–3.

36 Cf. J. D. Crossan, *The Birth of Christianity: Discovering what Happened in the Years Immediately After the Execution of Jesus* (Edinburgh: T. & T. Clark, 1998), pp. 445–76.

equality that did not observe distinctions between male and female, young and old.[37]

Furthermore, it is argued there is evidence that, in the early years of his mission, Paul was himself a proponent of egalitarianism. In this regard, the statement in Gal. 3.28 that 'there is neither Jew nor Greek, neither slave nor free, neither male nor female; for all of you are one in Christ Jesus' is regarded as programmatic, and reflects notions of equal status.[38] The metaphor of the body in 1 Cor. 12.12-27 may be adduced as additional support for the promulgation of an egalitarian community, with its focus on the values of each distinct member of the body.

In a sequence of two articles, John Elliott has rejected the proposition that locates either the existence or the ideal of an egalitarian society in earliest Christianity. He argues in the first article that Jesus did not clearly oppose patriarchalism, and that the pattern of the Jesus Movement was modelled rather on the household setting;[39] and, in the second, that the pre-Pauline, Pauline and post-Pauline phases of the Christian church each marked, not so much a gradual abandonment of early egalitarianism and return to patriarchalism, but a continuation of the pattern of those household structures that were fundamental to the earlier Jesus Movement.[40] The thrust of his argument, in both cases, is that egalitarianism is an Enlightenment ideal that is anachronistic to the first-century setting, and lacks crucial, supporting evidence, either in the early Christian tradition or in its contemporary Graeco-Roman context.

Elliott focuses his criticism of this view on Schüssler Fiorenza as one of the key proponents of egalitarianism both in the Jesus Movement and the earliest Christian, including the Pauline, communities. He identifies an unhelpful lack of definition about the notions, practicalities and areas of equality;[41] he addresses a number of the features of her treatment of what they both concur to be a pre-Pauline formula in Gal. 3.28,[42] especially the question as to whether the formula concerns equality, as she concludes, or unity, or inclusiveness. Additionally, he argues that she fails to account adequately for the wider context in Galatians 3, namely, the inclusion of

37   Cf. Peter's quotation of the prophet Joel in Acts 2.17-21.

38   Elliott, 'The Jesus Movement was not Egalitarian but Family-Oriented', p. 178.

39   J. H. Elliott, 'Jesus was not an Egalitarian: A Critique of an Anachronistic and Idealist Theory', *BTB* 32 (2002), pp. 75–91.

40   Elliott, 'The Jesus Movement was not Egalitarian but Family-Oriented', pp. 173–210. Cf. also the extended argument in R. W. Gehring, *House Church and Mission: The Importance of Household Structures in Early Christianity* (Peabody: Hendrickson, 2004).

41   Elliott, 'The Jesus Movement was not Egalitarian but Family-Oriented', pp. 174, 179–80.

42   Schüssler Fiorenza, *In Memory of Her*, pp. 208, 218–20, argues that the text shows evidence of Paul having changed the formula, and that the resulting changes, reflected in 1 Cor. 12.13; 7.17-24, leave his meaning somewhat opaque.

the Gentiles on the ground of faith. His fullest criticism, however, concerns the ways in which her egalitarian reading of this particular text raises significant inconsistencies across the Pauline corpus.

Elliott argues that the case for equality, in the sense of non-hierarchy, is questionable on the basis of the wider context of a second, and similar, core text, not tackled in detail by Schüssler Fiorenza, namely, 1 Cor. 12.13: 'For in the one Spirit we were all baptized into one body – whether Jews or Greeks, whether slaves or free – and we were all made to drink of one Spirit'. He notes that Paul's subsequent references to 'inferior' and 'superior', in his exposition of the metaphor of the body, are in part recognition of the inequalities that do exist. Paul's solution to this is not equal treatment, but, rather, unequal, preferential treatment or greater honour accorded to some over others, a practice that God himself has arranged in the body (1 Cor. 12.22-24). This is then followed in 1 Cor. 12.28-31 by what appears to be a ranking of gifts ('And God has appointed in the church first apostles, second prophets, third teachers; then deeds of power . . .'); and in 1 Corinthians 14 by a specific ranking of prophecy over tongues, reinforcing the view that Paul is not here speaking of equality.[43] There is a danger that unity or mutuality be confused with or interpreted as equality.

Elliott next draws attention to Paul's avoidance of a clear anti-slavery message elsewhere in his correspondence as evidence that he did not have a thorough-going 'equality' agenda that rejected the differentiations between slave and free.[44] It is true that Paul urges those slaves who can to purchase their freedom (1 Cor. 7.21), and that he reinforces that all, whether slave or free, are at the same time free in Christ and slaves to Christ (1 Cor. 7.22); but this falls a long way short of a concerted move to subvert so fundamental a principle of the Roman society as the slave economy. Furthermore, the injunctions that slaves continue to obey their masters reinforce the apostle's recognition that ongoing social inequalities are not, and are unlikely to be, dissolved.[45]

In regard to 'male nor female', Elliott disputes that Gal. 3.28 necessitates a dissolution of status distinctions between men and women. He finds in Paul evidence of an encouragement to mutuality, rather than equality. Indeed, language from the semantic domain of 'submission' in regard to head-coverings (1 Cor. 11.2-16) is an unavoidable characteristic of how Paul views the relationship between women and men. Such language can, of course, be juxtaposed alongside examples in the Pauline correspondence of women who appear to be regarded as having high status, possibly in leadership, including Junia, Prisca, and Phoebe.

---

43 Elliott, 'The Jesus Movement was not Egalitarian but Family-Oriented', p. 182.
44 Elliott, 'The Jesus Movement was not Egalitarian but Family-Oriented', p. 183.
45 Elliott, 'The Jesus Movement was not Egalitarian but Family-Oriented', p. 185.

However, in his view, it would again be wrong to take these instances as demonstrating egalitarianism. On the contrary, they are further examples of hierarchy within these communities.[46] Elliott sums up his critique:

> With the elimination of Gal. 3.28 as evidence of an egalitarianism prevailing among Jesus groups prior to Paul, the prime witness for such an alleged egalitarianism in the Jesus movement subsequent to Jesus' death and prior to Paul is eliminated. It has been shown ... that the movement inaugurated by Jesus prior to his death was by no means 'egalitarian' in nature, but was stratified economically and socially. New Testament texts alleged to express an 'ideal' or 'spirit' of equality are open to a differing interpretation and in any case are no proof that an equality was established in concrete social and economic terms. To pass off visions, ideas, and ideals as concrete realities is to engage in the idealist fallacy.[47]

In the later New Testament texts, particularly the household codes, Schüssler Fiorenza notes the absence of evidence for egalitarianism. Her argument here is, on the contrary, that patriarchalism is evident in the household structures, and that it is a regressive supplanting of the egalitarianism that had emerged and stemmed from the Jesus Movement. Elliott concurs with the lack of evidence for egalitarianism, but his analysis is that these texts also lack the residual evidence that this return to patriarchalism was a counter-move away from egalitarianism, or a late lamenting of the previous régime of equality. He writes:

> To imagine what amounts to two 'sea changes' within half a century – a revolutionary shift from traditionally patriarchally structured households to households structured as 'communities of equals' and then within a generation a reversion back to patriarchal arrangements – is as sociologically naïve as it is historically indemonstrable.[48]

In this way, Elliott criticizes those who confuse anti-patriarchalism in Paul with egalitarianism.[49] Elliott's reluctant refutation of a developed and thorough-going egalitarianism in the early New Testament period is compelling. Not only would some form of hierarchy have been expected in a community within so stratified a cultural context, but also there is little residual evidence in the New Testament for so remarkable a counter-cultural feature as thorough-going egalitarianism.

However, we have seen that the Christian communities, and not simply those of the late apostolic period, included elements of hierarchy, with recognized leaders. It seems to me, nonetheless, that there are a number of

---

46   Elliott, 'The Jesus Movement was not Egalitarian but Family-Oriented', p. 202.
47   Elliott, 'The Jesus Movement was not Egalitarian but Family-Oriented', p. 186.
48   Elliott, 'The Jesus Movement was not Egalitarian but Family-Oriented', p. 204.
49   Elliott, 'The Jesus Movement was not Egalitarian but Family-Oriented', p. 192.

aspects of Paul's ministry that are apparently egalitarian, but, in reality, should be regarded, instead, simply as non-hierarchical. These references need to be interpreted alongside, and in the light of, the evidence of an actual hierarchy that was endorsed in the Pauline communities, rather than against the supposition of egalitarianism. We should note three particular features of his language.

Paul's favourite term of address towards his correspondents is that of 'brother' (ἀδελφοί, often expanded in translation to 'brothers and sisters'), used in this metaphorical sense some 112 times in those letters commonly attributed to Paul, and significantly less frequently in the later letters.[50] This term is widely interpreted as egalitarian language, and in this regard may modify the force or consistency of the father-child language that is used much less frequently by Paul. However, in Graeco-Roman contexts, as in some contemporary oriental societies, 'brother' would not have been interpreted as an egalitarian term. Rather, there was a recognition that, in a family, brothers were ranked according to their inheritance rights, the first-born being the senior.[51] Brother language conveys mutual dependence, support and love, notwithstanding the status differentiations within the family context.

A second instance in which there is commonly held to be a sense of egalitarianism is Paul's widespread use of συν- as a prefix in nouns such as συνεργός, συναιχμάλωτος, συγκοινωνός, σύνδουλος, συστρατιώτης, σύζυγος, συνέκδημος.[52] Again, we might ask whether this language reflects equality or common fellowship, shared circumstances, or shared goals. It is clear that some of those whom Paul terms co-workers evidently have a subordinate relationship to him, and act as his envoys or ambassadors.[53] In 1 Thess. 3.2, Timothy is described as Paul's brother,

---

50 Cf. D. G. Horrell, 'From ἀδελφοί to οἶκος θεοῦ: Social Transformation in Pauline Christianity', *JBL* 120 (2001), pp. 293–311.

51 This argument is pursued in greater depth in A. D. Clarke, 'Equality Or Mutuality?: Paul's Use of "Brother" Language', in P. J. Williams, A. D. Clarke, P. M. Head and D. Instone-Brewer (eds.), *The New Testament in its First-Century Setting: Essays on Context and Background in Honour of B. W. Winter on his 65th Birthday* (Grand Rapids; Cambridge: Eerdmans, 2004), pp. 151–64, with an analysis of Plutarch's work 'Concerning Brotherly Love' (περὶ φιλαδελφίας or *de fraterno amore*) and a number of papyrological sources, all of which demonstrate the unequal use of brother language.

52 Cf. συνεργός in Rom. 16.3, 9, 21; 1 Cor. 3.9; 2 Cor. 1.24; 8.23; Phil. 2.25; 4.3; Col. 4.11; 1 Thess. 3.2; Phlm. 1, 24; συναιχμάλωτος in Rom. 16.7; Col. 4.10; Phlm. 23; συγκοινωνός in 1 Cor. 9.23; Phil. 1.7; σύνδουλος in Col. 1.7; 4.7; συστρατιώτης in Phil. 2.25; Phlm. 2; σύζυγος in Phil. 4.3; and συνέκδημος in 2 Cor. 8.19.

53 Cf. 2 Cor. 8.23 where κοινωνός is juxtaposed with συνεργός, and ἀδελφοί is juxtaposed with ἀπόστολοι (in the sense of ambassadors).

but God's co-worker (τὸν ἀδελφὸν ἡμῶν καὶ συνεργὸν τοῦ θεοῦ).[54] Similarly, in 1 Cor. 3.9, Paul and Apollos are together described as God's co-workers (θεοῦ γάρ ἐσμεν συνεργοί, θεοῦ γεώργιον, θεοῦ οἰκοδομή ἐστε).[55] In 1 Cor. 3.5, Paul describes himself and Apollos as servants (διάκονοι), presumably of 'the Lord', with tasks appointed by him. A likely reading in these instances is that 'co-worker' does not imply equality, but rather co-operation, that is, helping in a task where there is unity of purpose, rather than an equal worker with God.[56] Similarly, in 2 Cor. 1.24, Paul uses συνεργοί with a purposive genitive in the sense of a shared goal: 'Not that we lord it (κυριεύομεν) over your faith, but we are co-operating for your joy (συνεργοί ἐσμεν τῆς χαρᾶς ὑμῶν)'. The term can also be applied to a junior apprentice;[57] and the term 'fellow-soldier' need not imply equal rank, but endeavour in the same military campaign; and 'fellow-prisoner' may simply refer to similarly straitened circumstances.[58] Finally, in Phil. 2.25, Epaphroditus is identified as 'the brother and my co-worker and fellow-soldier' ('Επαφρόδιτον τὸν ἀδελφὸν καὶ συνεργὸν καὶ συστρατιώτην μου), where the use of the definite article suggests that the term brother is not here in relation specifically to Paul, and therefore no equality with Paul is assumed. In this particular instance, it is also evident that these terms seem to have an interchangeable quality: Epaphroditus is both a co-worker and fellow-soldier (Phil. 2.25).

Paul has a practice of naming co-senders at the head of his letters,[59] and it might be considered that this reflects an attempt on his part to project an element of egalitarianism. For the most part, however, this is not something that is explored in detail by commentators; instead, it is a commonplace that Paul is the sole author and that the letters reflect his theology (or at times an earlier stratum), rather than any significant

---

54   I am grateful to Peter Williams and my student, Karen Fulton, for discussion of these textual variants. Although the text 'co-worker of God' is not strongly supported (the first hand of D, four Old Latin witnesses and three Latin Fathers), it is nonetheless more probable than either, 'servant of God' (א, A, P – adopted by Westcott and Hort, and Tischendorf); and the conflated readings: 'servant of God and our co-worker' (D, M); and 'servant and co-worker of God' (G). Cf. B. D. Ehrman, *et al.*, *The Text of the New Testament in Contemporary Research: Essays on the Status Quaestionis* (Eugene: Wipf and Stock, 2001), pp. 337–9.

55   There is no significant textual variant here.

56   Cf. V. P. Furnish, 'Fellow Workers in God's Service', *JBL* 80 (1961), pp. 364–70, explores the term at length, and argues from 1 Cor 3.9 that Apollos and Paul have equal status before God (that is, equally 'nothing'), but different tasks, and that they are fellow-workers *for* God.

57   Plutarch, *Pericles* 31.2.

58   Xenophon, *Hist. Graec.* 2.4.20; Plato, *Republic* 8.556c.

59   Romans is a notable exception here.

influence of his co-senders.[60] A link between the citation of co-senders and consistent use of first person plural verbs and pronouns is not conclusive in these letters, and the suggestion of egalitarianism has to be regarded as somewhat forced.[61]

These three elements of evidence may give the appearance of egalitarianism in the Pauline mission; however, in the context of the clearly hierarchical relationships that not only existed, but were also endorsed by Paul, they should instead be viewed as instances of non-hierarchical language, within a framework that accommodates leaders and led.

4. *Servant Leadership*

The third arena of debate revolves around the metaphor of servanthood, and is clearly related to aspects of Paul's voluntary status inconsistency. The implication here is again of hierarchy, but significantly it is an inverted hierarchy where the so-called leader is at the bottom of the pyramid 'as one who serves'. Again, discussion of this aspect of community structuring is focused principally on the gospels; however, the Pauline texts also apply a number of words from the semantic domains of slave and serving both to the leader and the task of the leader. There are two questions that are especially pertinent to our discussion. The first is the meaning of the metaphor, especially in its Pauline usage; and, the second is the extent to which the metaphor can be consistently adopted, or is instead an oxymoron – in particular, if the notion of a slave/servant presupposes hierarchy, what is the hierarchical relation of the servant leader to those who are served?

A significant amount of research has been done on slaves and slavery both in biblical and Graeco-Roman studies in recent years. Studies have variously addressed the sociological questions concerned with the field, but also issues that emerge from the metaphorical use of this language. In biblical studies, there remains a key question as to whether the Graeco-Roman or the Jewish context is the more appropriate background for

---

60 E. R. Richards, *Paul and First-Century Letter Writing: Secretaries, Composition and Collection* (Downers Grove: IVP, 2004), pp. 33, 64, explores the likely input that a secretary might have in composing a letter, but notes that listing co-senders was a rarity. J. Murphy-O'Connor, *Paul the Letter-Writer: His World, His Options, His Skills* (Good News Studies, 41; Collegeville: Liturgical Press, 1995); and idem, 'Co-Authorship in the Corinthian Correspondence', *RB* 100 (1993), pp. 562–79, argues instead that the co-senders of Paul's letters had a definite contribution to the product.

61 I am grateful to my student, Karen Fulton, for her detailed work on this area.

understanding the metaphorical usage.[62] In sociological study, there has been continuing reflection on our general understanding of the master/slave relationship, and whether first-century slavery in the Mediterranean countries should be regarded as a predominantly brutal or a benign régime. One focus of particular value has been investigation of how the different types of primary source data should be evaluated. In particular, there has been discussion of the limitations of using legal texts as source data for our sociological understanding of slavery; and the ways in which the satirical characterisations of the stock-slave character inform our wider picture of the public's view of slaves and slavery.[63] This recent interest in the slave economy and the metaphorical use of slavery have significantly enhanced our ability to understand the broad range of uses of such language in the biblical texts, although there remain many areas of continuing debate.

One of the particular interests of this field of research is the wide range of uses of slave/slavery language in both the Old and New Testaments.[64] At root there is the awareness that this language carries menial and servile connotations; the associated status of the slave can clearly be one of degradation and punishment, a feature that characterizes the humiliation of the captured enemy.[65] However, the same language may be used, without any shame, merely to differentiate the person of comparatively lower status in relation to the person of comparatively higher status, for example, the subject in relation to his king.[66] Thirdly, slave language could even be a term of honour, especially in reference to the slave of a king or God. The description 'servant/s of the Lord' (עֶבֶד־יהוה) is widely used of the more honoured leaders of the Israelite people, principally Moses, but also Abraham, Isaac, Jacob, Joshua, Samuel,[67] David, the prophets,[68] and the Israelites in general.[69] Most distinctively, however, in the so-called Isaianic 'Servant-songs' a figure, who is expressly identified

---

62   J. Byron, *Slavery Metaphors in Early Judaism and Pauline Christianity: A Traditio-Historical and Exegetical Examination* (Wissenschaftliche Untersuchungen zum Neuen Testament, 2,62; Tübingen: Mohr Siebeck, 2003), has revived this debate, but reflects a minority position.

63   Cf. J. A. Harrill, *Slaves in the New Testament: Literary, Social, and Moral Dimensions* (Minneapolis: Fortress, 2006).

64   עֶבֶד ('slave'), and the verb עָבַד ('to work').

65   Deut. 28.68 'The LORD will bring you back in ships to Egypt, by a route that I promised you would never see again; and there you shall offer yourselves for sale to your enemies as male and female slaves, but there will be no buyer'.

66   1 Sam. 17.8; 29.3; 2 Sam. 19.5.

67   1 Sam. 3.9.

68   Ezra 9.11.

69   Lev. 25.55.

as the servant of the Lord, comes to the fore as one who rules.[70] This notion of being a divine servant is then repeatedly taken up also by Paul (Rom. 1.1, Παῦλος δοῦλος Χριστοῦ Ἰησοῦ; Gal. 1.10, Χριστοῦ δοῦλος; Phil. 1.1, δοῦλοι Χριστοῦ Ἰησοῦ; Tit. 1.1, Παῦλος δοῦλος θεοῦ),[71] but mixed with the contrasting metaphor of sonship (Rom. 8.15, 21; Gal. 4.7), the encouragement of freedom in distinction to the yoke of slavery (Gal. 5.1), and the notion in 1 Cor. 7.22 that a believer who is a slave when called, is nonetheless the Lord's freedman.[72] There is similar diversity when the phrases 'slaves of/to sin/unrighteousness' and 'being as a slave to the law', especially in Romans 6 and 7, are contrasted with the honourable status of being a 'slave of Christ'.

As with other aspects of the present study, there is the added hermeneutical issue about the background of interpreters affecting their reading.[73] In North America, the influencing baggage is all the more deep-seated, with inadvertent assumptions that North American slavery paralleled Graeco-Roman slavery. It seems that the majority of English translations of the Bible reflect something of this social conscience in their decision at times to translate δοῦλος and עֶבֶד as 'slave', and on other occasions as 'servant'.[74]

What has received rather less coverage as an integral part of these wider studies is discussion of the notion of leaders being slaves or enslaved, not simply within, but to the communities they lead. We have already noted the extensive and influential monograph of John Collins that has proved

---

70   That is, those songs in Isaiah that were identified by Duhm as referring to a servant as a single individual: Isa. 42.1-4; 49.1-6; 50.4-9; 52.13–53.12. Cf. especially (consistently employing עֶבֶד), 'Here is my servant (παῖς), whom I uphold, my chosen, in whom my soul delights; I have put my spirit upon him; he will bring forth justice to the nations' (Isa. 42.1); And now the LORD says, who formed me in the womb to be his slave (δοῦλος), to bring Jacob back to him, and that Israel might be gathered to him, for I am honoured in the sight of the LORD, and my God has become my strength – he says, "It is too light a thing that you should be my servant (παῖδά) to raise up the tribes of Jacob and to restore the survivors of Israel; I will give you as a light to the nations, that my salvation may reach to the end of the earth"' (Isa. 49.3, 5–6); 'And he said to me, "You are my slave (δοῦλός), Israel, in whom I will be glorified." ... See, my servant (παῖς) shall prosper; he shall be exalted and lifted up, and shall be very high. Just as there were many who were astonished at him – so marred was his appearance, beyond human semblance, and his form beyond that of mortals – so he shall startle many nations; kings shall shut their mouths because of him; for that which had not been told them they shall see, and that which they had not heard they shall contemplate' (Isa. 52.13-15).

71   Cf. also, 'servant of the gospel': Col. 1.23, 25 etc.

72   Although not exclusively applied by Paul to himself; cf. his recognition of Epaphras also as a slave of Christ: Ἐπαφρᾶς ὁ ἐξ ὑμῶν, δοῦλος Χριστοῦ [Ἰησοῦ] (Col. 4.12).

73   At the time of writing, the 200th anniversary of the abolition of the slave-trade in the United Kingdom has attracted significant media interest.

74   M. J. Harris, *Slave of Christ: A New Testament Metaphor for Total Devotion to Christ* (New Studies in Biblical Theology, 8; Leicester: Apollos, 1999), pp. 183–91.

valuable within this broader debate, but its brief focused on διάκονος language, rather than the δοῦλος semantic domain. Significant in our discussion, however, are not the references to 'slave of Christ', but rather those instances where Paul, or other leaders, are urged to be slaves of their fellow community members.

The language of serving and servanthood has long been associated with Christian leadership after the pattern of Jesus. The Gospels record at a number of points an explicit identification between serving and leading in Jesus' own mission. The principal verse is:

> You know that among the Gentiles those whom they recognize as their rulers lord it over them, and their great ones are tyrants over them. But it is not so among you; rather, whoever wishes to become great among you must be your servant (διάκονος), and whoever wishes to be first among you must be slave (δοῦλος) of all. For the Son of Man came not to be served but to serve (οὐκ ἦλθεν διακονηθῆναι ἀλλὰ διακονῆσαι), and to give his life a ransom for many.[75]

The Fourth Gospel includes the pericope of Jesus taking the role of a servant in washing the feet of the disciples, yet simultaneously and rightfully being recognized as teacher, lord and master.[76] This juxtaposition is also apparent outside the Gospels: Paul includes a hymn in his letter to the Philippians that highlights the serving focus (μορφὴν δούλου λαβών) of Jesus' mission.[77] Although this motif is now closely identified with Jesus, the notion of ruling through serving was clearly outlined to Rehoboam in the advice he solicited, and ultimately ignored, from his advisers: 'If you will be a slave (δοῦλος) to this people today and serve (δουλεύσῃς) them, and speak good words to them when you answer them, then they will be your servants forever'.[78]

It is clear, then, that the language of slavery carries an extraordinarily wide range of connotations, spanning both the dishonourable and the honourable. Furthermore, there are hermeneutical complications, not only with colonial histories, but also in regard to the transparency of the first-century primary source material. Finally, the oxymoron of a nexus between leaders who are enslaved is evident. In pastoral studies the sobriquet, 'servant leadership', was adopted in a book of that title by

---

75   Mk 10.42-45; cf. parallels, Mt. 20.25-28; Lk. 22.24-28.

76   Jn 13.13-17.

77   Phil. 2.5-11.

78   1 Kgs 12.7. The young men instead urged, famously, that the ruler should reinforce servile subjugation: 'Thus you should say to this people who spoke to you, "Your father made our yoke heavy, but you must lighten it for us"; thus you should say to them, "My little finger is thicker than my father's loins. Now, whereas my father laid on you a heavy yoke, I will add to your yoke. My father disciplined you with whips, but I will discipline you with scorpions"' (1 Kgs 12.10-11).

Robert Greenleaf, and the phrase is now a commonplace in much popular pastoral literature.[79] The evident difficulties with this phrase, however, include what was meant by, or is compromised by, the marrying of these two concepts; how did it play out in Christian communities that included the presence both of slaves and their masters; and to what extent was or is it practically achievable in Christian communities?[80]

Although Paul uses διάκονος and δοῦλος language extensively right across his corpus of letters, the vast majority of instances concern either those who were slaves in society, or the metaphorical slavery to sin or the law, or a relationship as slave to God, Christ or the gospel. Very few of these instances directly use the notion of leaders acting as slaves (using δοῦλος or δουλόω) in regard to those whom they lead. Of these, the key verses using δοῦλος language are: 1 Cor. 9.19, 'For though I am free with respect to all, I have enslaved myself (ἐδούλωσα) to all, so that I might win more of them'. Paul maintains that, although he is nonetheless free in respect of the Corinthians, he is voluntarily making himself their slave. This drawing attention to his actual freedom may suggest a note of caution on Paul's part, perhaps related to the status squabbles that were so endemic in this community. More wholehearted seems to be the statement in 2 Cor. 4.5: 'For we do not preach ourselves, but Jesus Christ as Lord, and ourselves as your slaves (δοῦλοι) for Jesus' sake', combining, as it does, language of the lordship of Christ, together with language about Paul and Timothy, his co-author, as slaves to the Corinthians. A third, potentially analogous, reference, already mentioned, is that in the Philippian hymn of Christ, in which Christ takes the form of a slave (Phil. 2.7: μορφὴν δούλου λαβών), prior to resuming his position of high exaltation.

Beyond these few references, others that may potentially be considered under the heading of 'servant leadership' employ διακονία, διάκονος and διακονέω language.[81] Although, these terms may well be relevant, indeed significant, there are two issues to be borne in mind. The first is the eventual formalising of διάκονος into a titled office (thus, 'deacon', as opposed to 'servant'), and the effect that this had on both the noun and associated language. The second is the extensive study of διακονία by

---

79   R. K. Greenleaf, *Servant Leadership: A Journey into the Nature of Legitimate Power and Greatness* (New York: Paulist Press, 1977). For Greenleaf, the term 'servant leadership' describes those whose primary desire is to serve others (thus, 'the Son of Man came not to be served but to serve'), and is followed by a secondary aspiration to lead. Closely associated is the sense that such a leader is a steward of resources in a given institution, and acts with appropriate integrity.

80   These issues are all the more difficult to grasp in contemporary ecclesiastical contexts that are not familiar with the humiliated status of the Graeco-Roman slave.

81   Cf. Rom. 12.7; 15.8, 25, 31; 16.1; 1 Cor. 3.5; 16.15; 2 Cor. 8.4; 9.1, 12–13; 11.8; Eph. 4.12.

John Collins, discussed in the previous chapter, in which he has in large measure overturned a consensus. We have seen that his principal theses are, first, that this domain did not, in general Greek usage, of necessity carry servile connotations; the notion of 'serving at tables' is not the root meaning, rather this term normally described the role of an ambassador or representative. Secondly, he maintains that Christian usage did not significantly add new content to this Greek usage. Collins has won many supporters to his view.[82]

I have already drawn attention to my hesitation over Collins' conclusions, particularly regarding those instances in which διάκονος language and δοῦλος language are juxtaposed or in close proximity, and presumably should be read as in some way qualifying each other.[83] In the present discussion, there are those instances in which Paul signals that he or others assume the apparent status of slaves or adopt menial tasks, perhaps without contiguous evidence of δοῦλος language. We have recognized that Paul writes from a position of high status that is associated with the gospel that he proclaims and the commission that he received. It is noteworthy, however, that in a number of ways he downplays the impact of that elevated status, without actually removing it. In this way, Paul is at pains to draw attention to aspects of status inconsistency, the most obvious of which are his readiness to pursue manual labour and his use of servant and servile language in regard to his ministry. Such language ought to be understood alongside the widespread sense in Graeco-Roman society that free people should not act like slaves by working with their hands, denying their dignity and self-respect.[84] In addition to δοῦλος and διάκονος language, Paul makes significant use of

---

82　Cf. P. Gooder, 'Diakonia in the New Testament: A Dialogue with John N. Collins', *Ecclesiology* 3 (2006), p. 33–56.

83　J. N. Collins, *Diakonia: Re-Interpreting the Ancient Sources* (New York; Oxford: Oxford University Press, 1990), p. 245, concedes that much usage in the Gospels does include menial connotations; cf. also Lk. 17.7-10; 22.24-27; Mk 9.33-35. I explored this at greater length in Clarke, *Serve the Community of the Church*, pp. 233–45.

84　Cf. the reference in Jewett, *Romans,* p. 53, to Cicero, *Off.* 1.150. For comparable, negative views of manual labour, cf. also Plutarch, *Pericles* 1.4–2.1, 'while we delight in the work, we despise the workman, as, for instance, in the case of perfumes and dyes; we take a delight in them, but dyers and perfumers we regard as illiberal and vulgar folk ... Labour with one's own hands on lowly tasks gives witness, in the toil thus expended on useless things, to one's own indifference to higher things ... For it does not of necessity follow that if the work delights you with its grace, the one who wrought it is worthy of your esteem'; and Philo, *Det. Pot. Ins.* 33–34, who contrasted the established of society with those who worked with their hands and were consequently without status: 'Those who take care of themselves are men of mark and wealth, holding leading positions, praised on all hands, recipients of honours, portly, healthy and robust, revelling in luxurious and riotous living, knowing nothing of labour, conversant with pleasures which carry the sweets of life to the all-welcoming soul by every channel of sense'.

other terms associated with toil or labour (κοπιάω, κόπος, πόνος, ἐργάζομαι, ἔργον, and ἐργάτης) in contexts both of manual labour and Christian mission. Furthermore, he applies these both to him and to other individuals or groups.[85]

The widespread use of such language is further supplemented by those instances where Paul draws attention to his own sufferings in the cause of Christian ministry, commends others for so suffering, and urges that they continue to endure resolutely such suffering.[86] There is, also, the unexpected inverted pyramid of 1 Cor. 3.21-23, in which Paul says, in the context of a repudiation of the Corinthians' boasting, 'So let no one boast about men. For all things are yours, whether Paul or Apollos or Cephas or the world or life or death or the present or the future – all belong to you, and you belong to Christ, and Christ belongs to God'. Finally, there are occasions when Paul denies exercising his rights to financial support (1 Cor. 9.1-23), and in other measures exposes his vulnerabilities, both in terms of his physical weaknesses and his lack of skill in certain areas.[87] In these ways, Paul lays aside the impression of unassailable strength and status on a number of occasions.

These aspects point to a status inconsistency that is, in large measure, voluntary for Paul, and is commended in and for others. Furthermore, Paul also criticizes situations where he, and others, are accorded an elevated status that is inappropriate, or certain individuals are apparently abusing their status. In these contexts, he adopts a number of moves that were presumably designed to limit the perception of his status, whilst not removing it. In regard to his own position, the apostle is at pains to reject the personality politics that epitomized the behaviour of the Corinthian Christians. We have noted that they were placing one or other leading figure on a pre-eminent pedestal (1 Cor. 1.10-12); in other words, they were according a greater status to Paul and his fellow apostles than he considered appropriate. Significant within this is Paul's particular repudiation of those who held him in unique regard (1 Cor. 1.13), or regarded baptism by him to be of supreme value (1 Cor. 1.14-17). He, instead, provides the starkly contrasting metaphor of the shameful

85 For Paul's manual labour, cf. 1 Cor. 4.12; 9.6; 1 Thess. 2.9; 2 Thess. 3.8; for his Christian ministry, cf. 1 Cor. 9.1; 15.10; Gal. 4.11; Phil. 1.22; 2.16; Col. 1.29; 1 Tim. 4.10; for the manual labour of others, cf. 1 Thess. 4.11; 2 Thess. 3.10-12; and, for the Christian ministry of others, cf. Rom. 16.6, 12; 1 Cor. 15.58; 16.10, 16; 2 Cor. 11.13, 15; Gal. 6.1; Eph. 4.12; Col. 3.23; 4.13 1 Thess. 1.3; 5.12-13; 1 Tim. 3.1; 5.10, 17–18; 2 Tim. 2.15, 21.

86 Rom. 5.3; 8.18, 35; 12.12, 14; 1 Cor. 4.8-13; 15.32; 2 Cor. 1.4-8; 4.8-12, 17; 6.4; 7.4-5; 8.2; 12.10; Gal. 5.11; Eph. 3.13; Phil. 1.17, 29; 3.10; 4.14; Col. 1.24; 1 Thess. 1.6; 2.14; 3.3-4, 7; 2 Thess. 1.4-7; 1 Tim. 5.10; 2 Tim. 1.8, 12; 2.3, 9; 3.11-12; 4.5.

87 In terms of ailments, cf. the thorn in the flesh (2 Cor. 12.7), and the possibility of an eye condition (Gal. 4.15); in terms of physical stature, cf. 2 Cor. 10.10; in terms of key skills, cf. his lack of ability in public speaking (1 Cor. 2.1-5).

position of apostles at the end of the victory parade, as those humiliated and reviled. These Corinthians were not only granting the apostles a more elevated status than was appropriate, but were themselves too conscious of the importance of even their own status (1 Cor. 4.8-13).

The greatest difficulty that inheres in the metaphor of 'servant-leadership' is whether or not it can be consistently applied. In surveying the Pauline material, it is evident that δοῦλος language is used in regard to the Christian ministry very rarely. On the other hand, διάκονος language is considerably more frequent, but it has been convincingly demonstrated that it does not always or necessarily carry servile connotations. A significant interpretative framework for understanding this language, however, has been other aspects of Paul's message that draw attention to status inconsistency. These serve well to suggest a vulnerable, serving, low status characteristic to Paul's view of Christian ministry.

However, this inconsistency in his status highlights the very problem with this portrait. It entails a mixing of metaphors, or a combining of otherwise incompatible structures. This serving nature of Christian ministry works within a structure that is otherwise marked by hierarchy, submission and a call to obedience – both appear to be integral to the Pauline theology of leadership. Paul's conception of the Christian leader is one who is the head of a household, and master of domestic slaves, and whose house-church in all probability includes other slaves. Accordingly, the message of servanthood as it appears in the Pauline corpus is not a thorough-going servanthood that inverts the normal hierarchy of the home; the head of the household remains the leader. Rather, the context of humility, vulnerability and service set a context for the exercising of authority, rather than its removal. This is consistent with the portrait of Jesus in the Gospels that shows a figure who was renowned both for his authority and his repudiation of authoritarianism.

5. Conclusion

These discussions in regard to the status and models of leadership are hotly contested and wide ranging. Of the three models, that of the presence and endorsement of an 'established, and arguably predictable, hierarchy is the most assured, and enjoys the widest body of supporting evidence from the Pauline letters. Significantly, the number and spread of relevant verses cited throughout the Pauline corpus serve to demonstrate some consistency, over time and across a range of contexts, for what Paul is saying. Clearly, it is a model that attracts criticism and is innately open to abuse, both in the first and twenty-first centuries. The second of the models, 'egalitarianism', finds no clear support within the first-century sources, although it happens to be the most palatable in today's Western societies. The third of the models is widely propounded in ecclesiastical circles, although a consistent outworking of the model is problematic. Difficulties include both the meaning of διάκονος, the infrequency with which δοῦλος language is used of community leadership, and the complex range of statuses associated with these terms.

It is concluded that the notion of the leader acting, on occasion, as a servant or slave is apparent in the Pauline text, and finds its source in Jesus' ministry. Paul is not averse, however, to mixing metaphors, or applying different notions in response to different situations. In this regard, the way in which servant leadership one-sidedly dominates so many pastoral and management books is perhaps unwarranted in light of the extent of its treatment in both the Pauline and dominical texts. The leader has a higher status within the hierarchy, but is not to abuse that status, and there will be occasions when the actions, vulnerabilities, sufferings and incessant toil of the leader reflect more the status of a slave. In this regard, Jesus, Paul and Peter are each presented as resisting the notion of leaders 'lording it over' their subjects.[88]

It is both the juxtaposition of these three arenas and the failure to juxtapose these three arenas that cause difficulties, both hermeneutically and in contemporary and historical, church contexts. The conundrum is apparent, not only in Paul's writings, but also in the portrayal of Jesus' life. Both are highly authoritative figures, with a widely recognized legitimacy. They act with authority and have followers or loyal supporters, on whom they make demands. However, they both adopt the language of serving, not only of themselves, but they also recommend it of others.

---

88 Cf. 2 Cor. 1.24 (κυριεύομεν); 1 Pet. 5.3 (κατακυριεύοντες); and Mt. 20.25; Mk 10.42; Lk. 22.25 ([κατα]κυριεύουσιν).

Chapter Five

THE POWER OF LEADERS

1. *Introduction*

Power and authority are profoundly contentious issues, not only in society at large, but also, and unfortunately, in many churches. They are no less controversial concepts in academic debate, both among social theorists, and also in the scholarly study of the apostle Paul. A major complication, not only in the dynamics of actual power interactions but also in academic debates about power, is the difficulty of defining what are, and what are the differences between, authority, leadership, power, influence, control and management. Each of these concepts is quite distinct, yet they are closely related; and, at times, the terms are used interchangeably. In a single, given, social context, each of these *may* be exercised by, or reside in, quite different people, or even in multiple, competing factions. And yet, theoretical analysis of power dynamics often over-simplifies these complexities, and occasionally presupposes that these concepts are co-extensive, co-located and unilateral – that is, an assumption that in a society or institution there are the leaders who manage, and possess authority, power, influence, and control; and there are the rest, who are led, and who don't.

This simplified perspective that there are the powerful, who exercise power, and there are the weak, who don't, is now widely applied in readings of the Pauline epistles. Paul is identified as a figure who exercises power and asserts authority, and the recipients of the letters are generally regarded as those that, Paul asserts, either are, or should be, subject to him. In this way, Elizabeth Castelli, in *Imitating Paul: a Discourse in Power*, is especially interested in the power strategy that underlies Paul's use of the imitation motif.[1] This Pauline injunction, and its anticipated effects, are analysed independently of any contrary power moves that are antagonistic to Paul, and to which he is responding. Similarly, Sandra Hack Polaski, in *Paul and the Discourse of Power*, while noting that there

---

[1] Cf. E. A. Castelli, *Imitating Paul: A Discourse of Power* (Literary Currents in Biblical Interpretation; Louisville: Westminster John Knox Press, 1991). Cf. also the more detailed discussion in Chapter 7 below.

is a wide range of asymmetric power relations that are reflected in the Pauline letters, including the relations between God and Paul,[2] nonetheless focuses almost exclusively on an analysis of Paul as the principal power figure, thereby ignoring leading figures other than the apostle. Cynthia Briggs Kittredge, in *Community and Authority: the Rhetoric of Obedience in the Pauline Tradition,* compares calls to obedience and submission made by the authors of Philippians, Ephesians and Colossians.[3] Framed in this way, her study analyses the relations between the one who demands obedience and those who should obey. It is, of course, in the nature of the extant evidence as exhortatory letters from a single figure that the *apostle's* exercising of power will surface as a key focus; consequently, investigations into the imitation motif, language of obedience and submission, and other power discourse are bound to concentrate on the particular dynamic of Paul's power in relation to his correspondents. Furthermore, studies of this kind of language, which is widely to be found in the Pauline correspondence, are bound to reinforce a picture of an authoritarian Paul precisely because of their focus on identifying and evaluating instances of this one individual's power rhetoric.[4]

Although this aspect of Paul's portrait has been a particular focus during the last two decades, over the longer history of interpretation the wider issue of Pauline social power has either been largely unidentified or it has been ignored. Indeed, Castelli suggests that there has been a longstanding tendency to 'skirt around' what may be regarded as the less palatable elements of power and authority in the text:

> For just as many commentators on the New Testament have skirted the question of power – to avoid the danger or for fear of controversy – so the question of power has continued to skirt both the text and commentaries upon it ... Though early Christian texts are full of references to, articulations of, and claims to power, paradoxically the interpretation of these texts rarely has taken up the question of the power relations underwritten or enabled by these texts, or examined the implications of power being enacted discursively. ... In Pauline scholarship on mimesis, at least two moves have been operative, both

---

2   S. Hack Polaski, *Paul and the Discourse of Power* (Gender, Culture, Theory; Sheffield: Sheffield Academic Press, 1999), p. 23.

3   C. Briggs Kittredge, *Community and Authority: The Rhetoric of Obedience in the Pauline Tradition* (Harvard Theological Studies; Harrisburg: Trinity Press International, 1998).

4   Hack Polaski, *Paul and the Discourse of Power*, p. 21, quotes Nietzsche's comment about Paul, 'Even what he himself did not believe, was believed in by the idiots among whom he spread his doctrine. What he wanted was power; with St Paul the priest again aspired to power, he could make use only of concepts, doctrines, symbols with which masses may be tyrannized over, and with which herds are formed'.

of which either remarkably skirt the question of power or reinscribe it unproblematically. The first move involves a spiritualizing gesture towards the text, one which, not incidentally, assumes the transparency of textual reference while remaining silent on the question of the interestedness of the text. The second move stems from an implicit investment in the notion of the tradition itself as authoritative, monolithic, and univocal.[5]

While recent discussions about power have corrected this blind spot, and have brought the topic of power into the public arena as an appropriate topic for discussion, it is now important that these power relations are not treated in simplified terms, essentially dealing exclusively with Paul's mechanisms of asserting power. Paul's power rhetoric and his power dealings need to be explored within their wider context, including the ways in which Paul defined the limits of his power, the ways in which he undermined the power that was inherent in his own position, how he responded to the power plays of others, and how, and when, he articulated what are appropriate power strategies for local leaders to adopt.

Social theorists are profoundly aware that power relations are often highly complex, and are rarely bi-polar and uni-directional. Consequently, they frequently predicate their deliberations with an apology that their discussions will, of necessity, over-simplify the issues.[6] Although in this chapter I shall highlight more of the complexities than are typically identified in Pauline discussions about power, authority and manipulation, I am no less aware that my analysis also, and of necessity, remains a simplification of what is both an inordinately convoluted debate and also a complex, and remote, underlying historical reality. It will be helpful, at the outset of our investigation into aspects of power both in regard to Paul and the Pauline communities, however, to consider a number of the complicating factors.

2. *Complicating Factors*

So much of the content of Paul's letters was composed in direct response to specific, historical situations of power conflict.[7] Sometimes Paul, as an

---

5   Castelli, *Imitating Paul*, p. 23.

6   Recognizing the lack of clarity in the scholarly research on leadership, A. Gini, 'Moral Leadership: An Overview', *J Bus Ethics* 16 (1997), p. 323, provides the following, unattributed, and presumably tongue-in-cheek quotation: 'next to economic theory, never has so much been written on the same topic – resulting in so little agreement on the most elemental propositions in the field'.

7   There has been a notable growth in interest in the study of Pauline community conflict in recent years; cf., for example, the following extended studies: J. A. Crafton, *The Agency of*

outsider, is seen to be addressing a conflict that was bilateral, and contained within a single Christian community, as, for example, between Euodia and Syntyche in the Philippian church.[8] At other times Paul was himself one of the two parties engaging in a conflict that had ramifications far beyond a single Christian community, exemplified in the theological dispute between the apostle and the Judaizers that had infiltrated the Galatian churches. On another occasion, supremely represented in the personality politics that is addressed in 1 Corinthians, it was Paul who was the object of discord within a community. In addition to the power engagements that are pursued within the letters themselves, Paul was also both a pawn and a key player in power dynamics in which his life and safety were at risk.[9] Consequently, we are engaging with power dynamics that were at times entirely at an apostolic or other trans-local level; at other times the power dynamics are at the nexus between the apostolic and the local levels; and at still other times the issues are entirely local, albeit involving external, apostolic attempts at conciliation. In the light of this, it is important not to focus exclusively on the Pauline power plays, but to ask whether Paul held that other Christian leaders ought to have a distinct set of reasonable values and parameters for exercising power, which might vary depending on their position within a hierarchy that spanned the domestic (house church), the local (groups across a city) and the trans-local contexts. Did Paul expect members of the Christian communities to respond differently to their local leaders than to an apostolic figure? Did Paul, in theory or in practice, anticipate that his own

---

the Apostle: A Dramatic Analysis of Paul's Responses to Conflict in 2 Corinthians (JSNTSup; Sheffield: JSOT Press, 1991); D. W. Kuck, Judgement and Community Conflict: Paul's Use of Apocalyptic Judgement Language in 1 Corinthians 3.5–4.5 (NovTSup; Leiden; New York: E. J. Brill, 1992); C. S. De Vos, Church and Community Conflicts: The Relationships of the Thessalonian, Corinthian, and Philippian Churches with their Wider Civic Communities (SBLDS; Atlanta: Scholars Press; Flinders University of South Australia, 1999); T. D. Still, Conflict at Thessalonica: A Pauline Church and its Neighbours (JSNTSup; Sheffield: Sheffield Academic, 1999); R. M. Grant, Paul in the Roman World: The Conflict at Corinth (Louisville; London: Westminster John Knox Press, 2001); D. K. Williams, Enemies of the Cross of Christ: The Terminology of the Cross and Conflict in Philippians (JSNTSup; London: Sheffield Academic Press, 2002); P. F. Esler, Conflict and Identity in Romans: The Social Setting of Paul's Letter (Minneapolis: Fortress, 2003); T. J. Burke and J. K. Elliott (eds), Paul and the Corinthians: Studies on a Community in Conflict: Essays in Honour of Margaret Thrall (NovTSup, 109; Leiden: Brill, 2003); M. Slee, The Church in Antioch in the First Century CE: Communion and Conflict (JSNTSup; Sheffield: Sheffield Academic Press, 2003); R. S. Dutch, The Educated Elite in 1 Corinthians: Education and Community Conflict in Graeco-Roman Context (JSNTSup; New York; London: T. & T. Clark, 2005); and P. Coutsoumpos, Community, Conflict, and the Eucharist in Roman Corinth: The Social Setting of Paul's Letter (Lanham: University Press of America, 2006).

8 Phil. 4.2-3.

9 Cf., for example, 1 Cor. 15.32; 2 Cor. 1.8.

parameters of apostolic leadership could be simply adopted, or should instead be adapted, when applied by a local church leader?

It is clear that the contending sources of power were diverse, and even the number of challenges to those in established authority (and to others who held influence) can no longer be identified on the basis of the limited texts available to us. Not only did Paul's letters raise and respond to issues of power distribution in the first-century Christian communities, but also many regard his letters as holding a normative status today. Those who offer their own interpretations of Paul's handling of these power conflicts, his views on local church leadership and authority, and his own exercise of power, are potentially raising significant implications for attitudes towards leadership and influence within contemporary social contexts. Both the parameters and conclusions of such research are in some measure defined by each interpreter's experiences, both positive and negative, of leadership, management and control, whether within ecclesiastical or other social contexts.[10] Similarly, those who read and evaluate such research, indeed the sources, methods, and conclusions of this publication, will do so influenced by their own experiences of power plays, in churches and other social contexts. It is because the issues are at the same time highly complex, and yet have significant, contemporary ramifications, that analysis, both within the academy and the church, of the distribution of power within the Pauline communities is rarely dispassionate, and perhaps even more subjective than many other fields of New Testament scholarship.

We are thus faced with multiple levels of complexity, many of which are not adequately outlined or fully appreciated by those who have engaged in these debates, both in historical research and in contemporary church contexts. First, specialists recognize that the field itself is conceptually complex, and that much of the discussion and many of the findings are necessarily simplifications. Secondly, the dynamics of power are far broader than simply assessing Paul's own qualities of leadership – power is normally held multilaterally; furthermore, Paul is dealing with multiple, discrete communities, each with their own leaders and peculiar power dynamics. Thirdly, our access to sufficient, informed, independent, yet relevant, historical data is far from ideal. Indeed, what we do possess derives from a single author, yet relates to a wide range of quite different social contexts with which Paul was engaging intimately yet often remotely; furthermore, each situation had its own particular conflicts and

---

10   Like many, my experiences have included being a leader, making decisions and acting in ways that have been both challenged or endorsed by others (and no doubt both responses have been justified). In other contexts, where I have not held a particular office, my behaviour and responses towards those in authority have at times been characterized by support or compliance, and at other times by challenge or even resistance.

dynamics of power. We shall see that this paucity of material, together with Paul's remoteness from the presenting problems, and our remoteness from Paul, reflect points of vulnerability in the study. Fourthly, it is difficult to map onto this complex matrix of power exchanges the effect on Paul of living a life that regularly faced punishment, imprisonment, distress, danger, and death threats, as he saw it for the sake of the gospel and the continuing faith of his spiritual children. Finally, our own personal interpretative frameworks influence our identification, or failure to identify, the key issues and questions; and they similarly influence our response to the findings of others. This daunting sequence of hurdles does not render the task itself futile; indeed it serves to reinforce aspects of its essential importance. It does, however, demand that a careful and judicious approach be adopted, seeking to reach conclusions that are both cautious and guarded.

A fully extensive comparison of the multiple contexts will not be attempted here. Rather, this chapter will focus on identifying and exploring from the Pauline sources a number of issues that impinge on the task of collating and evaluating evidence of the exercise of power in the Pauline communities. I shall seek to draw some conclusions as to the range of relevant evidence and the kind of findings that can be sustained from the text. I shall also outline Paul's own views on the nature and locus of power within Christian communities, and what he appears to characterize as reasonable or appropriate use of power within such contexts.

3. *Types of Power*

Power is a notoriously diffuse concept, and social theorists hold widely divergent views as to the principles and effects of power, and how, indeed even whether, power can be analysed.[11] For many, power is conceived according to the two, traditional categories of 'power to' achieve something, and 'power over' somebody, although this analysis is increasingly challenged as being too crude. Dahl's oft quoted maxim is that: 'A has *power over* B to the extent that he can get B to do something that B would not otherwise do.'[12] In other words, B is influenced to do something that, at the time, they believe to be contrary to their interests. Indeed, many would argue that for an individual to exercise power at all

---

11   S. Lukes, *Power: A Radical View* (Basingstoke: Palgrave Macmillan, 2005), p. 192, argues that, 'among those who have reflected on [power], there is no agreement about how to define it, how to conceive it, how to study it and, if it can be measured, how to measure it. There are endless debates about such questions, which show no sign of imminent resolution, and there is not even agreement about whether all this disagreement matters'.

12   R. Dahl, 'The Concept of Power', *Behavioral Science* 2 (1957), p. 80.

in a social context is, in its very essence, to act against the will or interests of another; and yet, the Foucauldian premise that power is everywhere is also deemed to be a truism. It is evident that, with such a perspective, 'power over' will normally be understood negatively. It may be associated with terms such as dominance, coercion, oppression and social manipulation, and it is likely to result in involuntary obedience, exacted by intimidation, threat or even physical force.

Interpreted alternatively, power may be beneficent – a 'resource' that can be a socially transforming positive, and may lead to the empowerment of others, or the redistribution of power to others; it may increase the capabilities of others, or enhance their freedoms. In other words, power has the potential to further the interests of others, rather than necessarily and exclusively act against, or in conflict with their interests. This kind of power has been termed 'power with', or co-action, in contrast to coercion,[13] or simply as a constructive form of 'power over'. Clearly, the positive changes in behaviour caused by this second category of power may at the same time also serve the interests of the one exercising power, and thus the benefits may be mutual.

Beneficent power, however, cannot simply be defined as the kind of influence that results in constructive changes in behaviour. Clearly, even such positive ends do not necessarily justify any means. The affirmative changes in behaviour may, perhaps, have been conceded with willing compliance; but they may, alternatively, have been exacted under inappropriate duress, constraint or threat; or the influence may simply have been unwelcome at the time. Under what circumstances is the application of coercion not only advisable, but also reasonable, and necessary? The notion of 'acting in another's interests' is surely a complex exchange, entailing analysis of both the ends and the means.

We may also see that the number of different types even of beneficent power is considerable. Paternal or maternal power, or the power of the teacher, to influence or broaden the capacities of their offspring or pupils is potentially beneficent power. These parental or pedagogic authorities *may* endeavour to exercise power while all the time seeking to maintain the dignity and gradually enhance the independence of their subjects. Their motives *may* even be altruistic. Significantly, both the teacher and the parent typically share the goal that their protégés eventually come to

---

13   M. P. Follett, *et al.*, *Dynamic Administration: The Collected Papers of Mary Parker Follett* (London: Pitman, 1941), pp. 101–5. Cf. the more recent discussion in S. Kreisberg, *Transforming Power: Domination, Empowerment, and Education* (SUNY Series, Teacher Empowerment and School Reform; Albany: State University of New York Press, 1992), in which pp. 29–53 describe 'power over' as the more common association with power, and pp. 55–90 explore the alternative model of transformative power, or 'power over'.

develop skills and abilities that surpass those of their mentors, and they use themselves as role models in the pursuit of those goals.

A second type of beneficent power may be seen in the rigorous and disciplinary regimes imposed by a football coach or a military commander. Unlike the child and pupil, the footballer or soldier *may* well be a volunteer; these players or subordinates *may* of their own free will submit and acquiesce to the power of the commanding officer or trainer; and that exercising of power *may* be in the interests of their players or more junior ranks. However, these regimes do not share the same goals as the teacher or parent; namely, gradually to enhance the independence or self-determining autonomy of individuals within the team or armed force.

The biblical analogy of the shepherd, in so far as his goals are to protect, care for and feed his flock, presents a further model of potentially beneficent power. Clearly, in both the biblical and ecclesiastical expositions of the metaphor of shepherd and sheep, the figure of speech is typically not developed to its ultimate destiny in slaughter or sacrifice.[14] A core focus of the good shepherd is the well-being and safety of his flock, and in this regard both his leadership and exercising of power may be deemed to be beneficent. The goals of the shepherd may be compared to those of the sports coach and the military commander in that the self-determination, liberty and autonomy of the sheep are not aspirations. On the other hand, the pastoral context is quite different in that his flock is not a group of willing volunteers. The shepherd also differs from the parents and teacher, in that he does not model qualities for the sheep to emulate; but, on the other hand, so the parables tell us, he may, like the parent, be quite altruistic in the extent to which he will go to secure the safety and nurture of those in his care. Thus, while each of these may be considered examples of beneficent power, there are notable differences in their ends and means – albeit that, framed in this way, both the ends and means might be said to be beneficent.

Of course, each of these types of power relationship – the familial, the pastoral, the military and the athletic – employs its own mechanisms of coercion, whether in the form of incentives, inducements or negative sanctions.[15] It is also all too evident that domination or other forms of relationship abuse in each of these contexts nonetheless can, and unfortunately do, occur. However, it should be clear from these theoretical examples alone, that power need not, of necessity, always be a tool of oppression.[16] It is not the presence of coercion that marks the

14 Contrast, e.g. Zech. 11.16.

15 Cf. T. Parsons, 'On the Concept of Political Power', *Proc Am Philos Soc* 107 (1963), pp. 238–9.

16 Although Foucault is often cited as an exponent of the view that power is a negative force, in M. Foucault, *Discipline and Punish: The Birth of the Prison* (London: Allen Lane,

boundary between a beneficent and an oppressive power structure, but it is the nature of any coercion (or threatened or otherwise potential coercion) that defines the power relationship. Appropriately exercised power may indeed be a means of liberation and life enhancement for those who are led. The twin difficulties remain, however, of determining the boundary and overlaps between coercion and consent, and what defines the parameters of appropriate coercion.[17] The very diffuseness of the concept of power, however, means that both this boundary and these parameters will necessarily vary from context to context and from relationship to relationship.

It may be noted that each of these metaphors of power relations, the parent, the teacher, the shepherd and the team leader, is used by Paul to describe either his own role or that of others in the Christian communities.[18] We cannot determine simply from Paul's use of these titles, however, whether Paul, or others, exercised coercion in ways that were beneficent. Paul does, however, identify isolated examples of inappropriate coercion by the Judaizers and by his opponents. He notes with a sense of victory that Titus had not been compelled to be circumcised (Gal. 2.3), in contrast to those Galatians and those in Antioch who had been subject to a measure of compulsion (Gal. 2.14; 6.12).[19] It is also interesting to note those instances in which Paul does appear to apply compulsion, and yet denies that he is doing so – although in the following instances the goal may be said to be to the benefit of a third party. In 2 Cor. 9.7 he urges the Corinthians to give to the collection in a way that is generous, willing, and not under compulsion, and yet the implicit comparison that is made with the generosity of the Macedonians must have afforded a measure of pressure. Similarly, in his dialogue with Philemon, Paul clearly applies some emotional pressure, although he denies that it is his intention to achieve a forced response (Phlm. 14).

The scholarly debate in regard to Paul and power has been significantly

---

1977), p. 194, he urges that, 'We must cease once and for all to describe the effects of power in negative terms: it "excludes," it "represses," it "censors," it "abstracts," it "masks," it "conceals." In fact, power produces; it produces reality; it produces domains of objects and rituals of truths. The individual and the knowledge that may be gained of him belong to this production'.

17   Cf. Parsons, 'On the Concept of Political Power', p. 232.

18   For the parent, cf. 1 Cor. 4.14-15, 17; 2 Cor. 6.13; 12.14; Gal. 4.19; Phil. 2.22; 1 Thess. 2.7, 11; 1 Tim. 1.2, 18; 3.4; 2 Tim. 1.2; 2.1; Tit. 1.4; Phlm. 10; for the teacher, cf. Rom. 2.20-21; 6.17; 12.7; 16.17; 1 Cor. 4.17; 12.28; 14.6, 26; Eph. 4.11, 21; Col. 1.28; 2.7; 3.16; 2 Thess. 2.15; 1 Tim. 2.7; 3.2; 4.6, 11, 13, 16; 5: 17; 6.1; 2 Tim. 1.11; 2.2, 24; 3.10; 4.2; Tit. 1.9; 2.1, 7; for the team leader, cf. the use of the words κυβέρνησις in 1 Cor. 12.28, and προϊστάμενος in Rom. 12.8; 1 Thess. 5.12; 1 Tim. 5.17; and for the shepherd, cf. Eph. 4.11 and 1 Cor. 9.7.

19   Cf. also the use of ἀναγκάζω in 2 Cor. 12.11.

and provocatively furthered by Elizabeth Castelli,[20] in her application of a Foucauldian theory of power and power's ubiquity to Paul's use of the motif of imitation. Her argument is that the call to imitation essentially establishes and enshrines a permanently asymmetrical, hierarchical and necessarily non-egalitarian relationship – by definition, a power relationship that is coercive.[21] Castelli regards Paul's framing of the relationship between him and his correspondents in this way as illegitimate – because it lacks appropriate legitimation, it consequently resorts to manipulative discourse in order to privilege Paul's position as 'truth'.[22] Understanding the imitation relationship as one of permanent inequality[23] contrasts with my own exposition of the parental and pedagogical metaphors as ones that encourage advancement, in an environment in which the child learns and matures, and which, both the parent and teacher hope, will encourage the child to exceed the abilities of their mentor.[24] The relationship of both the parent and the teacher is initially, and necessarily, one that highlights a difference in status. This is evident in Paul's description of the Corinthians as those who are immature (1 Cor. 3.1-2; 14.20). Eventual maturity is a goal that Paul and Epaphras are said to have pursued in regard to those at Colossae (Col. 1.28; 4.12); furthermore, Paul certainly writes elsewhere as though maturity were something that has either been attained or is obtainable (1 Cor. 2.6; 14.20; 2 Cor. 13.9; Eph. 4.13; Phil. 3.15). Although the metaphor of imitation may be power discourse, it is not evident that such power discourse is always and only negative – especially when applied by a father figure.

Castelli's reading focuses on the reader's reception of the text, rather than seeking to reconstruct the now inaccessible intention of the author, and it is presented as self-interested, but plausible, and, she hopes, persuasive.[25] Castelli demonstrates something of the complexity of the field, but, following Foucault, her assumptions are that power, even paternal power, is repressive. Although I shall interact with Castelli's treatment of the imitation motif more in chapter 7, mention of her at this point serves in a number of ways. First, it demonstrates from Pauline scholarship something of the diversity of views on the principles, purpose and effects of power. Secondly, it exemplifies in regard to Paul how one's

20   Cf. also the recent and detailed critique of Castelli in V. A. Copan, *Saint Paul as Spiritual Director: An Analysis of the Imitation of Paul with Implications and Applications to the Practice of Spiritual Direction* (Paternoster Biblical Monographs; Milton Keynes: Paternoster, 2007).

21   Castelli, *Imitating Paul*, p. 116.

22   Castelli, *Imitating Paul*, pp. 32, 54, 57.

23   Castelli, *Imitating Paul*, p. 80.

24   Cf. also Copan, *Saint Paul as Spiritual Director*, p. 206, who draws a similar conclusion.

25   Castelli, *Imitating Paul*, pp. 120–1.

understanding of power as potentially beneficent or essentially manipulative and oppressive has a significant impact on one's reading of the Pauline text. Thirdly, it raises our next question, namely, that of how power can be or is measured.

4. *Measuring Power*

It is clear that power is complex, both conceptually and in its exercise. We may note that it is rarely held unilaterally, but is a commodity that is often challenged, enhanced or vitiated, through negotiation and the exchange of resources or other incentives.[26] In a given social context, the powerful are not always the leaders, and power is not a constant or fixed quantity resource, such that a loss of power in one person or group is directly proportionate to the gaining of power in another.[27] We have also seen that different types of power are not defined according to a simple dichotomy between the coercive and the consensual, where the one is always and necessarily oppressive, and the other is by definition beneficent.[28] With these provisos in mind, we may be able to consider how or whether it may be possible to identify, measure and evaluate the power that Paul possessed and exercised, challenged or endorsed.

a. *Power and its Effects*
There is a widely held assumption that power can only be identified and evaluated in terms of its actions and effects. Indeed, social theories are often demonstrated either by experimentation or observation. Although this view is now rightly contested as too narrow, it nonetheless remains the case that changes in behaviour as a consequence of the exercising of power are the principal means by which one observes and therefore evaluates that power. In this regard, power is clearly quite different from authority, which cannot be observed behaviourally.

When it comes to the Pauline evidence, however, to the extent that the exercising of power or influence is measured or analysed with regard to changes in behaviour, we are necessarily faced with a fundamental

26   The presence and implications of such a power exchange are not factored into Castelli's analysis of the Pauline discourse.

27   Parsons, 'On the Concept of Political Power', pp. 250–7, adopting economic theory, uses the term 'zero-sum', and explores the fallacy of equilibrium between power inputs and power outputs.

28   Parsons, 'On the Concept of Political Power', p. 258, writes, 'I think [I] can advance a claim to present a resolution of the old dilemma as to whether (in the older terms) power is "essentially" a phenomenon of coercion or of consensus. It is both, precisely because it is a phenomenon which integrates a plurality of factors and outputs of political effectiveness and is not to be identified with any one of them'.

limitation in our source data. These individual letters, the majority without sequels, and all lacking extant responses from the recipients, provide very little measurable evidence of changes of behaviour, either in Paul or in others, from which to extrapolate or determine the use of power or influence, either by Paul or others.[29] This limited record of measurable changes in behaviour places key constraints on our ability to isolate and evaluate the effects of any such power, and therefore the nature of such power.

It is tempting for interpreters, in view of this deficiency, instead to evaluate Paul's power in terms of the reactions that his correspondence now elicits in their own, quite different, cultural and psychological contexts. In this regard, measurable, contemporary responses to Paul's correspondence are substituted for the inaccessible, and consequently unmeasurable, original reception. Where I identify that a Pauline statement either challenges aspects of my behaviour, or elicits a change in my behaviour, or draws some negative or affirmative response from me, I have also identified or observed something of his power to influence me. I may then either expressly argue for commensurability or simply assume it, and suppose that the ways in which Paul exercised power in the first instance, and, indeed, his influences on all subsequent readers, can be reconstructed on the basis of my own contemporary reactions.

However, there are two bases that render such an approach either unreasonable or unreliable grounds for extrapolating backwards. Reactions in one context, historically and culturally remote from our own, are likely to be quite different from reactions in any of a range of subsequent settings, especially those of the twenty-first century. Furthermore, since the Pauline statements were expressly directed to individuals, identified by and known to Paul, it is far from appropriate to measure their impact and influence by means of how a quite different, and unintended, individual receives those statements. In other words, it may be problematic if Paul's specific and occasional power engagements with personal acquaintances are inadvertently, and inappropriately, regarded as generically and universally intended.

We might note, by way of limited analogy, how parents develop an instinctive awareness that the ways in which they educate, influence or discipline their children have to be modified depending on each child's particular personality type and character. A parent learns that what is a

---

29 Cf. K. M. Dowding, *Power* (Concepts in the Social Sciences; Buckingham: Open University Press, 1996), p. 4, 'The problem for studying power is that we may have to discover the power of actors without actually seeing them wield that power. This is partly because they do not always use all their power, and partly because, even when they do, the nature of the political process and the social world means that some actors may try to exercise that power away from the prying eyes of those trying to study them'.

proportionate attempt to exercise control in one set of circumstances and for one child may be either ineffective for another, or possibly quite disproportionate. It is reasonable to hold that in most instances when Paul sought to exercise power in regard to certain individuals or small groups, he did so conscious of the particular contexts and people he was addressing. If so, it would be a mistake to read the force of those engagements as intended for all audiences in some indiscriminate sense. In a more limited sense, Paul's interactions with larger groups, even whole communities, will also have been tailored to his awareness of the context of those groups and the seriousness of the situations he was addressing.

If the parental analogy still holds, it is also clear that well-meaning parents do, on occasion, entirely misjudge a situation and apply disproportionate control that is immediately or later regretted. There may be identifiable evidence of momentary regret on the part of Paul, but the medium of the formal letter at one level ought to eliminate or limit hasty over-reactions on his part, and at another level the letter makes it less likely that we will see *postscriptum* evidence of subsequent regret. One potential instance of momentary regret on the part of Paul, speaking *in loco parentis,* may be his statement: 'I am not writing this to make you ashamed, but to admonish you as my beloved children' (1 Cor. 4.14). Clearly what he has just written (1 Cor. 4.8-13) runs every risk of being interpreted as biting criticism, which is highly likely to have pricked the heart of more than simply the most sensitive members of the Corinthian church. Thiselton, however, argues that the thrust here in Paul's confessed desire not to humiliate is to give the Corinthians a sense of realism.[30] This is not to suggest that Paul is averse to using shame as a tool of persuasion, indeed he even encourages it in others, and he almost certainly holds there to be occasions when inciting shame may be considered a fitting action.[31] It is nonetheless clear that it may be hermeneutically inappropriate for interpreters to associate their own reactions to Paul's persuasive techniques with the assumed reactions of his originally intended audience, presupposing not only a comparable psychology in both audiences, but also that Paul would have taken the same tone with all such audiences.

Secondly, we note that the historical and cultural gap that spans between our contexts and those of Paul's correspondents adds a distance, additional to the psychological, which should caution against an ill-considered transposing of the apostle's interactions to a quite different context. It is clear that where an act of power may be deemed to be

---

30   A. C. Thiselton, *The First Epistle to the Corinthians: A Commentary on the Greek Text* (NIGTC; Carlisle; Grand Rapids: Paternoster; Eerdmans, 2000), p. 368.

31   Cf. 1 Cor. 6.5; 15.34 (ἐντροπή); 2 Thess. 3.14; Tit. 2.8 (ἐντρέπω).

unequivocally tyrannical both in a generic, first-century context and ours, our assessment, indeed critique, may be reasonably straightforward and entirely justified. In other circumstances, for example, where Graeco-Roman social mores are not only clearly different to ours, but we can also no longer identify the likely reaction of a first-century audience, our task is rather more difficult. Where the specific circumstances and individuals of the historical context are unknown, their reactions are unrecorded, and our general understanding of their social context suggests that a given action would not have been regarded as unreasonably oppressive, our task is very complex – and surely demands considerable caution in drawing critical conclusions. In this regard, the interpreter must adopt caution before criticizing Paul for adopting a stance that much later generations and cultures have come to critique.

Much of this applies to those contexts in which interpreters are unable to gauge the response of Paul's original audience to his expression of power, and have opted to substitute their own reaction. From a different standpoint, however, Paul's correspondence does occasionally record or reflect his own reactions to the influences of others, and, in this regard, we clearly do possess behavioural data, but in rejoinder to the power dynamics of others, where Paul is the butt. At a number of points, his letters contain evidence of his responses to the challenges and criticisms of others – although, of course, in these instances we have comparatively little by which to reconstruct their power gambits. Fee, for example, has argued that much of 1 Corinthians is framed as Paul's defence in the face of challenges to his authority and rights as an apostle.[32] 2 Corinthians records further evidence, especially in chapters 10–12, of his contested apostleship. In both instances, Paul provides a robust response to the challenge, and defends his own, superior, position of authority, conceding nothing to those who would contest his position. It is clear to Paul that he considers himself to be in a position of authority over the Corinthians (2 Cor. 10.8); indeed, in the light of this challenge, he maintains that he holds the right both to expect their obedience and 'to punish [their] every disobedience' (2 Cor. 10.6). That said, Paul identifies that his authority (ἐξουσία) is to be channelled only towards 'building you up and not ... tearing you down' (2 Cor. 10.8) – a criterion that the Corinthians can use to evaluate his actions, even if later interpreters cannot. The grounds for Paul's self-defence in 2 Corinthians 10–11

---

32 G. D. Fee, *The First Epistle to the Corinthians* (NICNT; Grand Rapids: Eerdmans, 1987), pp. 4–14, 392–4, especially, p. 393, in regard to 1 Cor. 9.1-27, 'Since a crisis of authority lies behind much of this letter (cf. 4.1-5; 5–6; 14.36-37), Paul takes this occasion, which arose directly from their letter to hit it head-on'. Although it may well be considered that Fee has too narrowly defined the purpose of the letter, it is nonetheless evident that important sections of 1 Corinthians are a defence of his authority.

appears to be prompted by a similar concern to that recorded in Galatians, namely his concern for the ongoing faith and salvation of his correspondents. In 2 Cor. 11.3-4 Paul expresses his fear that the Corinthians will be led astray, to a different Jesus, a different spirit and a different gospel, and it is in the light of this challenge that Paul responds robustly to the challenge to his apostleship.

In the opening sections of Philippians (Phil. 1.15-18), however, Paul's response to personal opposition appears to be quite different. While he is in chains, there are many who are preaching the gospel – some from good motives, and others who want to stir up trouble for Paul. In both cases, the gospel is being proclaimed, although in the process some are seeking to cause trouble and increased suffering for Paul. In this instance, Paul expresses no personal concern for his own reputation and discomfort, and there is no attempt at self-defence in the face of opposition. Likewise, the catalogues of suffering, which Paul reports in 1 Cor. 4.8-12; 2 Cor. 1.3-11; 4.8-12; 6.3-10; 12.10; Eph. 3.13; Phil. 3.10; Col. 1.24; 1 Thess. 3.7; and 2 Tim. 1.8, 12; 2.8-9; 3.10-12, show an apparent disregard for his personal safety and reputation; rather, a commitment repeatedly to face such difficulties in the cause of preaching the gospel. In these instances it is clear that Paul's particular response to the powerful opposition of others depends primarily on whether or not the gospel or the faith of his fellow believers is threatened. In the one instance, he will vehemently defend himself as the proclaimer of the true gospel; in the other, he appears to be almost ambivalent about the impact the opposition has on him, and will continue his mission regardless.

On both of these counts, we have seen that our New Testament evidence provides difficult, if not hazardous, grounds on which to isolate and evaluate the behavioural responses of Paul's original audiences to some of his power stratagems. In some instances the evidence provides a more reliable basis than others, but the interpreter needs to be aware of the deliberate, or inadvertent, assumption that the original context is commensurable, either culturally or psychologically, to a later and necessarily different one. In a few instances, however, Paul provides his own record of his behavioural response to the power dynamics of others; and, accordingly, we variously see his robust and defensive counter-challenges, and his impervious determination to continue his ministry notwithstanding any amount of personal opposition or hazard.

b. *Power as a Disposition*
This focus on measuring power by examining behavioural responses to power, however, is now termed the 'exercise fallacy'. It is widely considered inappropriate only to detect the presence of power by means either of identifiable and measurable demonstrations of power, or their

corollaries of behavioural responses to the powerful.[33] The Latin abstract noun, *potentia,* is suggestive that power may also be defined as a disposition.[34] The political and social theorist, Steven Lukes, argues that power 'identifies a capacity: power is a potentiality, not an actuality – indeed a potentiality that may never be actualized'.[35] Accordingly, power need not simply be measured either by its own actions or its reactions in others. In this vein, he points out that, although 'observing the exercise of power can give evidence of its possession, and counting power resources can be a clue to its distribution ... power is a capacity, and not the exercise or the vehicle of that capacity'.[36]

Accordingly, it may be noted that power is linked to responsibility; thus, those who have a responsibility are necessarily powerful in potentiality, even if they choose to neglect their responsibility and not exercise their power. Indeed, in this sense, a failure to exercise power may have consequences for which the powerful is nonetheless accountable.[37] It is also evident that the very powerful may especially be those who achieve outcomes even through inaction.[38] In any of these instances, the status of a particular figure may in and of itself exert a powerful influence, and obviate the need for measurable words or action.

In this second aspect, however, the New Testament evidence again provides only a slight basis from which to measure how Paul's contemporaries perceived the potentiality of his power, or indeed how Paul responded to the powerful positions and dispositions of others. If we lack the ability to observe the behavioural responses of Paul's readers, we also have only limited grounds on which to identify the dispositional extent of Paul's power. However, a few instances may be instructive.

Paul's interactions with both the Galatians and the Jerusalem authorities, recorded in Galatians 1–2, suggest an interesting series of power dynamics. Paul opens his letter with a stark criticism of the Galatians' adoption of a different gospel (Gal. 1.6). He writes, both assuming and stating his authority, which is based on this gospel. Should he, or indeed

33 Cf. P. Morriss, *Power: A Philosophical Analysis* (Manchester: Manchester University Press, 2002), pp. 20–9, where power is categorized as a disposition.

34 Cf. Lukes, *Power*, pp. 73–4, where, by contrast, *potestas*, is regarded as 'power over'.

35 Lukes, *Power*, p. 69.

36 Lukes, *Power*, p. 70; cf. also Morriss, *Power*, pp. 20–9, for his elucidation of the so-called 'vehicle fallacy' that power is measured in terms of its resources or structure, as for example when identifying wealth as power, when it need not be.

37 Cf. Lukes, *Power*, pp. 66–7, 77; and Morriss, *Power*, pp. 38–40.

38 Thus, Lukes, *Power*, pp. 77–8, 'the features of agents that make them powerful include those that render activity unnecessary. If I can achieve the appropriate outcomes without having to act, because of the attitudes of others towards me or because of a favourable alignment of social relations and forces facilitating such outcomes, then my power is surely all the greater'.

an angel, diverge from this gospel, then the authority of either of them is immediately dissipated (Gal. 1.8), for this gospel derives neither from him, nor any other human source, but was received by Paul through a revelation of Jesus Christ (Gal. 1.12). Alternative interpretations are held as to whether Paul's reference to a personal revelation is in effect to present him as holding a privileged and powerful position in regard to this gospel – that is, the stress may be on Paul as recipient of this prized revelation. On the other hand, it may be that the source of the revelation in Jesus Christ, not the recipient of the revelation, is the intended focus. In which case, Paul would thereby be underlining that the gospel, not he, is the defining control or yardstick, from which not even he may diverge with impunity. This latter reading strikes me as the more probable, and, indeed, one that is regularly and typically rehearsed when expositors present a challenge that derives ultimately from a source more authoritative than them. It is clear, however, that we cannot, here or elsewhere, isolate or analyse the behavioural responses of the Galatians in response to this power exchange. Neither, indeed, can we identify any action on the part of Paul either carried out or even threatened. The Galatians are, nonetheless, threatened with dire consequences – ἀνάθεμα ἔστω (Gal. 1.9). I am assuming in my discussion that in these words a power disposition is established in regard to the Galatians – although we cannot measure its effects, and, interestingly, Paul presents himself as merely the channel, rather than the source, of the threat. If some or all of the Galatians had viewed Paul's words either as an empty threat – not something that could or would be fulfilled – then they are not likely to have regarded this in any sense as a power exchange. Our difficulty with the evidence is that it is an insufficient basis on which to identify the presence or impact of a power disposition.

In regard to the Jerusalem authorities, we see a different dynamic. Paul begins by outlining what might be deemed to be remarkable credentials in the eyes of the Jerusalem authorities (Gal. 1.13-14). He then underlines that, following his revelation, he became quite independent of them, neither consulting them nor others, nor visiting Jerusalem (Gal. 1.15-17). After a notable period of time, he then visits both Cephas and James in Jerusalem (Gal. 1.18-19) – but he stresses that this is a limited visit; it was for only a brief period, during which he saw none of the other apostles, nor did he allow himself to become a recognizable figure in Judea (Gal. 1.19-22). It is difficult to reconstruct from these verses what Paul is endeavouring to convey to the Galatians in terms of the power dynamic between him and his correspondents. It is all the more difficult to isolate the nature of any power dynamic between Cephas, James and Paul in the Jerusalem encounter that Paul is recording. No actions or reactions on either part are recorded – whether in or as a result of the Jerusalem visit, or in or as a result of the letter to the Galatians. In both contexts, the letter and the visit, however, there is undoubtedly a power disposition, albeit unmeasurable – and that between the apostles is clearly the more complex.

Galatians 2 alludes to a yet more complex exchange. After a remarkably long interval, a full fourteen years, Paul returns to Jerusalem. It appears to be important for him to highlight that on this occasion he is accompanied – by Barnabas and Titus; that his visit is in response to a revelation; that his meeting was private, and was with τοῖς δοκοῦσιν; and that the purpose of the visit was to lay before them the gospel that he was preaching, 'in order to make sure that I was not running, or had not run, in vain' (Gal. 2.1-2). This series of important factors, starting with the statement about the long time interval, appears to set up a complex dynamic between Paul and the Jerusalem apostles in which both his authority and theirs are counterposed, although not necessarily with a view to contesting which is the superior. In one sense, Paul's visit is in clear recognition of the authority of the Jerusalem apostles, indeed he appears to be seeking their endorsement of his mission and gospel. Yet, at the same time, we get the impression that he would have continued his mission, confident of the revelation of Jesus Christ, even if he had not secured their approval. Indeed, Paul is explicit that he, at no point, submitted to them; at no point was Titus compelled to be circumcised in response to them; and, furthermore, he states to the Galatians that he did not in any sense regard James or Cephas as authoritative over him, using the remarkable phrase that they are only apparently leaders (ἀπὸ δὲ τῶν δοκούντων εἶναί τι), and that he is indifferent to their actual position (Gal. 2.2, 5-6). In the process of the meeting, he concedes almost nothing to them from his own authority. The fourteen year interval suggests that Paul had no sense of dependence on Jerusalem; indeed his visit was not prompted either by his needs, nor their summons, but by revelation. Furthermore, Paul's power base was enhanced by the accompanying presence of his own established team of Barnabas and Titus. We appear to have here a record of an extraordinary encounter between two parties, each of which holds a significant power potentiality. Both appear to have recognized in some measure the status of the other, and yet neither has conceded power to the other. There is no statement about a change in behaviour on either part – even the demand by James, Cephas and John, that Paul and Barnabas remember the poor is not framed as a concession, but rather as something that Paul would have done regardless of those in Jerusalem (Gal. 2.10).

Clearly, our evidence is limited by virtue of being the record of only one of the two parties. This record, however, is being presented to a third party, the Galatians, as further evidence of Paul's power disposition – namely, that although he does not need the endorsement of Jerusalem, he nonetheless can present that he has it; and, although he recognizes that they do hold a measure of authority (οἱ δοκοῦντες στῦλοι εἶναι, Gal. 2.9), he is in no sense accountable to them. (It is notable that on three occasions in this short exchange he has used the verb, δοκέω, to describe their apparent status; Gal. 2.2, 6, 9.) There is no explicit threat to the Galatians here, but this report of the Paul–Jerusalem dynamic is an intangible, and unmeasurable expression of Paul's power, and presumably paves the way for the issues that Paul will tackle in the ensuing chapters of his letter. These are two extraordinarily charged power encounters, in the visit and in the letter, and yet neither is recorded as developing beyond a potentiality.

Of course, in the subsequent section, Gal. 2.11-14, the recorded dynamic between Paul and Cephas develops significantly. Paul's stance in regard to Cephas is expressly oppositional, prompted by what is presented as Cephas' hypocritical and fear-inspired behaviour in regard to table-fellowship with the Gentiles. Again, we know nothing of the outcome of this exchange between Paul and Cephas. In the context of the letter, this scenario simply furthers the introduction of his central point, namely the grounds of and response to justification. However, it would seem evident that recording this exchange in the course of the letter may well have been intended to bolster Paul's power potentiality. He is one who not only roundly confronted and criticized the renowned Cephas, but is conse-quently the one who has grounds to criticize the Galatians on issues related to the inclusion of Gentiles. As with the earlier exchanges recorded in the letter, we have no access to the response of the Galatians, but we may conclude in each of these instances that the absence of *evidence* of power need not imply the absence of power. However, the task of reconstructing the impact of this potentiality on the Galatians, on the basis simply of the Pauline text, is tenuous.

To a significant extent it is this dispositional nature of power that has to be the focus of Castelli's analysis of the imitation motif in Paul.[39] Whether Paul's repeated calls to imitation were either intended or interpreted as an oppressive tool of manipulation is not, of course, measurable since the impact of any such power exchange cannot be reconstructed, and neither, Castelli maintains, can a confident reconstruction of authorial intention be reached. It seems to me incontrovertible that the call to imitation is potentially power discourse, albeit that it only has credible potentiality if exercised within a context in which it is either likely or potentially to have an impact. Castelli reasonably argues for that potentiality, although she does not account for the suggestion in Paul's own correspondence that any such potentiality was mitigated by those who challenged and either rejected his authority, or subjected it to the greater authority of other

---

39   Castelli, *Imitating Paul*, p. 176.

apostolic figures. In this regard at least, Paul's disposition to power over his correspondents faced competing models.

The greater difficulty with *Imitating Paul*, however, is the argument that such power discourse is and was clearly oppressive and unacceptable. The limited, available evidence, and our distance from the original contexts, cannot produce a certain answer to this question. However, Castelli combines her stance about the unknowability and irrelevance of intentionality,[40] with conclusions that presuppose and are dependent on a particular intentionality on the part of Paul; and, in the process, she criticises other interpreters who have failed to put 'any ironic distance' between themselves and the Pauline text.[41] If we are to ask the question about whether or not Paul's discourse was power discourse, then it is necessary to take a stance in regard to the apostle's intentionality, even though this has to be regarded as ultimately uncertain. This unrecoverability of authorial intention simply puts boundaries around the certainty of any conclusions. The particular stance an interpreter might take in regard to Paul's intentions in employing the call to imitation – and the associated question of the implicit potentiality of his power – will be informed by whether or not one regards that such a call is, or was, by definition unacceptable, and would have been universally regarded at the time as neither welcome, nor beneficent. In regard to this, one might ask whether Castelli's ideology that diversity should be valued above sameness holds universally, or whether there are circumstances in which a call to emulation is reasonable, indeed normal and expected.[42] On occasion, Paul presents himself as a champion of diversity, even defending the otherwise vulnerable position of others, including those who hold an alternate view to his;[43] and this advocacy of diversity ought to influence one's interpretation of the apostle's intentions behind the call to imitation.[44]

It is clear that power is often to be regarded as a disposition, rather than necessarily and exclusively as an action. However, in regard to the Pauline evidence, it is difficult to measure the potentiality of power by anything other than broad comparisons; and in many remote circumstances it may even be difficult to identify the presence of such power with confidence. Clearly, however, any potentiality will cause a different reflex in different

---

40   Castelli, *Imitating Paul*, p. 121.

41   Castelli, *Imitating Paul*, p. 32; cf. also ibid., p. 113, 'Paul ... has constructed a hierarchy which, above all else, undergirds and reinforces his own privileged position'; and ibid., pp. 127, 130.

42   Cf. Castelli, *Imitating Paul*, p. 21.

43   Phil. 3.15 is an instance where Paul considers that those who hold an alternative view to his are evidently wrong. 1 Cor. 8.7-13, on the contrary, highlights an instance where the weak, who hold a different view to Paul, are to be protected from the strong.

44   E.g. 1 Cor. 8.12.

individuals and across different interpersonal relationships. It is reasonable to deduce from the extent of opposition to Paul that his call to imitation did not prompt a universally compliant response from his correspondents, and consequently that this language was not interpreted as universally and effectively manipulative.

c. *Power as a Resource*

If observation of influenced changes in behaviour is one key means of assessing power, and a second is the identification of power as a potentiality or a disposition, a third approach is to recognize that power may be identified in terms of quantifiable resources. Such resources might, for example, include money, military prowess, or the size of a workforce. Clearly, these resources do not always or necessarily equate to power in that they may not be used or may not be effectively used in a power exchange, or as a power resource. For example, some individuals who possess considerable wealth, and are economically very shrewd, may nonetheless choose to employ their finances for reasons other than the enhancement or exercise of their power, as for example using their resources in the pursuit of leisure or the enjoyment of aesthetics. The political theorist, Peter Morriss, has sought to show that, although power is often usefully assessed in terms of measurable resources, many theories of power fail to observe crucial components, and, therefore, they necessarily draw faulty conclusions. He observes, 'the main difficulty with resources is that a resource is not an empirical datum . . . : we cannot observe resources directly. We have to infer that things are resources by observing other people's reactions to them; one cannot simply measure resources since the worth of a resource is determined by the effects it produces.'[45] In regard to assessing the power resources available to and used by Paul, it is clear that we will again face limitations. Ideally, we would first need to identify the nature of the power resources available to him; and, secondly, we would then seek to determine from our source material both the effectiveness with which he used those resources, and how other people viewed those resources.

It is clear that Paul lacked many of the standard, more readily observable, power resources. He seems to have been aware that his poor or unreliable financial resources laid him open to being a pawn of the Corinthians, indebted to them and potentially in their control. Furthermore, in the eyes of a number of the Corinthians, he cut a figure that was far short of being powerful and impressive.[46] It is clear also that he worked with a comparatively small and changing team of co-workers

---

45   Morriss, *Power*, p. 139.
46   1 Cor. 2.1-3; 2 Cor. 10.1, 10; 12.7.

and travelling companions, rather than a large and established entourage, as was the measurable resource of the politically influential figures in his contemporary cities. He also appears to have lacked the unqualified or enthusiastic support of the Jerusalem hierarchy as an endorsing resource; indeed, at times, he even stressed his independence from them. In these ways, Paul lacked the standard power resources that might have been identifiable, perhaps measurable, and were universally recognized.

Paul did, however, present himself as one who had been called by none other than Christ and set apart by him.[47] He also took the opportunity to draw attention in his letters to his influence among the Pauline communities and across the Pauline mission.[48] (However, he also reports that on all of these counts he faced significant opposition.) Our conclusions have to be that those resources that he may have possessed were not tangible; furthermore, they were challenged and questioned by others, and their effectiveness was proportionately limited. Key to Paul's self-portrait, however, is his stance that his authority, and consequently his power, lay beyond himself. In his letters, Paul regularly invokes a higher authority in defence of his own position, beliefs and actions. He describes himself as an apostle of Jesus Christ,[49] and an ambassador of Christ (2 Cor. 5.20), sent from God (2 Cor. 2.17), and commissioned by him. It is of material significance to the argument he presents in his letter to the Galatians that he is neither sent by a human authority, nor immediately answerable to other people; and the particular gospel which he proclaims is not man-made; indeed, it is independent of the authorities in Jerusalem (Gal. 1.1, 11-12). When writing to the Thessalonians Paul reminds them that the instructions that he gave them came with the very authority of Christ (1 Thess. 4.2). And when he first preached in Corinth, it was his determination that the faith of the Corinthians might not rest on his own ability to communicate in the vein of the contemporary sophists, but on God's power (1 Cor. 2.5); accordingly, he distinguishes between those commands that he considers issue from the Lord himself, and others which come merely with his own authority (1 Cor. 7.10, 12, 25; 14.37) – indeed, so much of what Paul teaches is, in his judgement, revealed by the Spirit (1 Cor. 2.13; 7.40; Gal. 1.12).

These statements do point to a significant power resource, although it is neither tangible nor measurable. Arguably this resource serves to place Paul in an unassailable category. Significantly, however, there are

47   Rom. 1.1; Gal. 1.15.

48   1 Cor. 7.17; 11.16; 16.1; 2 Cor. 11.28; 2 Thess. 1.4.

49   Paul describes himself as an apostle in the opening verse of the majority of his extant letters: Rom., 1 and 2 Cor., Gal., Eph., Col., 1 and 2 Tim. and Tit. Cf. A. Bash, *Ambassadors for Christ: An Exploration of Ambassadorial Language in the New Testament* (Wissenschaftliche Untersuchungen zum Neuen Testament; Tübingen: J.C.B. Mohr, 1997).

occasions when Paul appears to moderate any picture of personal power by means of a number of qualifiers. The first is that Paul describes himself both as a slave[50] and a servant.[51] As in the case of a high-ranking imperial slave, to be selected by the master to serve as a slave of God is no menial task, but rather a position of great honour, and even notable status. While it is clear that Paul considers it a privilege to be a slave of Christ, it is noteworthy that he appears not to demand from others the reflected respect and honour that might reasonably be his as a result of his association with Christ. Indeed, he downplays his own significance and describes both himself and Apollos, a fellow apostle, as nothing in their ministry, where God is the one who makes things grow (1 Cor. 3.5-9).[52] Furthermore, if a slave might choose to bask in the reflected glory of his master, it is noteworthy that Paul also describes himself as one who is a servant to the *churches* (2 Cor. 4.5) – an association from which he can expect little reflected glory; yet he insists that to serve one another in the church is in effect to serve Christ (Rom. 14.18; Gal. 5.13; Col. 3.24).

So, to be an apostle is not always to enjoy an authoritative position of unassailable glory and honour, but it is to be placed by Christ at the end of the procession, to be fools, to be weak, to be dishonoured, indeed to be the refuse of the world (1 Cor. 4.9-14). It is likely that Paul is here speaking with more than a hint of irony; but the irony is only effective when his portrayal of the apostles' role is compared with what might reasonably have been expected of one who enjoyed honoured status in contemporary society. Certainly, the Corinthians had been wielding power over Cephas, Apollos and Paul by variously placing them on a pedestal or deposing them. But Paul's point is that God has neither placed apostles on a pedestal nor wielded power over them in a humiliating way by selectively deposing them. Rather, he places *all* of the apostles at the end of the procession.

To be in a position of authority often implies a degree of autonomy. The second qualifier to Paul's authority is that it is decidedly constrained. His ministry is constrained by the love of Christ (2 Cor. 5.14), by his fear of the Lord (2 Cor. 5.11), and supremely by the gospel, which has been given to him and which he preaches (Rom. 1.1-2). The Thessalonians are praised for receiving the gospel as from God, although it was presented to

50   The term δοῦλος is used in Rom. 1.1; Phil. 1.1; Tit. 1.1. In 2 Cor. 4.5, Paul describes himself as a δοῦλος of the Corinthian Christians.

51   The term διάκονος is used in 1 Cor. 3.5; 2 Cor. 3.6; 6.4; 11.23; Eph. 3.7; Phil. 1.1; Col. 1.23, 25. All believers are to serve one another (Gal. 5.13).

52   Cf. the discussion in A. D. Clarke, *Secular and Christian Leadership in Corinth: A Socio-Historical and Exegetical Study of 1 Corinthians 1–6* (Paternoster Biblical Monographs; Milton Keynes: Paternoster, 2006), pp. 119–21, and idem, *Serve the Community of the Church: Christians as Leaders and Ministers* (First-Century Christians in the Graeco-Roman World; Grand Rapids; Cambridge: Eerdmans, 2000), pp. 216, 241.

them by Paul (1 Thess. 2.13). The content of this gospel is non-negotiable. He writes that even if he or an angel from heaven were to preach a gospel other than the one that he had originally received then he would be accursed (Gal. 1.8). Thus, while Paul lacks the standard currencies of power resource, he draws attention both to his divine commissioning and the surpassing power inherent in the gospel (Rom. 1.16), but he also declares there to be constraints on his personal power and position.

There is then a clear tension within Paul's presentation of his own authority. He is, on one level, one of few within the ecclesiastical hierarchy who can claim to have seen the Lord; his authority is at times recognized by Jerusalem; and he is qualified to issue edicts to the churches that he has founded, edicts that he can expect his readers to obey. Yet on a second level, he is a man under authority, that of God, and he has little freedom either in the message he proclaims or the contexts to which he must proclaim that gospel. And on a third level, he is a servant to many, and is frequently called upon to suffer deprivation or even physical abuse for the sake of those in the church; and yet while he is playing the role of a servant he does not abdicate his position of authority within the church, nor even leave a power vacuum.

As in other aspects of the Pauline portrait of leadership, we are left with either a sense of inconsistency or an inherent instability in the patterns that he presents. This tension within Paul's presentation of his own authority is arguably also a source of some confusion within the churches. There are those who question his credentials and his stature. Within the Corinthian context in particular, we have seen that there are those who were critical of his lack of presence, and of the way in which he failed to conform to a standard picture of authority. There is confusion that he is occasionally timid, while at other times he is bold (2 Cor. 10.1, 10). Where there was a popular expectation that authority would normally be legitimated either on the basis of electoral mandate or social standing (and these two were often closely connected), Paul seems, at times at least, to have adopted a quite different model of authority. Rejecting both popular appeal and the standard measures of status and honour, it appears that he has not infrequently thrown his readers.

In part, this inconsistency in the extant record reflects the variety and range of circumstances that he is addressing; but, in part, it also reflects an inherent tension in his understanding of the nature of the power resources of the Christian leader. The number of occasions on which Paul parades his own weakness undermines his ability to parade and exercise those power resources that are available to him as if they were his own power resources. He can and does draw on such resources at times, while on other occasions he instead refers to his weakness. On a number of occasions he draws attention to the contradiction of power through weakness that is inherent in the message of Christ and is reflected his own position.[53] More consistent, however, is the portrayal that power is something that is a resource that derives from God, from the Holy Spirit, or from Jesus – and is not, therefore, a resource that is exclusively accessible to him;[54] others have access to the power of God available in the gospel.

d. *Power as an Exchange*

One of the observations about power in the preceding discussion that has been too often neglected in Pauline discussions about power, is that power is rarely held unilaterally. Rather, we have noted that it is often held multi-laterally and from counterposed directions. We may further note, however, that even where power is regarded as apparently residing in one party, that power is rarely absolute. Rather, it is often exercised within a complex matrix of relative and negotiated power exchanges. Commonly, B has something that A wants or needs. This may be called the 'dependency model'. In this sense, power is not limited to those in office and is not even necessarily in proportion to office; those not holding an authoritative office can sometimes exercise significant sanctions or other forms of resistance or non-compliance. Even in contexts of apparently consensual influence, there is often an implicit negotiation or exchange between the person in power and the person who is subject. If a powerful individual is to receive my willing support, as opposed to my grudging co-operation, or my resistance, then he or she must concede something to me. An acceptable concession may be in the form of payment, promotion, protection, reward, or some other benefit or means of inducement. This negotiated exchange aspect of a power dynamic is clearly evident in the patron-client relationships so widespread in the first-century Graeco-Roman context. Both parties had a mutual dependence – where the one needed financial support, the other needed a popular following. In this regard, it must be recognized that power is not something that is exclusively held by those who are in a legitimated position of leadership – power and authority are not necessarily co-extensive. Rather, power tends to be distributed, so that, just as an appointed authority may or may not effectively exercise power, so also that leadership may or may not be challenged by the power moves, demands or resistance of others.

We have noted that Paul did not hold a position of unilateral and

---

53   Cf. also, in regard to Paul, 1 Cor. 9.22; 2 Cor. 11.29-30; 12.5, 9–10; 13.3-4.

54   δύναμις θεοῦ (Rom. 1.16; 1 Cor. 1.18, 24; 2.5; 6.14; 2 Cor. 4.7; 6.7; 12.9-10; 13.4); δύναμις πνεύματος (Rom. 15.13, 19); δύναμις τοῦ Ἰησοῦ (1 Cor. 5.4; 2 Cor. 12.9-10). He does refer to the 'power' of his opponents in 1 Cor. 4.19; and to those who are workers of power (miracles) in 1 Cor. 12.10, 28, 29; and that the working of power is a sign of a true apostle (2 Cor. 12.12).

unopposed power. His relationship with the Jerusalem authorities reflected a counterposed power dynamic; similarly, the opposition that he faced from the false or the super apostles was a challenge to his authority; and the competing groups in Corinth, variously endorsing Apollos, Cephas and Paul, each had their own relationship in regard to Paul's power position. In addition, however, even those Christians who acknowledged and endorsed Paul's authority may also have been part of an implicit power exchange.

We shall see in Chapter 7 that Paul, on occasion, needed to negotiate the compliance of his correspondents by careful persuasion, often appealing to their emotions. On a number of counts, however, Paul seems to avoid, or distance himself from, situations in which he might have 'bought' the support of key individuals. In 1 Cor 1.13-16, it is clear that his exceptional baptizing of Crispus, Gaius and the household of Stephanas was counter to his normal practice of not being personally involved in the baptizing of converts, thereby, presumably, avoiding setting up special relationships on which he might be able to count in the future for support. In the same context, he objects to those who have placed him and other apostles on competing pedestals, where he might instead have sought to build on this power base as insurance against future negotiated power exchanges. We see little evidence of Paul specifically appointing certain individuals to positions of authority in the communities. In 1 Thess. 5.12-13 the endorsement of those who are leaders is generic, rather than specific; and, where he mentions the names of three leaders in 1 Cor. 16.15-18, this is supplemented by a general comment that the Corinthians should submit to any individual who labours in the work in similar fashion to Stephanas, Fortunatus and Achaicus.

This feature of power as a negotiated exchange between parties serves to show instances in which Paul's power is clearly limited and compliance has to be negotiated rather than demanded. It also shows instances in which Paul distances himself from clear opportunities to build credit into his relationships in order to purchase future negotiating power. In some measure, Paul's position as an ambassador, rather than a unilateral power, means at one level that his negotiations are on behalf of another, and at another level, he is representing the one with whom there can be no negotiation.[55]

---

55   Cf. the non-negotiating phrase ἀνάθεμα ἔστω in Gal. 1.9.

5. *Conclusion*

Although Pauline power has been a neglected issue in Pauline studies throughout much of the history of interpretation of the epistles, more recently the taboo has been removed, but it has been treated in ways that are too simplified. The contemporary scholarly focus has often been exclusively on aspects of Paul's exercising of power as if his power were unilateral, without recognizing that power is normally exercised in a more complex exchange. Additionally, there has been a tendency to overlook the extent to which the Pauline epistles provide a limited evidence base for a detailed analysis of Paul's power interactions; conclusions have been too categorically and simplistically reached. Furthermore, key elements of any study of Paul's use of power must include his reaction to the power plays of others as well as the ways in which he enhances the power of others, and circumscribes his own exercising of power. Indeed, for Paul, while leadership entails the exercising of power, the task of leadership is not about power. This conclusion is contrary to those who either hold that Paul is preoccupied with the exercising of power or that true leadership should not seek to influence or manipulate.

Significantly, this chapter has shown the truth of Morriss's dictum with regard to the Pauline evidence:

> we do not *observe* power: our evidence is used in *indirect* ways to establish the truth of, or reasonableness of asserting, counterfactuals that cannot be tested directly. And there is no easy, mechanical way of establishing how much power someone has; the connection between a justifiable assertion that someone has power and the evidence for this assertion is often complex and subtle.[56]

---

56 Morriss, *Power*, p. 145.

Chapter Six

THE TASK OF LEADERS

1. *Introduction*

The preceding chapters have explored the dominant issues of contemporary debate in regard to Pauline leadership and church order, including: the methodological and hermeneutical questions of first accessing, then interpreting the Pauline record, and, perhaps also transposing elements of it to contemporary contexts; secondly, the development of Pauline church order over the New Testament period, including in particular the titles and distinctions between church officers; and thirdly, the debates concerning the status of leaders, and their use of power, especially the status and power of the apostle Paul.

The concerns of these next chapters, namely the task of Pauline leaders and the tools of leadership at their disposal, are much more neglected issues. In part this is because answers to these issues are not systematically treated in the Pauline letters and are, therefore, not readily accessible. We have already noted that the instances in which official titles occur are not only few and far between, but they reveal comparatively little about the function of the postholders; consequently, there have been fundamental uncertainties, for example, as to whether the overseer has a role distinct from the elders, or whether the deacons' responsibilities are administrative or pastoral. Indeed, it is noteworthy that Paul rarely, either in his early or his later congregational letters, explicitly instructs local leaders as to their tasks and responsibilities.[1] In part, however, this neglect of the task and tools of leadership is also because these issues have not prompted, either in the church or the academy, the same degree of contention as questions about the titles, status and power of church officers.

It is clear that the task of church leaders is closely linked to the mission

---

1 Frequently this is taken as grounds that Paul implicitly endorsed a congregational form of government that was not facilitated by leaders; but it is neither a necessary conclusion, nor is it consistent with Paul's evident awareness and endorsement of leaders in the congregations with which he corresponded.

of the church.[2] Accordingly, our exploration of their function will be pursued in connection with Paul's understanding of the church. The apostle adopts a number of metaphors for the church, two of which we shall identify and explore with a particular view to understanding what they imply about the associated functions of their leaders and of the apostle Paul. The primary Pauline metaphor for the church is that of the body of Christ. Paul's adoption of this image articulates elements of his understanding not only about the church but also about the relationships between its members. Significantly, it is in the context of this metaphor that key responsibilities of leaders are identified.

A second important metaphor for the church is that of the household. We have already seen, however, that the household is not simply a Pauline way of conceiving of church, but it is also the setting that dominates both the meeting context and the organizational structure of these early Christian communities.[3] The household consequently defines much of the focus, scope and character of the task of the leaders; and in consideration of both this domestic context and metaphor, we shall therefore further identify how Paul defines the role of the leader in a particular community.

We should not, of course, conceive of the household in terms of the contemporary, Western nuclear family. It is for this reason that 'household' is a more helpful term than 'family'. A core feature of the Graeco-Roman household that must not be overlooked is slavery and its concomitant expectations of hierarchy and status. This impinged on the Pauline churches not only because of the presence of slaves within the house-churches, but also the unexpected, metaphorical use of slave and servile language in regard to aspects of the role of the leader.[4] The metaphors of the slave and servant have already been explored both in regard to the status of leaders and also in discussion of the title διάκονος. Here it will be further developed in terms of the task of leaders.

---

2 This is, of course, evident also in contemporary churches. The core mission of a particular church community is most clearly reflected in the core functions of its appointed leaders.

3 R. W. Gehring, *House Church and Mission: The Importance of Household Structures in Early Christianity* (Peabody: Hendrickson, 2004), p. 408, has demonstrated at length that the domestic setting is integral to the mission of both Jesus and the early church. There are a significant number of domestic terms in the New Testament associated with the context of the οἶκος and οἰκία: οἰκιακός, οἴκημα, οἰκεῖος, οἰκονομέω, οἰκοδεσποτέω, οἰκοδεσπότης, οἰκουργός, οἰκέτης, οἰκετεία, οἰκητήριον.

4 There are a number of reasons why the Pauline setting for church cannot and should not be reconstructed in the twenty-first century setting; for example, the Graeco-Roman household context in which slaves co-existed with a *paterfamilias* who, in turn, should serve the others as a slave.

2. *The Body*

The metaphor of the body is a dominant image in Paul, and, flexibly used, it most clearly characterizes the heart of early Pauline ecclesiology and encapsulates Paul's concept of ministry.[5] Indeed, Roger Gehring argues that this metaphor brought 'a new ecclesiological accent in the history of Christianity ... and it can be seen as the central idea of Pauline ecclesiology'.[6] For the apostle, the church *is* the body of Christ (Rom. 12.5; 1 Cor. 10.17; 12.27; Eph. 4.12; 5.23). In a particular sense, however, it is when it is gathered in assembly (ἐν ἐκκλησίᾳ) that it is most visibly the body of Christ.[7]

Scholars have traditionally held that there are two principal, but counterposed, elements to reconstructions of models of New Testament church order: on the one hand, Paul's use of the metaphor of the body; and, on the other hand, a structured organization, marked by an established hierarchy of church offices. We have also noted the view that Paul's omission of references to specific church officers in his early correspondence together with his use of the 'body' metaphor reflected either a more egalitarian order, or a more fluid hierarchy, dominated by the immediate authority of the Spirit. In this vein, Eduard Schweizer argued that in the early Pauline communities there was, 'no fundamental organization of superior or subordinate ranks, because the gift of the Spirit is adapted to every Church member. Whenever such working of the Spirit actually takes place, superiority and subordination will always follow'.[8] Schweizer conceived that at one moment in a gathering of the church, it is the prophet who holds authority, while at another, the prophet retires to the background and the teacher might become the more prominent.[9] Thus, none of these ministries is to be considered inferior to another, and each is dependent on all the others, rather than merely on a special few.[10] The Spirit distributes gifts to all members of the congregation, and accordingly all 'are fundamentally equal, and superiority and subordination are to be regarded as only incidental'.[11] It is for this reason

---

5   Cf. J. D. G. Dunn, *Unity and Diversity in the New Testament: An Inquiry into the Character of Earliest Christianity* (London: SCM Press, 1977), pp. 109–10, and idem, *The Theology of Paul the Apostle* (Grand Rapids: Eerdmans, 1998), pp. 548–64.

6   Gehring, *House Church and Mission*, p. 162.

7   This phrase was especially used in relation to the Corinthian community (1 Cor. 11.18; 14.19, 28, 35); and there were particular problems and guidelines for when they 'came together as a church' (συνερχομένων ὑμῶν ἐν ἐκκλησίᾳ, 1 Cor. 11.18; cf. also, ἐὰν οὖν συνέλθῃ ἡ ἐκκλησία ὅλη, 1 Cor. 14.23).

8   E. R. Schweizer, *Church Order in the New Testament* (Studies in Biblical Theology; London: SCM Press, 1961), p. 99.

9   Schweizer, *Church Order in the New Testament*, p. 99.

10   Cf. Dunn, *Unity and Diversity in the New Testament*, p. 111.

11   Schweizer, *Church Order in the New Testament*, p. 100.

that Paul does not appeal, in contexts of disorder such as the Lord's Supper or the actions of an immoral brother, to specific leading individuals, but to the church as a whole.[12] At the heart of this image of harmonious co-operation is the understanding that each and every member of the community is gifted by the Spirit to perform different ministries.

This picture of aspects of ministry distributed among and throughout the members of the community, however, appears at first to be in tension with the conclusions we have already identified that even the early Pauline communities in Corinth, Thessalonica and Philippi had leaders who were variously endorsed by Paul for their leadership or who were, by virtue of their social status as householders, nonetheless exercising a dominating influence within their congregations. It is also significant, however, that Paul's expositions of the body metaphor are integrated with lists of leading positions within the Pauline communities (Rom. 12.4-8; 1 Cor. 12.4-31; Eph. 4.7-16). Consequently, a coherent understanding of the metaphor of the body and of Pauline ministry has to be able to accommodate an ecclesiology with leading figures, including prophets, pastors, teachers and deacons.

In large measure following Schweizer, Dunn argues that gifts in some people may have been occasional, that is acts of ministry, whereas in others they may have been more regular. Indeed, he suggests that some areas of ministry may have become grouped together and been exercised by overseers or deacons (Phil. 1.1).[13] It is essential to note, however, that the body metaphor is neither proposing a new egalitarianism, nor reinforcing an existing egalitarianism. Rather, the focus in 1 Corinthians 12 is on an essential diversity of function, in which all roles are necessary, and the core ethos simultaneously reflects unity, diversity and mutuality, rather than equality.[14] Indeed, there appears to be an implicit hierarchy of ordering that is significantly linked with a reinforcement that the full range of gifts or body parts is essential to the functioning of the body.[15] The metaphor of the body should not, therefore, be viewed as an alternative model to that of a structured leadership with offices and titles. Paul's tendency to refer to positions of leadership alongside his use of the

---

12 Schweizer, *Church Order in the New Testament*, p. 101.

13 We have noted that Dunn, *Unity and Diversity in the New Testament*, pp. 111–13, does not argue that these should be regarded as directly analogous to the later offices of these names.

14 These elements of unity, co-operation and harmony are also consistent elements of the metaphor of the body among Paul's contemporaries and antecedents; equality was not a feature of these other conceptions, and neither is it a feature that is introduced by Paul into his use of the metaphor. I am particularly grateful to my student, Mark DeNeui, for his detailed exploration of Greek and Roman conceptions of the body metaphor.

15 1 Cor. 12.27-31.

body metaphor demonstrates that hierarchy is not incompatible with the body metaphor. Furthermore, while the earlier articulations of the metaphor of the body are juxtaposed alongside such ranked lists of positions of leadership,[16] the later articulations even more explicitly draw attention to the hierarchy that is inherent in the concept of the body by specific reference to a governing head.[17]

Paul does, however, argue for one aspect of equality within the community. In 1 Cor. 12.7 he presents the case that the Spirit equips *all* within the community and for the sake of *all* the community.[18] The charismatic community of the body is precisely one in which tasks are variously distributed to all by the Spirit and grace of God. All have a function or ministry, yet these ministries differ from each other in their nature and significance. As Paul's argument develops it is clear that each person is equipped differently (1 Cor. 12.8-11, 28-30; Eph. 4.7), but nonetheless all are equipped, and are equipped according to God's grace and distribution, rather than personal abilities. Accordingly, all have a part to play (Eph. 4.16). Indeed, the metaphor of the body that Paul develops in 1 Corinthians 12 reinforces the case that variety within the community does not reflect comparative honour or dishonour. Those parts that might otherwise be deemed unworthy, actually receive special honour (1 Cor. 12.23). Concern is equally felt for all (1 Cor. 12.25). This neither requires that all members therefore have the same authority within the community, nor precludes that leadership be exercised by those who are, by virtue of being householders, in any case socially dominant. It is not, therefore, a picture that is in contrast to, incompatible with or usurped by what many have described as the later institutionalization of the Pauline communities.

It is significant, in fact, that Paul's adoption of this key metaphor is precisely because there was a danger that dominant leaders were not recognizing the essential gifts or functions of others. Thus, while Paul's use of the metaphor in 1 Corinthians is most definitely not reflecting egalitarianism as the existing pattern of church order,[19] neither is it seeking to impose egalitarianism as a remedy for the problem that those exercising authority were ignoring the weak or otherwise marginal. Rather, the metaphor of the body highlights the mutual dependence of each member, and the essential requirement and inherent value of each person exercising a role within a fully functioning body. In this regard,

16 Cf. 1 Cor. 12.28; Rom. 12.7-8.

17 Cf. Eph. 1.22-23; 4.15-16; 5.23, 30; Col. 1.18; 2.10, 19. Note, however, that there is a head to the body in 1 Cor. 12.21; also the descriptions of Christ as the head in 1 Cor. 11.3 are followed by exposition of the body of Christ in 1 Cor. 11.17-31.

18 Cf. also Rom. 12.4-6; Eph. 4.7.

19 The mistake of reading the metaphor as descriptive of the Corinthian situation, rather than instructive of what should be happening is widespread.

Paul's hymn about love (1 Corinthians 13) sets out to determine the parameters within which people in the church should exercise their various ministries. Just as the gifts are to be exercised in love, their goal is to serve or edify the body of Christ (1 Cor. 14.3-5, 12; Eph. 4.12).

Implicit within the metaphor of the body, therefore, are notions both of hierarchy and mutuality.[20] Those who are leaders have a responsibility both to teach and ensure that the body reflects such mutuality and that each person exercises their prescribed function. These two aspects not only define a strategic element of the leaders' task, but at the same time they limit both the function and importance of the leader. The functioning of the body requires and is *equally* dependent on those who are not leaders.

A key aspect of this is Paul's reinforcement of the governing ethic of mutual upbuilding. The word οἰκοδομή may refer either to the process or the product of construction – that is, either a building or an upbuilding. Accordingly, this word is closely associated with the metaphor of the body, yet it also comprises a parallel metaphor of the church as an edifice. Thus, in Eph. 4.12, Paul refers to the building up of the body of Christ (εἰς οἰκοδομὴν τοῦ σώματος τοῦ Χριστοῦ), and in 1 Cor. 3.9 the same noun is used in the phrase, 'you are God's building' (θεοῦ οἰκοδομή ἐστε).[21] 1 Corinthians, in particular, focuses on the mutual responsibility of each person to ensure that others are built up, and that such an ethic should govern all actions. Thus, in 1 Cor. 8.1, knowledge and individual rights in regard to eating meat that has been sacrificed to idols have to be subjugated to love, for love builds up.[22] Similarly in 1 Corinthians 14, the gifts of the Spirit have to be exercised according to the criteria of building up (1 Cor. 14.3-5) – indeed, 'all things must be done for the purpose of building up' (1 Cor. 14.26).[23]

Although the injunctions in 1 Corinthians 12 and 14 have addressed the congregation as a whole,[24] it may be assumed that it is the responsibility of the leaders in the Corinthian congregation to reinforce this teaching. In

---

20　Contra Gehring, *House Church and Mission*, p. 263, both of these notions are also apparent in the household and *familia*.

21　The noun and its related verb (οἰκοδομέω) each occur most often in 1 Corinthians; but the noun occurs with the greatest frequency in Ephesians and 2 Corinthians. Both the noun and verb occur occasionally in Romans (14.19; 15.2, 20); and the verb also occurs in Gal. 2.18 and 1 Thess. 5.11.

22　Cf. also 1 Cor. 10.23.

23　Cf. 1 Cor. 14.3, ἐκκλησίαν οἰκοδομεῖ; 14.5, ἵνα ἡ ἐκκλησία οἰκοδομὴν λάβῃ; 14.12, πρὸς τὴν οἰκοδομὴν τῆς ἐκκλησίας.

24　Cf. also the explicit injunction to the church in 1 Thess. 5.11 'Therefore encourage one another and build up each other (καὶ οἰκοδομεῖτε εἷς τὸν ἕνα), as indeed you are doing', which is immediately followed by an injunction in regard to the leaders of the Thessalonian church. Cf. also Rom. 14.19; 15.2.

2 Corinthians, however, that building up is seen explicitly as a defining parameter of the function of the leader. In 2 Cor. 10.8 and 13.10, Paul uses the same phrase as a definition of the goal of his own God-given authority, namely to build up, not tear down, the Corinthians (εἰς οἰκοδομὴν καὶ οὐκ εἰς καθαίρεσιν); indeed, 'everything we do . . . is for the sake of building you up (ὑπὲρ τῆς ὑμῶν οἰκοδομῆς)' (2 Cor. 12.19). In Ephesians 4, the metaphor of the body and the goal of building up are brought together: gifts of leadership are given to the church 'in order to equip the saints for the work of ministry, for building up the body of Christ (εἰς οἰκοδομὴν τοῦ σώματος τοῦ Χριστοῦ)' (Eph. 4.12).[25]

The building up of the body of Christ is, thus, a key motif across a number of Pauline letters. This upbuilding should not only govern the behaviour of its members, but should also be both the goal and the function of its leaders. In 1 Corinthians 12, the upbuilding is expressed in terms of giving recognition and honour even to the apparently less prominent, presumably non-leading, members of the community; and in ensuring that all members are able to contribute to the functioning of the body. In Rom. 14.19, 15.2, 1 Cor. 8.1 and 1 Thess. 5.11 the focus is on a regard for others. In Eph. 4.12 the work of ministry (ἔργον διακονίας) is the building up of the body of Christ; and, in 2 Cor. 10.8, 12.19, 13.10, the primary goal of Paul's ministry is to build up. This portrait of aspects of Christian ministry has to qualify aspects of leading, and contrasts with notions of ruling.

3. *The Household*

The organic metaphor of the body differs significantly from the metaphor of the household, and yet the responsibilities of leaders in regard to the body similarly qualify the functions of the leaders of the household. We have seen that the household setting for the early Christian communities provided models for its leadership structures, in which heads of households became the overseer of a local Christian house-church.[26] The

---

25 The relation between the prepositions πρός ... εἰς ... εἰς ... is problematic. A. T. Lincoln, *Ephesians* (WBC; Dallas: Word Books, 1990), pp. 254–5, argues that it is the leaders themselves who are responsible for the building up of the body of Christ, whereas E. E. Best, *A Critical and Exegetical Commentary on Ephesians* (ICC; Edinburgh: T. & T. Clark, 1998), pp. 396–9, and H. W. Hoehner, *Ephesians: An Exegetical Commentary* (Grand Rapids: Baker, 2002), pp. 547–9, hold that it is the responsibility of the leaders to train the saints to build up the body of Christ. The latter is more probable, and is consistent with the reflexive sense in Eph. 4.16 εἰς οἰκοδομὴν ἑαυτοῦ ἐν ἀγάπῃ, and the corporate command in 4.29, πρὸς οἰκοδομὴν τῆς χρείας; but in either reading, building up is the ultimate goal of the leaders, even if indirectly.

26 H. Moxnes, 'What is Family?': Problems Constructing Early Christian Families', in H. Moxnes (ed.), *Constructing Early Christian Families: Family as Social Reality and Metaphor*

household was also, however, a key Pauline metaphor for his conception of the church. At the heart of this metaphor is the understanding that God is father, and fellow Christians are his sons and each other's siblings.[27] Significantly, all of the letters in the Pauline corpus open with an acknowledgement of God as father, although in each of the Pastoral Epistles and Philemon, this is the only use of this language in reference to God.

For Paul, however, it is this relationship to God as father that characterizes all those who belong to Christ. He insists that for all those who are truly of Christ, God uniquely becomes their father, and the Holy Spirit instils both the right and inclination to address God as *abba* (Rom. 8.15; Gal. 4.6). In this phrase there is clear dependence on dominical tradition. Paul is emulating Jesus' preference to address God as father, and thereby encouraging his correspondents to view their relationship to God as his sons and children. By extension, all believers are not simply members together of a single household, but more specifically they are members of *the* household of faith/God – an understanding of church that is presented both in the earlier and later letters of the Pauline corpus (οἰκεῖοι τῆς πίστεως, Gal. 6.10;[28] οἰκεῖοι τοῦ θεοῦ, Eph. 2.19; ἐν οἴκῳ θεοῦ, 1 Tim. 3.15).[29]

Paul's understanding of the church is not only of a single fictive household or family, however, but also of individual groups that meet within houses and with many of the connotations of household. In parallel fashion, the 'body of Christ' is not only universal, but also has multiple, local embodiments. This combination of the household as both a metaphor for the church, but also a setting for the church and a model for its governmental structures results in an inevitable confusing and

---

(London: Routledge, 1997), p. 26, writes, 'the institution of the household within a system of patronage and structures of personal authority ... provided the setting for the first Christians and ... circumscribed their possibilities for social behaviour'.

27   Further note, however, that Abraham is described as the 'father' of all who have faith, including both those who are circumcised and those who are uncircumcised (Rom. 4.11-12, 16-18); and Paul also uses the term of the patriarchs, in the sense of our forefathers (Rom. 9.5, 10; 11.28; 15.8); also our fathers more generally (1 Cor. 10.1).

28   Cf. the discussion of this metaphor in Gal. 6.10 in P. F. Esler, 'Family Imagery and Christian Identity in Galatians 5.13 to 6.10', in H. Moxnes (ed.), *Constructing Early Christian Families: Family as Social Reality and Metaphor* (London: Routledge, 1997), pp. 121–49.

29   Gehring, *House Church and Mission*, p. 261, argues with regard to the Pastoral Epistles that the '"house or family of God" becomes the model for responsible behavior as well as for church order and leadership structures, and thus the central, all-guiding image for the self-understanding and organization of the church'; however, he also notes, ibid., p. 263, that 'the notions of the family of God and of the house of God are both clearly an important part of Paul's understanding of the church'.

overlapping of categories. God is the father of this household,[30] but Paul also categorises himself as a father (1 Cor. 4.15; Phil. 2.22; 1 Thess. 2.11); he encourages the leaders of house-churches to function as good heads of their households;[31] and he encourages Timothy to treat all older men as father figures.[32] Furthermore, consistent with his self-understanding as a father, Paul addresses his correspondents as his 'children' (τέκνα);[33] and yet his most common way of addressing them is as his 'brothers' (ἀδελφοί); moreover, Paul even recognizes one individual as having been as a mother to him (Rom. 16.13). All of this has to be combined with the presentation of himself as the slave of the Corinthians for the sake of Jesus (2 Cor. 4.5). In all, the model of the household is widespread, and important; but is not consistent, and it entails much mixing of categories.

a. *The Father*
We have seen that 'father' language is principally used in the New Testament in reference to God, who is regarded as the supreme father with sovereign authority and power over his family.[34] Notwithstanding the Matthaean tradition 'call no one on earth your father' (Mt. 23.9),[35] on a number of occasions Paul adopts a parental metaphor or simile to describe his relationships with some fellow believers.[36] It is noteworthy that Paul is the only writer in the New Testament who explicitly uses 'father' metaphorically of the relationship between one believer and another.[37] This language gives the impression of an exclusive, privileged and protected relationship. The concept is conveyed explicitly by means of

30 He is described as the master (δεσπότης) of the household in the parable of 2 Tim. 2.21. In 1 Tim. 6.1-2 and Tit. 2.9, slaves are given instructions as to how they should act in regard to their masters (δεσπόται). Related terminology is used of the younger widows in 1 Tim. 5.14, who must 'manage their households' (οἰκοδεσποτεῖν).

31 1 Tim. 3.4, 12.

32 1 Tim. 5.1.

33 He does not describe individuals as either his son or daughter; contrast the use of 'sons of God' (Rom. 8.14, 19), sons of Israel (Rom. 9.27; 2 Cor. 3.7, 13), son of Sarah (Rom. 9.9), sons of Abraham (Gal. 3.7), and sons of disobedience/destruction/light/day (Eph. 2.2; 5.6; Col. 3.6; 1 Thess. 5.5; 2 Thess. 3.3).

34 Such a view is reflected most clearly in Eph. 3.14-15; but see also some of the introductions to Pauline letters, for example, Rom. 1.7; 1 Cor. 1.3; 2 Cor. 1.2; Gal. 1.4; Phil. 1.2; 1 Thess. 1.3; Phlm. 3; cf. also Gal. 4.6.

35 Cf. also *Agrapha* 57, 'Therefore, do not call yourselves "father" upon the earth, for masters (δεσπόται) are on the earth, but the Father is in heaven, from whom is all lineage in heaven and on the earth'; and 1 Cor. 8.6; 2 Cor. 6.18.

36 Cf. E. M. Lassen, 'The Use of the Father Image in Imperial Propaganda and 1 Corinthians 4.14-21', *TynBull* 42 (1991), p. 127.

37 The writer of 1 John repeatedly refers to his readers as his children, but not to himself as father (1 Jn 2.1; 2 Jn 1.4). Note, however, that a father/son relationship between a teacher and pupil is presented in the Wisdom literature (Prov. 1.8-10; 2.1; 3.1, 11, 21).

'father' or other parenting language, and implicitly, by means of 'offspring' (τέκνον) or 'begetting' (γεννάω) language.

Significantly, however, Paul does not refer to such a relationship in all his extant letters. Indeed, he only uses this metaphor in regard to the churches in Corinth,[38] Galatia and Thessalonica.[39] In addition, there are repeated references to his father–child relationship with Timothy, Titus and Onesimus; in each of these instances an additional measure of tenderness is conveyed.[40] Notably, therefore, Paul does not use this language of fatherhood in addressing either the Christians in Rome, or the majority of named individuals in the corpus.[41] It seems likely that he exclusively applied this title and conceived of this relationship only in regard to communities that he had founded or in whose establishment he had played a major role, and only in regard to individuals whom he had led to Christ,[42] or over whom he had exercised a formative influence. Presumably, it would have been considered inappropriate to use language of fatherhood in relation to a congregation that was very distant in terms of relationship. Paul also appears to make distinctions in his relationships with familiar individuals. In Phil. 2.22 he refers to Timothy as his child, but immediately thereafter he refers to Epaphroditus as his brother (Phil. 2.25);[43] and yet on other occasions Paul refers to Timothy as his brother.[44] Paul addresses Philemon as a partner (Phlm. 17), but in the same letter he refers to Onesimus as his child (Phlm. 10). These distinctions are not based on familiarity, in that all four individuals, Timothy, Epaphroditus, Philemon and Onesimus, appear to have been close associates of Paul. It may, therefore, be that the distinction was simply that Paul's role in each of their lives had not been equally formative, or that Paul was of a similar

38 Notably in 2 Cor. 11.2, Paul views himself as the one who promises the Corinthians to Christ as a father might promise his daughter to a future husband.

39 1 Cor. 4.14-15; 2 Cor. 6.13; 12.14-15; Gal. 4.19; 1 Thess. 2.11; Paul is like a mother in 1 Thess. 2.7; Gal. 4.19. These are the same churches that he urges to imitate him; although Paul also uses the metaphor of imitation in relation to the Christians in Philippi.

40 1 Cor. 4.17; Phil. 2.22 (contrast the brother Epaphroditus in 2.25); 1 Tim. 1.2, 18; 2 Tim. 1.2; 2.1; Phlm. 10. In none of these instances does Paul use the term 'son'.

41 Although, as we have seen, the mother of Rufus, associated with the church in Rome, was regarded as a mother figure also to Paul (Rom. 16.13).

42 Cf. Phlm. 10, 19. N. R. Petersen, *Rediscovering Paul: Philemon and the Sociology of Paul's Narrative World* (Philadelphia: Fortress, 1985), p. 131, concludes incorrectly that Paul's language of fatherhood in the letter to Philemon is related to the indebtedness of Onesimus (and Philemon) to him, rather than to the conversion of the slave under Paul's ministry.

43 Epaphroditus had clearly been ill, nearly to the point of death, which may suggest significant age. Perhaps on account of Epaphroditus' age Paul considered it inappropriate to address him as father.

44 2 Cor. 1.1; Col. 1.1; 1 Thess. 3.2; Phlm. 1.1.

age to Epaphroditus and Philemon, and therefore paternal imagery would have seemed somewhat incongruous.[45]

It is clear, therefore, that Paul's use of the father metaphor stands out in the New Testament as untypical. Secondly, Paul appears not to use the term indiscriminately, but only in certain cases. Although we cannot be categorical, there appear to be patterns to his usage, both in regard to communities and individuals. He considers himself a father to communities that he has founded or with which he has had a close and formative relationship; and he considers himself to have been a father to individuals whom he has brought to Christ, especially, perhaps, where they may be significantly younger than he. Thirdly, the metaphor is not, indeed perhaps cannot, be applied consistently.

Having noted that it is only in the Pauline corpus that we find father language used in this way, it is important to determine whether he was establishing an exclusive set of relationships, or whether his 'children' could simultaneously relate to more than one person as a father. Clearly the possibility of multiple fathers would signal that the analogy had to be interpreted flexibly, but we have already seen that the household or familial metaphor is in any case compromised at a number of points and not intended to be applied strictly. Just as Timothy can be both Paul's child and brother,[46] here we investigate the possibility that an individual, or a community, might have more than one father. Paul uses a maternal simile in relation to the Thessalonians, comparing himself with a nurse/ mother (τροφός) handling her children.[47] Significantly, however, he deems to have shared this role with other apostles, presumably Silas and Timothy as his companions in Thessalonica. Furthermore, in 1 Thess. 2.11, Paul uses the term 'father', again as a simile – 'as a father is with his children, we encouraged, exhorted and charged each one of you'. Once more, Paul's co-writers, Timothy and Silas, are included in the analogy. In both of these verses, therefore, the Thessalonians are encouraged to regard, indeed recall, a number of people, in addition to Paul, as their spiritual parents.[48]

---

45   Age certainly is a factor in his advice to Timothy to address an older man or woman as though he were Timothy's father or mother (1 Tim. 5.1-2).

46   Cf. for child, cf. 1 Cor. 4.17; 1 Tim. 1.2, 18; 2 Tim. 1.2; contrast for brother, cf. 2 Cor. 1.1; Col. 1.1; 1 Thess. 3.2; Phlm. 1.

47   1 Thess. 2.7. There is a textual difficulty here as to whether ἤπιοι ('gentle') or νήπιοι (children) is intended. In defence of the former, cf. C. A. Wanamaker, *The Epistles to the Thessalonians: A Commentary on the Greek Text* (NIGTC; Grand Rapids; Exeter: William B. Eerdmans; Paternoster Press, 1990), p. 100; for a defence of the latter (and the necessary interpretative punctuation and mixed metaphor), cf. J. A. D. Weima, '"But we Became Infants among You": The Case for νήπιοι in 1 Thess 2.7', *NTS* 46 (2000), pp. 547–64.

48   We can again note Paul's injunction to treat all older men as though they were fathers (1 Tim. 5.1).

It is this possibility of multiple fathers and mothers raised by these two passages that offers an interpretative solution to Paul's unexpected turn of phrase in a further passage. 1 Cor. 4.14-21 is the most extended section concerning Paul's fatherly relationship with any of his correspondents. Here Paul refers to both the Corinthians and Timothy as his children; he illustrates a range of ways in which a father might respond to his children; and he contrasts two different types of children: the Corinthians on the one hand who deserve to be shamed, and faithful Timothy on the other. Additionally there are two anomalous statements regarding fatherhood. First, Paul describes himself as one who begat the Corinthians through the gospel; and secondly, he introduces the puzzle that the Corinthians do not have *many* fathers (1 Cor. 4.15).

This phrase 'not many fathers' is normally interpreted to mean 'only one father',[49] and therefore taken to circumscribe Paul's exclusive role among the Corinthians. However, such exclusivity sits uneasily with the thrust of the case that he has made consistently until this point in the letter. In the face of party division, Paul has gone to great lengths to criticize the Corinthian tendency to develop preferential relations with one or other of the apostles, not least with himself.[50] To this end, Paul demonstrates that there is no tension between him and Apollos. Both apostles are fulfilling for the Corinthians roles that had been assigned by Christ – namely that one planted, and another watered. There is no difference between them in that both are, in relation to both Christ and the Corinthians, mere servants.[51] Paul has urged the Corinthians not to boast about particular leading figures (1 Cor. 3.3-4, 21). It is then unexpected to see him appeal in 1 Cor. 4.15 to the apparently exclusive relationship that he had with them as their 'father', thereby outlining for himself a privileged position over others – that is, *he* is their father, and *he* should be the object of their imitation.

A number of commentators are puzzled by this and consider that the apparently conciliatory tone of the preceding chapters is somewhat anomalous in the light of the authority that Paul now wields in this section.[52] Brian Dodd, for example, has unconvincingly argued that 1 Cor. 4.14 marks a shift in tone and that Paul's reference in the verse to 'these things (ταῦτα)' refers to the succeeding, rather than the preceding, section. Hereafter, Paul begins to assert his authority more conspicuously,

---

49   Cf. the later, and evidently exclusive, phrase: ἐγὼ ὑμᾶς ἐγέννησα (1 Cor. 4.15).

50   Cf. 1 Cor. 1.10-17; 3.4.

51   1 Cor. 3.5-14.

52   A. C. Thiselton, *The First Epistle to the Corinthians: A Commentary on the Greek Text* (NIGTC; Carlisle; Grand Rapids: Paternoster; Eerdmans, 2000), p. 370, does not discuss the apparent anomaly of multiple fathers; and G. D. Fee, *The First Epistle to the Corinthians* (NICNT; Grand Rapids: Eerdmans, 1987), p. 185, simply talks of the 'unique' relationship that Paul has with the Corinthians.

both by reminding the Corinthians of his role as father and in the disciplining of the incestuous man in 1 Corinthians 5.[53] Eva Maria Lassen suggests that the father metaphor is contrasted ironically with the preceding picture depicted in 1 Cor. 4.8-13. She suggests that Paul's invoking of the father image in v 14, immediately following the outburst in vv 8–13, was in order to drive home 'the irony of the situation – the father experienced inferior status and degrading treatment while his children enjoyed the very best'.[54] Although, the effect of this irony might well have been to shame and humiliate the Corinthians, Paul urges that his professed aim was neither.[55]

Regarding his phrase 'through the gospel I begat you', however, the principal contrast is not with other fathers, but with other non-fathers, that is other παιδαγωγοί. Nonetheless, it is puzzling that Paul avoids the opportunity to make his argument considerably more convincing, and more natural, by saying, 'you have many guardians/pedagogues, but *only one father*'. Arguably, such a statement would not have been indefensible in that Paul did regard himself to have been the first to preach the gospel to the Corinthians (2 Cor. 10.14). Yet, on the other hand, in 1 Cor. 9.11-23 Paul recognizes that there are others who have sown among the Corinthians, and consequently share in the right of material reward; and we have already noted the role of Apollos as the one who 'watered', after Paul's planting.[56] It is significant, however, that in this particular phrase in 1 Cor. 4.15 he neither excludes the possibility of other 'fathers' nor insists on being exclusively the one 'father' of the *whole* church.[57] There were many in the church, and Paul is not claiming sole resp-onsibility for having 'fathered' all of them in the faith, although he is well aware of his influential role in the initial founding of the church.

Thus, instead of couching his argument in the somewhat more persuasive frame, 'you may have a myriad guardians, *but only one father*', his key thrust is rather that the tens of thousands who may have been guardians differed in motivation from the few who could call themselves fathers, among whom Paul certainly counted himself. The Corinthians might conceivably have had any number of 'guardians' (ἐὰν γὰρ μυρίους παιδαγωγοὺς ἔχητε) in Christ (1 Cor. 4.15); but however many there might have been, they would all have had a limited basis for appeal to the

---

53 B. J. Dodd, *Paul's Paradigmatic "I": Personal Example as Literary Strategy* (JSNTSup; Sheffield: Sheffield Academic Press, 1999), p. 65.

54 Lassen, 'The Use of the Father Image in Imperial Propaganda and 1 Corinthians 4.14-21', pp. 135–6.

55 Cf. Thiselton, *1 Corinthians*, p. 368, who notes that the thrust of the 'irony was to achieve *realism, not low self-esteem*'.

56 1 Cor. 3.6.

57 Contra Fee, *1 Corinthians*, p. 185, who stresses, with other commentators, the uniqueness of Paul's relationship with the Corinthians as their *only* father.

Corinthians on the grounds of their relationship merely as guardians or supervisors, that is those slaves or paid employees who were appointed to protect and accompany the master's children to their place of education.[58] Paul's appeal is that, on the contrary, he had a particular relationship with them based on his bringing the gospel to them, thus making him a 'father' to them, and not merely a guardian.

This suggestion that Paul is not an exclusive father is consistent with his statement in 1 Cor. 1.13-16 that he lays claim to having baptized only Crispus, Gaius, and the household of Stephanas. Thus, just as he made no attempt in previous chapters to further his own cause to the detriment of other apostolic figures in Corinth, so here also he does not exclude the possibility that some may have viewed Apollos (or Cephas) as an additional 'father'. This further reinforces the case that his quarrel was not with the other apostles, and a wedge could not be driven between him and them. Paul's plea is that a father's relationship with his children provides a unique basis for appeal, a unique authority, but also a unique motivation. The possibility of there being more than one 'father', however, did not proportionately diminish Paul's grounds for appeal, authority or motivation. In any case, Paul's distinction here lies not between himself and other 'fathers', but between himself and those who were mere guardians. Thus, although the extant New Testament sources show that the father metaphor is used exclusively by Paul, it is not used by him in an exclusive way; he acknowledges that others might share a similar relationship.

A further key area of debate among scholars, however, is whether Paul uses the metaphor of the father with a particular force. As a 'father', with authority over his children, there were a number of ways in which Paul might have acted. This is most clearly highlighted by Paul in 1 Cor. 4.21 as part of this extended discussion. He states that he could have adopted the domineering tone of an authoritarian *paterfamilias* and exercised harsh discipline. Alternatively, he could have appealed on the basis of moderation and love, and provided for his children an example for them to follow.[59] It emerges that the option not reasonably available to one who is a father is inaction stemming from a lack of concern. In 1 Cor. 4.14-17, therefore, Paul lays down an appeal to those he loves, exemplified by his love for another of his 'children', namely Timothy. His goal is that his 'children' should conform their lifestyle to that of the gospel, and with this he would be satisfied. Timothy *is* 'faithful in the Lord', and is, therefore, able to exemplify 'life in Christ Jesus' and offer in Paul's absence an appropriate model for the Corinthians.[60] Thus, Paul is not

---

58   Thiselton, *1 Corinthians*, p. 370, suggests that the role of the pedagogue was in some measure as a 'corrector'.

59   1 Cor. 4.16-17.

60   1 Cor. 4.17.

here enforcing his own authority as superior to that of other appropriately qualified 'fathers', nor offering his own manner of life as the only one appropriate. Indeed, Timothy can be used as a means of reminding the Corinthians of what is appropriate behaviour.[61]

It may be argued that his continued adoption of the metaphor of fatherhood in 1 Cor. 4.21, however, is different. Here there is a threat of judgement on those who were exercising leadership in an arrogant fashion.[62] As a 'father', he can either come to them 'with a whip, or in love and with a gentle spirit'. Thus, Paul's normally non-combative approach does not mean that those in the congregation should arrogantly assume that he carries no authority among them and will not come to them.[63] He is a 'father', and not a mere guardian, and thus he will not, indeed cannot, ignore his paternal instincts. While the implication is that Paul would prefer to come to them 'with love and a gentle spirit', the choice is theirs. He insists on his authority as a father, without wishing to be forced to carry it out in an authoritarian manner. As a father, he could come to them with a stick (ἐν ῥάβδῳ), as also could the guardians; however, unlike the guardians, the father was also able to come to them in love (ἐν ἀγάπη, 1 Cor. 4.21). This portrait of the father is consistent with what we have already noted in 1 Thess. 2.11-12, where Paul reminds his readers that the fatherly characteristics that were demonstrated to them were encouragement and exhortation – 'as a father is with his children, we encouraged, exhorted and charged each one of you'. A similar characteristic is seen in the pain that parents endure when witnessing the suffering of their offspring. This is strikingly highlighted in Gal. 4.19 when Paul combines the language of children with that of the pain of childbirth. This is a maternal, rather than paternal, image, and clearly combines the idea of the birth of the community with an ongoing parental concern and suffering.

Thus, although the model of father/child was inherently, and especially at the time of the early Roman empire, a superior/inferior relation,[64] this does not necessarily entail an authoritarian relationship; indeed, in the case of Paul, this dynamic is clearly modified by love. The metaphor of the father includes the notion of authority, but this is combined with an emphasis on the love, concern and pain that a father feels for his children. In return, the children are to respond with loyalty and respect, as

---

61   It is also noteworthy that in the context of other epistles Paul does not claim to be the only model for his congregations to emulate; cf. the discussion in A. D. Clarke, '"Be Imitators of Me": Paul's Model of Leadership', *TynBull* 49 (1998), pp. 329–60, and in chapter 7.

62   1 Cor. 4.19, these 'leaders' are viewed, by some at least, as having 'power'.

63   1 Cor. 4.18.

64   E. E. Best, *Paul and His Converts: The Sprunt Lectures 1985* (Edinburgh: T. & T. Clark, 1988), p. 29.

exemplified by Timothy. We might also conclude that the 'father' metaphor is sometimes used without any overtone of authority or indeed implication of leadership – as in the exhortation to Timothy that he treat all older men with the respect which should be accorded to fathers.[65] However, the core notion of the metaphor is evidently one of authority exercised in love.

Although we have explored this metaphor with particular regard to Paul as a father, we have noted that he does not regard that he has a unique claim to this title, and he appears to consider other apostolic figures who might equally claim this role. In addition to this material, however, we have also noted the domestic setting for these early Christian communities, with specifically named individuals such as Stephanas, Gaius, Phoebe, Aquila and Prisca as heads of households. Furthermore, we have discussed how the later Pauline letters explicitly make a connection between acting as a *paterfamilias* and leading a house-church, specifically in terms of the relationship between a father and his children (1 Tim. 3.4-5, 12).

Further treatment of the nature of the relationship between a father and the members of his household may be seen in the so-called household codes.[66] Of particular significance in this regard are the statements about fathers not provoking their children (ἐρεθίζω, Col. 3.21; παροργίζω, Eph. 6.4), but rather bringing them up 'in the discipline and instruction (ἐν παιδείᾳ καὶ νουθεσίᾳ) of the Lord' (Eph. 6.4); and the statements about masters (κύριοι) treating their slaves justly, fairly and without threat, even as their Lord (κύριος) in heaven does (Col. 4.1; Eph. 6.9). A much disputed question in regard to these codes, however, is their purpose. Harold Hoehner has argued that the overall theme of Ephesians is the unity of the church, and the outworking of that unity;[67] accordingly, the codes reflect a challenge towards peaceable, communal living within the church,[68] and are likely to have been applied not simply in Christian households, but also in the household that was the church.[69] It seems to me that such teaching is very likely to have been applied in terms of the

---

65   1 Tim. 5.1.

66   The Pauline Household Codes are regarded as Eph. 5.22–6.9; Col. 3.18–4.1; 1 Tim. 2.8-15; 6.1-10; Tit. 2.1-10.

67   Hoehner, *Ephesians*, pp. 727–29.

68   Cf. Lincoln, *Ephesians*, p. 360, 'The household codes of Colossians and Ephesians can be seen as part of the process of stabilizing communal relations in the Pauline churches'.

69   Thus, not simply domestic codes, but church codes, cf. J. D. G. Dunn, *The Epistles to the Colossians and to Philemon: A Commentary on the Greek Text* (NIGTC; Grand Rapids; Carlisle: Eerdmans; Paternoster, 1996), p. 245, 'the model of the well-run household provided precedent for the well-run church'; contra D. C. Verner, *The Household of God: The Social World of the Pastoral Epistles* (SBLDS, 71; Chico: Scholars Press, 1983), p. 182; and, less certainly, Gehring, *House Church and Mission*, pp. 259–60.

house-church context, although explicitly directed towards the family. The setting of the house-church, together with the explicit application of familial language within the church community,[70] and the familial mix of older, younger, free and slave people within the church, are likely to have brought a significant measure of continuity between the two contexts. Accordingly, we have here further guidelines as to the function of leaders within their house-churches.

It is this context of the *paterfamilias* that sets the parameters for Paul's injunctions to obedience and submission. Following Louw and Nida, Cynthia Briggs Kittredge classifies instances of ὑποτάσσομαι (middle and passive) alongside ὑπακούω, within the semantic domain 'guide, discipline, follow'; but ὑποτάσσω (active) is classified alongside βασιλεύω and δουλεύω, within the subdomain 'control, rule'.[71] The middle and passive form occurs seventeen times in the Pauline corpus; the active form occurs six times, in each of which it is God who subjugates.[72] Furthermore, Briggs Kittredge argues that Paul uses words from the first semantic domain in much the same way as his contemporaries; that is, with connotations of benevolent patriarchalism within a clearly hierarchical social context.[73]

Core elements of the household codes are a call to submission and obedience: slaves and children should obey their masters and fathers, and wives should submit to their husbands.[74] Similarly, Paul's correspondents are urged to submit to their leaders (1 Cor. 16.16),[75] indeed, also to obey Paul (2 Thess. 3.14; Phlm. 21). The evident difficulty in these verses is that the required obedience of a believer to the gospel, of a citizen to an imperial ruler, of a child to her father, of a slave to his master, of a wife to her husband, of a church member to his leaders and of one Christian to another are all presented as analogous, using the same semantic domain.[76] Furthermore, the obedience and submission required seem to be total and

70   Cf., again, 1 Tim. 5.1-2.

71   C. Briggs Kittredge, *Community and Authority: The Rhetoric of Obedience in the Pauline Tradition* (Harvard Theological Studies; Harrisburg: Trinity Press International, 1998), p. 40.

72   Rom. 8.20; 1 Cor. 15.27; Eph. 1.22; Phil. 3.21.

73   Briggs Kittredge, *Community and Authority*, pp. 50–1. In this, she reasonably rejects the notion that Paul is using ὑπακούω without the conventional connotations of subordination.

74   Cf. Eph. 6.1, 5; Col. 3.20, 22; 1 Tim. 3.4; Tit. 2.9. It is in the same contexts that Paul refers to submission of the wife to the husband; cf. Eph. 5.24; Col. 3.18; 1 Tim. 2.11; Tit. 2.5; 1 Cor. 14.34. Cf. also the Petrine code in 1 Peter 3.

75   Cf. also the respect that is urged towards the Thessalonian leaders.

76   Except that the words ὑπακοή and ὑπακούω are not used of a wife in regard to her husband.

indiscriminate, with little in the way of defining parameters.[77] Although
the suggestion has been made that the semantic domain of Paul's usage in
each of these instances is that of guidance and discipline, rather than
ruling and controlling, it is evident that the relationships are unequivocally hierarchical, even though described as 'benevolent patriarchalism'.[78]

Paul frequently frames the parameters of obedience in regard to the
gospel and Christ.[79] Evidently, this may be a subtle bid for power or a
rhetorical strategy that, intentionally or otherwise,[80] further enhances the
apostle's underlying authority by aligning his demands to those of God,
and manipulating his readers towards conformity. Conformity to Christ
and the gospel are, however, key issues here, especially if seen in terms of
the cross at the heart of the Christian gospel. It is not simply that Paul
calls others to conformity to him, but that his own ministry must conform
to the message of weakness and vulnerability that is epitomized in the
gospel of the cross of Christ. Accordingly, as we have seen, the upbuilding
of the body of Christ is a governing ethic not only for Paul, but indeed for
all leaders and members of the Christian communities.[81] Within the
context of this governing ethic that is presented across the Pauline corpus,
there are further qualifying parameters. Although the obedience and
submission appear to be indiscriminate, the context has tight parameters.
Paul's call for the obedience of Philemon is in order that Onesimus be
welcomed back as a brother, not simply a slave (Phlm. 17–21). In 1 Tim.
3.2-5, the requirement that an overseer have a submissive and respectful
household is couched within the context of universally moderated
character qualifications. Children are to obey fathers who in turn are
not to provoke or exasperate their offspring (Col. 3.21; Eph. 6.4); slaves
are to obey their masters in everything, and masters are to be fair, just and

---

77   Cf., for example, 'in full submission (ἐν πάσῃ ὑποταγῇ)' (1 Tim. 2.11); 'be submissive
in everything (ὑποτάσσεσθαι ἐν πᾶσιν)' (Tit. 2.9); 'submissive with all reverence (ἐν
ὑποταγῇ, μετὰ πάσης σεμνότητος)' (1 Tim. 3.4); 'obey in everything (ὑπακούετε κατὰ
πάντα)' (Col. 3.20, 22); 'obey ... in everything (ὑποτάσσεται ... ἐν παντί)' (Eph. 5.24); 'you
have obeyed always (πάντοτε ὑπηκούσατε)' (Phil. 2.12); 'whenever your obedience is
complete (ὅταν πληρωθῇ ὑμῶν ἡ ὑπακοή)' (2 Cor. 10.5); 'the obedience of you all (τὴν
πάντων ὑμῶν ὑπακοήν)' (2 Cor. 7.15); 'submit to ... everyone (ὑποτάσσησθε ... παντὶ)'
(1 Cor. 16.16).

78   It is remarkable that Paul does indeed state that, in principle, he could come to the
Corinthians with a whip; furthermore, the whip was no stranger to the contemporary master/
slave relationship (1 Cor. 4.21).

79   Rom. 1.5; 6.17; 10.16; 16.26; 2 Cor. 9.13; 10.5; Gal. 2.5

80   E. A. Castelli, *Imitating Paul: A Discourse of Power* (Literary Currents in Biblical
Interpretation; Louisville: Westminster John Knox Press, 1991), pp. 116–17, recognizes that
Paul may be unaware of the effects of his rhetoric. Of course, in suggesting this, Castelli is
also cleverly disarming those who disagree with her reading.

81   Cf., for example, 2 Cor. 12.19, 'everything we do, beloved, is to build you up (ὑπὲρ
τῆς ὑμῶν οἰκοδομῆς)'.

non-threatening (Col. 4.1; Eph. 6.9); and a husband is to love, care for, and not be harsh to his wife (Col. 3.19; Eph. 5.25-29).

Both the fictive and the natural father and head of household clearly operated within a hierarchical, non-egalitarian context. The obedience and submission of members of the church and household are required, apparently in all things. However, strict limitations are placed upon the character of the father and leader, and the governing parameters of the gospel of Christ and the upbuilding of his body are held by Paul to be paramount. It is significant that the very reason Paul introduced in 1 Corinthians 10–12 the metaphor of the body was because of a situation in which leaders had adopted an abusive and disrespectful relationship in regard to their fellow church members. The solution, for Paul, was not to alter the organizational structure of the church community, but to highlight its organic qualities, emphasizing its dependence on mutuality and mutual respect. The same constraints apply to the authority that Paul himself received – it must not be destructive, and can only be used for the task of upbuilding (εἰς οἰκοδομήν, 2 Cor. 10.8; 13.10).

b. *Domestic Service*

It has been clear that Paul does not consistently apply the metaphor of family relationships. Although there are some congregations and individuals over whom he exercises the authority of a father, his favoured term of address is the generic word 'brother'[82] – he regards and addresses all believers as his siblings, whether or not he knows them well, and whether or not he is their 'father'.[83] A still more puzzling conundrum, however, is Paul's application of terms of domestic service to himself and others.[84]

Most prominently, Paul describes himself as both a slave and servant of Christ/God.[85] It has been argued that the notion of bondage is not associated with this usage; rather, it is a position of honour and leadership

82 Cf., for example, Rom. 1.13; 7.1, 4; 8.12; 14.10, 13, 15, 21; 1 Cor. 5.11; 6.1, 6; 7.12, 15; 8.11; 2 Cor. 8.18. Cf. also the opening phrase in Paul's speech reported in Acts 22.1, ἀδελφοὶ καὶ πατέρες.

83 Rom. 16.23; 1 Cor. 1.1; 8.13; 16.12; 2 Cor. 1.1; 2.13; 8.22; Phil. 2.25; 1 Thess. 3.2. Cf. my argument that ἀδελφός language does not project egalitarianism, but brotherly love: A. D. Clarke, 'Equality Or Mutuality?: Paul's Use of "Brother" Language', in P. J. Williams, A. D. Clarke, P. M. Head and D. Instone-Brewer (eds.), *The New Testament in its First-Century Setting: Essays on Context and Background in Honour of B. W. Winter on His 65th Birthday* (Grand Rapids; Cambridge: Eerdmans, 2004), pp. 151–64.

84 Paul uses a wide-range of slave/servant-related vocabulary: δοῦλος, δουλεία, δουλόω, δουλεύω, σύνδουλος, καταδουλόω, δουλαγωγέω, οἰκονόμος, οἰκέτης, λειτουργία, λειτουργός, λειτουργέω, ὑπηρέτης, διάκονος, διακονία, διακονέω, ἀντίλημψις.

85 Cf. δοῦλος (Rom. 1.1; 1 Cor. 7.22; Gal. 1.10; Phil. 1.1; Tit. 1.1) and διάκονος (2 Cor. 6.4; Col. 1.7; 1 Tim. 4.6). Note that Epaphras is described as both in the same letter (Col. 1.7; 4.12).

that is generally only applied by Paul to himself.[86] Murray Harris challenges this view, describing it as 'instrumentality without servility'.[87] Rather, he argues that 'Septuagintal usage made it antecedently probable that in the New Testament the figurative and titular use of *doulos* would not be restricted to leaders of God's people'.[88] Paul regards all believers as slaves,[89] and Jesus as the master.[90] This is indeed a privileged status, but it is not reserved for the leader. In a contradictory depiction, Paul also states that all believers are no longer slaves; rather, they are sons of God (Gal. 4.7).[91] This mixing of slavery and sonship language in regard to God is reflected also in Paul's unexpected turn of phrase about Timothy who is commended because 'how like a child with a father he has served as a slave (ἐδούλευσεν) with me in the work of the gospel' (Phil. 2.22). This coexisting of otherwise incompatible states, however, is just one inconsistent application of Paul's metaphorical slave language.

It is clear that Graeco-Roman society considered slavery in general to be degrading and avoided. Paul objects to those who would enslave (καταδουλόω, 2 Cor 11.20; Gal. 2.4) his correspondents, for they have been called to freedom, and should not allow themselves again to be enslaved (Gal. 5.1). Indeed, he frequently counterposes slavery and freedom (1 Cor. 12.13; Gal. 3.28; Eph. 6.8; Col. 3.11). Paul is said to punish and enslave (δουλαγωγέω, 1 Cor. 9.27) his body in order to discipline it and make it fit for service. Notwithstanding both the honoured status of being a slave of Christ, and yet the generally negative connotations of bondage in all other regards, Paul on occasion uses elements of slave language to describe both his own ministry and that of other Christian leaders. In the preceding chapter, we considered the relationship between δοῦλος and διάκονος language, in which the latter

---

86   The few exceptions include the references to Epaphras (Col. 1.7; 4.12) and Timothy (2 Tim. 2.24); the collaboration with Timothy (Phil. 1.1), and with other co-workers in Corinth (2 Cor. 6.4); and the one instance in which Paul identifies all believers who are free, nonetheless to be slaves of Christ (1 Cor. 7.22; cf. also the implications in Rom. 6.16, 22).

87   M. J. Harris, *Slave of Christ: A New Testament Metaphor for Total Devotion to Christ* (New Studies in Biblical Theology, 8; Leicester: Apollos, 1999), pp. 128–33.

88   Harris, *Slave of Christ*, p. 133.

89   Cf. the phrase 'enslaved to righteousness (ἐδουλώθητε τῇ δικαιοσύνῃ)' (Rom. 6.18); 'slaves to righteousness (δοῦλα τῇ δικαιοσύνῃ)' (Rom. 6.19); 'enslaved to God (δουλωθέντες δὲ τῷ θεῷ)' (Rom. 6.22); 'enslaved to the Lord (ᾧ κυρίῳ δουλεύοντες)' (Rom. 12.11); 'enslaved to Christ (δουλεύων τῷ Χριστῷ)' (Rom. 14.18; 16.18); and 'enslaved in newness of spirit (δουλεύειν ἡμᾶς ἐν καινότητι πνεύματος)' (Rom. 7.6); the Thessalonians had turned from idols to become slaves to the living and true God (δουλεύειν θεῷ, 1 Thess. 1.9).

90   Cf. the test of all Christians that they can declare Jesus to be master (Κύριος Ἰησοῦς, 1 Cor. 12.1).

91   Cf. also Rom. 8.14-16, where slavery is replaced by sonship (υἱοθεσία) and becoming children of God (τέκνα θεοῦ).

sometimes, but not always, has associations with the first.[92] A number of other nouns denoting service are also employed by Paul; some are in service of Christ,[93] but a few, in addition to the term διάκονος, portray service of others. In addressing the Corinthians, Paul significantly describes 'ourselves as your slaves (δοῦλοι)' (2 Cor. 4.5); and he regards himself, indeed, as enslaved to all (πᾶσιν ἐμαυτὸν ἐδούλωσα, 1 Cor. 9.19); Epaphroditus is recognized to be a servant of Paul's needs (λειτουργός, Phil. 2.25); and Epaphras is a fellow slave with Paul (σύνδουλος, Col. 1.7).[94]

These terms are not frequent but they simultaneously express an important element of the ministry of leaders as well as an inherent conundrum. An attitude of service, indeed enslavement, is exemplified by Jesus who 'took the form of a slave (μορφὴν δούλου λαβών)' (Phil. 2.7), was a 'slave of all (πάντων δοῦλος)' and 'came not to be served but to serve (διακονηθῆναι ἀλλὰ διακονῆσαι)' (Mk 10.45).[95] Paul takes up this language in regard to Christian ministry, and yet, slaves, by definition and by Pauline injunction, should yield to their masters;[96] should be obedient and submissive;[97] are captive;[98] live in fear;[99] and should gain their freedom, if at all possible.[100] In this regard, the analogy breaks down. Paul and other leaders, indeed all Christians, should follow the example of Christ in serving one another, but the overarching hierarchical relationship remains in which Jesus is still the 'master and teacher',[101] and the leaders must continue to lead their households, which include slaves.[102] For Jesus, as for Paul, their task of leadership is nonetheless one of vulnerability and meeting the needs of others.[103]

---

92   Harris, *Slave of Christ*, p. 179, 'All *douloi* are *diakonoi*, but not all *diakonoi* are *douloi*; *diakonos* is the broader term'.

93   Apollos and Paul are together classed as ὑπηρέται Χριστοῦ καὶ οἰκονόμοι μυστηρίων θεοῦ (1 Cor. 4.1) (note that in Gal. 4.1, οἰκονόμοι are considered in derogatory terms); and in Tit. 1.7, an overseer is considered a θεοῦ οἰκονόμος; in endorsing the weak, Paul reminds his readers that they are οἰκέται of a Lord (Rom. 14.4); and Paul is a λειτουργός of Christ for the Gentiles (Rom. 15.16).

94   Note also that the Galatians are all charged to serve as each other's slaves (δουλεύετε ἀλλήλοις, Gal. 5.13).

95   Cf. also Jn 13.1-17.

96   Rom. 6.19.

97   Rom. 6.16-17; Eph. 6.5-7; Col. 3.22; Tit. 2.9.

98   Rom. 7.6.

99   Rom. 8.15.

100   1 Cor. 7.21-23.

101   Jn 13.13-14.

102   1 Cor. 12.13; Gal. 3.28; Col. 3.11.

103   2 Cor. 6.11-13; 7.2-3.

4. The Teacher

The household functions of Christian leaders span from leading to serving. Both of these responsibilities are governed by the metaphor of the body with its inherent goal that everything should be done for the sake of building up the body of Christ. In addition to these functions, however, we have identified one further function of many, but not all, leaders, namely, teaching. Indeed, Paul includes many words that refer either to the act of teaching or what is taught, with the greatest concentration of these words in the Pastoral Epistles where there is a particular concern to guard against heresy.[104] In the light of this, it may be argued that, for Paul, teaching is of supreme importance and a key function of the leader in the church.

The apostle Paul not only describes himself as a teacher,[105] but is survived in his extant letters by a significant body of his teaching.[106] Clearly there were many who regarded Paul as an authoritative teacher; indeed they specifically sought his advice on a number of matters.[107] However, teaching is a responsibility that Paul encourages other appropriately equipped individuals to pursue. He is confident that the Christians in Rome are competent to instruct each other (Rom. 15.14); he urges the Christians in Galatia to point out each other's shortcomings (Gal. 6.1); he encourages the Christians in Corinth to judge each other's behaviour to ensure that it is consistent with the gospel (1 Cor. 5.12; 6.1-2).[108] In 1 Tim. 3.2, an essential qualification of the overseer is that he can teach (διδακτικός);[109] similarly, those elders who are also overseers should be rewarded for labouring in the message and teaching (οἱ κοπιῶντες ἐν λόγῳ καὶ διδασκαλίᾳ, 1 Tim. 5.17); Timothy is urged both to command

104   The following words are used by Paul in reference to teaching, spanning all of the letters in the corpus except for Philemon [the number of occurrences where this is the particular meaning are listed in square brackets]: διδασκαλία ('teaching' [19]); διδάσκω ('to teach' [16]); παραλαμβάνω ('to take' [9]); διδάσκαλος ('teacher' [7]); νουθετέω ('to warn/ admonish' [7]); διδαχή ('teaching' [6]); παραδίδωμι ('to deliver/deliver over' [4]); παιδεύω ('to instruct/discipline' [4]); παράδοσις ('deliverance/tradition' (4); κατηχέω ('to instruct' [4]); νουθεσία ('warning' [3]); διδακτικός ('able to teach' [2]); διδακτός ('taught' [2]); παιδεία ('instruction/discipline' [2]); ἑτεροδιδασκαλέω ('to teach different doctrine' [2]); ὑποτίθημι ('to point out' [1]); θεοδίδακτος ('taught by God' [1]); καλοδιδάσκαλος ('teacher of good' [1]); νομοδιδάσκαλος ('teacher of the law' [1]); ἐντρέφω ('to feed on' [1]); παιδευτής ('instructor/corrector/ [1]); ὀρθοτομέω ('to use correctly' [1]); σωφρονίζω ('to train' [1]).

105   1 Cor. 4.17; 14.6; Col. 1.28; 2 Thess. 2.15; 1 Tim. 2.7; 2 Tim. 1.11; 2.2.

106   Paul, the teacher, urges that his teaching be heeded (2 Thess. 2.15; 3.6).

107   Cf., for example, the approach of some of the Corinthians for Paul's instruction on key matters: 1 Cor. 7.1; 8.1; 12.1.

108   Paul explains that, after all, believers will one day be expected to judge angels (1 Cor. 6.3), and, accordingly, even the least in the congregation is appropriately equipped to do this task (1 Cor. 6.4).

109   Cf. also 2 Tim. 2.24.

and teach those in his congregation (1 Tim. 4.11-13); and older women are urged to teach younger women (Tit. 2.3-4). Additionally, both in Rom. 12.7 and 1 Cor. 12.28-29, Paul refers to those who appear to have the office of teacher. This concentration and spread of references serve to demonstrate that Paul held the task of teaching in high regard, and sought to entrust the responsibility of instruction to others.

Paul is confident in the trustworthiness of his teaching, indeed he urges Timothy to hold onto the pattern of teaching that was passed on to him by Paul (2 Tim. 1.13; 2.2). He believes his teaching to be consistent with the Old Testament and the gospel that he had received from Christ (Rom. 16.17; Gal. 1.12; Eph. 3.2-5). As such, he speaks of the gospel even as 'my gospel' (Rom. 16.25; cf. 1 Thess. 1.5; 1 Tim. 1.11) or as 'our testimony about Christ' (1 Cor. 1.6; cf. 2 Thess. 1.10). This is in distinction to other versions of the gospel that conflict with the gospel he received (2 Cor. 11.4; Gal. 1.6-9, 11-12). The gospel is not something about which Paul is prepared to compromise. He will, for example, not give in to the Jerusalem authorities; the reason being that the gospel might remain with the Galatians (Gal. 2.5). Equally he is prepared to confront Cephas, to his face, where he believes that his fellow apostle to the Jews is acting in a way that compromises the truth of the gospel (Gal. 2.11-14). At stake is nothing less than the salvation of individuals (Gal. 4.11) – and this lies at the heart of the heated debate that Paul launches into in the course of his letter to the Galatians.

Significantly, there are two instances when Paul appears to forbid women to teach. In particular, the statements: 'I do not permit a woman/ wife (γυνή) to teach (διδάσκειν) or act in a domineering fashion (αὐθεντεῖν) over a man/husband (ἀνήρ), but to be quiet' (1 Tim. 2.12); and, 'women/wives should be silent in the churches. For they are not permitted to speak, but should be subordinate, as the law also says. If there is anything they desire to know, let them ask their husbands at home. For it is shameful for a woman to speak in church' (1 Cor. 14.34-35) – an injunction that is apparently raised in all the congregations, and not just the Corinthian one. The scholarly debates and quantity of secondary literature dealing with each of these verses have been detailed and heated, and are unlikely to reach a consensus. Dominant issues regarding 1 Cor. 14.34-35 are whether or not these verses are a non-Pauline interpolation or reflect a textual displacement; whether they reflect a Corinthian stance, rather than a Pauline; and whether Paul's instructions are reacting against a peculiarly Corinthian disruption, and consequently they are not intended to contradict his expectation that women will pray and prophesy. In the case of 1 Tim. 2.12, it is clear that Paul is responding more generally to a situation in which false teaching is rife.

The ecclesiastical context that I have defended lies behind both the early

Pauline letters and the Pastoral Epistles is that of a house-church, in which the head of the house is the appointed overseer, responsible for all teaching. In the majority of instances, a married couple are likely to have hosted such a house-church as, for example, in the case of Aquila and Prisca. It seems to me that a married couple was also the general assumption, although not the instruction, of Paul when he stipulates that an overseer should be the 'husband of one wife' (1 Tim. 3.2). The requirement of an orderly household is then that a wife should not usurp the position of her husband, just as nobody should usurp the position of the *paterfamilias*. The situation is not envisaged where either a man or woman is addressing a large ecclesiastical context; rather it is a smaller domestic setting in which the head of the household has been appointed as the head of a house-church with the specific responsibility of teaching. There are, of course, other contexts in which teaching takes place, as evidenced in Tit. 2.3-4, and in these instances the position of the head of the household is not usurped. Furthermore, there were contexts in which the head of a household was an unmarried woman (perhaps Lydia or Phoebe), and in these instances, she would be expected to teach within her household.

5. *Conclusion*

Although there are many functions of leaders identifiable within the Pauline corpus, only a few are handled repeatedly and widely. We have seen the metaphor of the body most significantly expresses the heart of Pauline ecclesiology; it frames Paul's concept of ministry, and sets parameters for the functioning of church leaders. Significantly, however, the metaphor of the body seeks to accommodate, not remove, the existing hierarchical structure. The governing ethic throughout is mutual upbuilding.

The household provides for Paul both a second metaphor and the context for church. Within this household context, Paul recognized that leaders would have the responsibilities of the *paterfamilias,* and similarly Paul considered that he had a paternal relationship with a number of those among whom he had worked and ministered. This metaphor underlines the hierarchical nature of the Pauline communities, but also the paternal motivations of its leaders. Obedience and submission are expected, but within the parameters of moderation and the gospel of Christ.

Associated with the metaphor of the household, Paul also occasionally uses language of service or slavery in regard to both his own ministry and that of others. There is evidently a mixing of categories here, exemplified in Jesus' own characterization as servant, yet also master (κύριος). Just as he forbade leaders to lord it over others (κυριεύω, κατακυριεύω), so in turn, the church is not to be master over their leaders. Again, the hierarchical relationship is not usurped.

Of all the functions of leaders, however, Paul gives greatest focus to their responsibilities in regard to teaching the gospel. The importance of this is seen not only in the urgency with which he conveyed his message, but also the refusal to compromise on the content of the gospel. It is essential that the overseer 'must have a firm grasp of the word that is trustworthy in accordance with the teaching, so that he may be able both to preach with sound doctrine and to refute those who contradict it' (Tit. 1.9).

Chapter Seven

The Tools of Leaders

1. *Introduction*

An essential corollary to exploring Paul's theology of leadership is to identify *how* the Pauline leader should lead; that is, what are the tools of leadership. Persuasion is a core instrument of leadership in any sphere. To the extent that someone is successful in persuading or influencing the lives of others, that person is by definition also a leader. Such persuasion can be verbal or physical; it can be intimidating or gentle; it can be threatening or affirming. Similarly, persuasion may be one of the core tools of a pastor who leads.[1] In recent decades, however, persuasion and influence have been viewed as essentially controlling or manipulative, and consequently unwelcome; indeed, there is an inherent reluctance either to influence or be influenced, which is in no small measure a consequence in the first instance of the self-reliance and independent spirit that characterize modernism, and more recently of the distrust and suspicion of authority that characterize postmodernism. As a result, congregations tend to resist the notion of an external authority, whether it resides in a person, a tradition or a shared text, and they are reluctant to defend a pastor's duty to challenge or confront. Where this is the case, pastoral persuasion is restricted to the spheres of affirmation and encouragement; and such a pastor is neither given, nor assumes, a position of leadership within a congregation.

This contemporary world view has many characteristics that are at odds with the portrait of leadership that has emerged from the Pauline corpus. In his quite different cultural context, it is clear from his surviving letters that the Apostle Paul unequivocally sought to persuade: 'knowing the fear of the Lord, we try to persuade others (πείθομεν)' (2 Cor. 5.11). In this chapter, we shall consider two particular aspects of how Paul framed his

---

1   I am grateful to the Highland Theological College, at the University of the Highlands and Islands Millennium Institute, for their kind invitation to deliver part of this chapter as the 2006 F. F. Bruce Lecture, entitled: 'The Parameters of Pastoral Persuasion: a Pauline Perspective'.

attempts to persuade – that is to effect in his readers a shaping, reinforcing or change in their behaviour, beliefs or attitudes.

Plutarch, a writer of Roman and Greek history and younger contemporary of Paul, held that 'leadership of a people is leadership of those who are persuaded by speech'.[2] In this vein, we shall explore those methods of verbal persuasion that were adopted by Paul, as well as those that he criticized. A core element of this is Paul's own aptitude with and dependence on the spoken and the written word, and his reaction to those who regarded him as unskilled in public oratory. Whether addressing churches or individuals, his letters present material that was intended in part to inform, but, in large measure, to instruct, encourage or correct his readers; that is to effect in his readers a change both in their thinking and action. The apostle could choose to frame his arguments and actions in either a threatening or non-threatening way; and, in part dependent on his rhetorical skill, his communication might be to a greater or lesser degree effective.

A second essential tool in the Pauline conception is the leader's character or lifestyle. We have noted the stress in the Pastoral Epistles on the temperament and disposition of the overseer, deacons and elders.[3] Significantly, these character attributes are not simply pre-requisites of leadership; rather they determine the style and method of leadership. In addition to his written instructions, Paul also drew attention on a number of occasions to his own actions and lifestyle with the intention of seeking to effect a change in behaviour in the lives of others. This imitation motif has attracted significant scholarly attention in recent years, and will be a key focus of the present chapter.

It is important to note, however, that the scope of our enquiry is necessarily limited in a number of ways due to the historical distance and the limitations posed by written communication where access to the original author and recipients is impossible. We have little means of assessing the reception accorded by the original readers to the apostle's instructions or exhortation.[4] Consequently, the extent to which we might regard Paul's attempts to persuade as successful or unsuccessful is very limited. On the one hand, his extant letters, and their continuing use in churches, suggest that his written word has had significant abiding influence; on the other hand, the opposition that Paul faced, the issues raised in the correspondence and the very need for such correspondence in the first place suggest that this travelling apostle was only partially successful in his attempts to persuade in person. Judgements about the

2   Plutarch, *Moralia* 802.E.
3   1 Tim. 3.2-12; 4.12; Tit. 1.6-9.
4   We faced a similar issue in seeking to assess, on the basis of the Pauline texts, the locus and extent of power within the Pauline congregations.

reception of Paul's correspondence cannot, however, be reliably made, and any such reconstructions are at best tenuous. Consequently, we shall focus on Paul's methods of persuasion, rather than their effectiveness.

Secondly, this chapter will also not endeavour to second guess Paul's motivations in seeking to persuade his readers. While I do not hold that the recovery of a singular meaning in a text is necessarily and altogether futile, I do recognize that intentionality in an author is often complex, and the recovery of that intentionality may be fraught with difficulty given that it can be partially or fully concealed from or within an author's chosen wording. By extension, our task of establishing the motivations of Paul as an ancient author, who is not known, and whose audiences are not known to us, is arguably impossible. Scholars are divided over whether it is appropriate to assume that Paul's motives are laudable, and are clearly and transparently presented by him in his letters, or that those motives are malicious and are deliberately hidden from his audiences in order that his underlying, manipulative agenda might be all the more effective, or, indeed, that there may be mixed motives, only some of which are transparent. We have seen that a way forward in this debate is hard to identify in that scholars adopting the first approach may be viewed as naïve and deluded – proof indeed that, to this day, Paul continues to be a successful manipulator – while those adopting the second are considered inherently and unnecessarily suspicious, unable to accept a surface reading of the text. I shall argue that determining intentionality is at the least problematic, and that an individual's motives are normally, highly complex, even fluctuating.[5] Accordingly, the motives of Paul are not a key question in this chapter.

Thirdly, I do not propose to argue that Paul applied his methods of pastoral persuasion in the same manner in all contexts; nor that a generic set of parameters, applicable in different contexts, with different pastors and congregations, can be determined. A careful reading of the Pauline letters reveals that his tone and techniques of persuasion varied considerably, apparently in relation both to the seriousness of the situations that he was addressing, the urgency of the presenting issue, and the nature of the relationship that existed between him and his readers.

Fourthly, the content of Paul's message will also not be our focus here. His ethical teaching and its theological grounding are the legitimate focus of quite separate studies. Indeed, scholars and pastors alike have tended to focus on this rather more accessible material. Rather, this chapter is restricted in large part to a consideration of those *methods* of persuasion that can be detected in his letters, irrespective of their effectiveness and content, or, indeed, Paul's underlying motivations.

---

5   The biblical narrative in any case recounts that not all the motives of all leaders in the Bible were always and thoroughly unimpeachable.

I have identified that rhetoric and personal example are the two principal tools of persuasion adopted and promoted by Paul. We shall first consider Paul's attitude towards and use of rhetoric; and secondly, we shall look at the ways in which he draws attention to and commends his own example. Although it is inevitable that on both of these issues the focus will be on Paul as leader, we shall see that he exhorts other leaders to adopt the same tools of persuasion.

2. Rhetoric

There is much confusion and misunderstanding surrounding the term rhetoric. Not only do scholars use the term in a wide range of senses that are not always explicitly defined; but also, even in regular conversation, we might praise a politician's speech for its rhetoric, or criticize it as being 'mere rhetoric'.[6] Philip Kern lists four identifiable uses of the term, ranging from the general sense that rhetoric describes any verbal communication that has a strategic goal of persuading or influencing an individual or an audience to the more restricted sense of the highly developed, grand style of Graeco-Roman public discourse as described in the ancient rhetorical handbooks.[7] Since the 1960s the development of rhetorical criticism as a hermeneutical method has resulted in a widely adopted distinction between rhetoric as descriptive of the skills of the ancient orator, and rhetoric as a literary term. In this more recent sense rhetoric describes the art of persuasion by the use of words, and is not necessarily restricted to the context of oratory and public declamation, but can be applied to analysis of narrative and epistolary genres. The two uses are not exclusive; indeed, occasionally, one comes across the literary and classical senses of the term used concurrently.[8]

a. *Paul and Oratory*
Paul's own rhetorical skills as well as his attitude towards the misuse of rhetoric in the proclamation of the gospel have been a focus of scholarly attention in recent decades.[9] How is it that Paul can in the same

---

6 In the *Oxford English Dictionary Online* (Oxford: Oxford University Press, 2000), 'rhetoric' is defined as both 'The art of using language so as to persuade or influence others'; and 'the body of rules to be observed by a speaker or writer in order that he may express himself with eloquence'.

7 Cf. P. H. Kern, *Rhetoric and Galatians: Assessing an Approach to Paul's Epistle* (SNTSMS; Cambridge: Cambridge University Press, 1998), pp. 7–34.

8 The new genre of rhetorical commentaries on New Testament texts occasionally reflects such a combining of these senses.

9 Cf. e.g. A. D. Litfin, *St. Paul's Theology of Proclamation: 1 Corinthians 1–4 and Greco-Roman Rhetoric* (SNTSMS; Cambridge; New York: Cambridge University Press, 1994);

correspondence demonstrate an impressive ability to construct a persuasive argument and yet, by his own estimation, and that of his first-century opponents, he not only lacks rhetorical skill but he also rejects its use in the presentation of the gospel? In this debate the Corinthian correspondence has been a key focus.

It is widely recognized that there were internal divisions within the early Corinthian church. Paul's statements in 1 Cor. 1.10-17 and 3.1-4, in which he refers to party allegiances focused around a number of apostolic individuals, together with those passages in the epistles in which he seeks to defend himself and his ministry, suggest that the apostle faced personal opposition from significant and influential quarters of the community.[10] Although the presence of such parties is clear, scholars dispute the severity and extent of these divisions and their particular cause or focus. In 1 Cor. 2.1-5 Paul raises the spectre of his own lack of rhetorical abilities and explicitly rejects the use of rhetoric in the presentation of the gospel – 'my speech and my proclamation were not in persuasive words of wisdom, but in demonstration of the Spirit and of power, so that your faith might not rest in human wisdom but in the power of God' (1 Cor. 2.4-5). Furthermore, in 2 Cor. 11.6 Paul openly concedes the charge that he was neither trained nor skilled in public speaking.[11] On the basis of this it is assumed by many that a number of the Christians in the early Corinthian community were critical of his skills in public declamation. This view is reinforced by Paul's extended criticism of the Corinthians' preoccupation with worldly wisdom in 1 Cor. 1.18–4.21, where that wisdom is equated with the contemporary sophistry of the ancient public orators.[12]

Furthermore, it is widely accepted that one specific factor in the Corinthian dissension was that a number of the local Christians were making unfavourable comparisons between Apollos and Paul in regard to their skills in public speaking. Duane Litfin describes the Corinthians as those who, 'Though they were themselves on the outside – or perhaps even in some cases still more tantalizingly, on the fringe – of the circles of

---

B. W. Winter, *Philo and Paul among the Sophists: Athenian and Corinthian Responses to a Julio-Claudian Movement* (Grand Rapids; Cambridge: Eerdmans, 2002); M. A. Bullmore, *St Paul's Theology of Rhetorical Style: An Examination of I Corinthians 2.1-5 in Light of First Century Graeco-Roman Rhetorical Culture* (San Francisco: International Scholars, 1995); D. D. Walker, *Paul's Offer of Leniency (2 Cor 10.1): Populist Ideology and Rhetoric in a Pauline Letter Fragment* (Wissenschaftliche Untersuchungen zum Neuen Testament; Tübingen: Mohr Siebeck, 2002); T. H. Tobin, *Paul's Rhetoric in its Contexts: The Argument of Romans* (Peabody: Hendrickson, 2004).

10   Cf. especially 1 Corinthians 9; 2 Corinthians 10–12.

11   The term ἰδιώτης, (ἰδιώτης τῷ λόγῳ, 2 Cor. 11.6) may either refer to someone who was not trained in public declamation, or to someone who was no longer a practising orator.

12   See also 2 Cor. 1.12; 11.19.

status, influence and sophistication in Corinth, they exalted those on the inside and themselves put on the airs of the aristocracy, affecting the stance of sophisticated critics as best they could.'[13] Largely on the basis of Luke's portrait of Apollos in Acts,[14] it is inferred that this apostle from Alexandria had more accomplished rhetorical skills than Paul, and that these were especially attractive to a significant section of the Christian community in Corinth. The portrait of the apostle Paul that predominates is, thus, one of a timid and faltering public speaker, who opposes the use of rhetoric in the presentation of the gospel. In contrast, the predominant portrait of the Corinthian community is one in which many of its members regarded themselves as sophisticated critics of public oratory who viewed Paul unfavourably in this regard.

There are, however, certain problems with this reconstruction that are too often overlooked, and result in either an inconsistent or a selective picture of Paul's attitude towards and abilities in the use of rhetoric. First, an assumption that the apostle Paul lacked accomplishment as a public speaker is at odds with the portrait presented by Luke in Acts. Both in public and private contexts, the apostle is repeatedly shown to be one who is able to deliver a highly skilled defence of himself and exposition of the gospel, and is clearly able to influence and persuade his audiences.[15] Indeed, some of the Pauline speeches in Acts have been assessed to be sophisticated examples of forensic rhetoric;[16] for example, it has been pointed out that Paul's speech in the Athenian Areopagus is a cleverly constructed piece of persuasion.[17] Clearly it can be argued that the writer of Acts may here be presenting an idealized portrait of the apostle, and that the speeches are largely editorial constructs; the presentation of Paul in this accomplished guise may simply be the fictional creation of the author of Acts. However, it is often overlooked that the argument that almost universally presents Apollos as contrastingly skilled in the use of rhetoric is based solely on the limited evidence found in Acts 18.24-28. Indeed, Luke's assessment of Apollos lacks any supporting documentation of examples of his rhetoric, whether in his own hand or in Luke's. Thus, Luke presents the reader with Paul who delivers persuasive speeches

13   Litfin, *St. Paul's Theology of Proclamation*, p. 245.

14   Acts 18.24-26.

15   Cf. Luke's presentation of the Pauline speeches in Acts 17.22-31; 20.18-35; 22.1-21; 24.10-21; 26.2-27.

16   Cf. B. W. Winter, 'The Importance of the *Captatio Benevolentiae* in the Speeches of Tertullus and Paul in Acts 24.1-21', *JTS* 42 (1991), pp. 505–31.

17   Cf. B. W. Winter, 'On Introducing Gods to Athens: An Alternative Reading of Acts 17.18-20', *TynBull* 47 (1996), pp. 71–90; also the discussion by S. Walton, *Leadership and Lifestyle: The Portrait of Paul in the Miletus Speech and 1 Thessalonians* (SNTSMS, 108; Cambridge: Cambridge University Press, 2000), p. 264, of the Pauline speech to the Ephesian elders at Miletus.

with fervour, and Apollos who is described as eloquent (λόγιος), bold (παρρησιάζομαι), accurate (ἀκριβῶς) and convincing (διακατελέγχομαι, ἐπιδείκνυμι) as a speaker.[18] Nevertheless, it is confidently held that Luke's portrait of Apollos is accurate, but his presentation of Paul is stylized. In this regard, the evidence in Acts is handled somewhat inconsistently, and those who argue, on the basis of Paul's own testimony, that he was not a convincing public speaker have to dismiss the Lukan material regarding him, if not the rather more sparse Lukan material regarding Apollos.

Secondly, whether or not scholars are correct in assuming that Apollos had more accomplished skills than Paul with regard to public speaking, in the Corinthian correspondence it should be noted that Paul does not oppose Apollos in any regard; in particular, he is not critical of Apollos' proficiencies in public speaking, nor does he even raise the issue of his fellow apostle's oratorical abilities. On the contrary, Paul's criticism is of those in the Corinthian church who were making such comparisons.[19] Thus, it is not that Paul was somewhat ashamed of both his timidity in public and his all too apparent lack of polish in the art of public declamation, and is consequently embarrassed by the unfavourable comparison with the highly accomplished Apollos. Rather, Paul roundly rejected the use of rhetoric in the presentation of the gospel, but made no public criticism of his fellow apostle's public speaking. We have already seen that Paul is not averse to offering frank criticism of apostolic figures. Where he believes one of his fellow apostles to be acting contrary to the ethos of the gospel, as in the case of Cephas recorded in Gal. 2.11-14, he roundly confronts the issue; where the Corinthians were elevating skilled rhetoric, Paul roundly opposes them; and yet, he raises no objection to the skill in public speaking of his fellow apostle, Apollos.

The third problem to be considered is that, if Paul positions himself in an anti-rhetorical camp, how is it that his own letters reflect considerable skill in the art of framing a persuasive argument? In this regard, the rhetoric displayed in the Pauline writings may appear to be more consistent with the Pauline speeches in Acts, than with his own statements that the presentation of the gospel should not be occluded by a reliance on rhetorical skills. While it may be held that Paul was accomplished with the written word, although not with the spoken word,[20] this does not resolve his apparent rejection of the use of 'wise and persuasive words' in the presentation of the gospel 'lest your faith might not rest on human wisdom, but on God's power' (1 Cor. 2.5).

Consequently, the evidence in Acts has to be partially dismissed for it not to contradict Paul's view of his abilities. Additionally, Paul's

---

18　Cf. Acts 18.24-28.
19　1 Cor. 3.1–4.7.
20　Cf. the accusation in 2 Cor. 10.10.

conviction that the use of rhetoric in the presentation of the gospel is inappropriate must apply only to the spoken, and not the written context. Conceivably Paul's stance is a defensive strategy; for pragmatic reasons, rather than out of a genuine conviction, Paul rejects the use of rhetoric in the presentation of the gospel, and it applies only in regard to the written word.

One solution to these contradictions, which avoids either treating the evidence selectively or considering Paul to be inconsistent, is to define more narrowly what is meant by rhetoric – in particular to avoid the situation where rhetoric is at some points used in a general sense, while at other points it is used in a more restricted sense. Michael Bullmore has proposed that the Corinthians wished to see in their leading figures public speakers who confidently declaimed with flourish and display, according to the grand style taught in the rhetorical handbooks of the time. In contrast, Paul's own conviction was that the presentation of the gospel should not be diluted by the use of such ornamentation, and this applied to both the oral and the written contexts.[21] Bullmore argues in 1 Cor. 1.18–2.5 that God, in his wisdom, has provided a message of the cross that in the eyes of the world is foolishness. Consequently, such a message of foolishness cannot effectively be presented when dressed up in the wisdom favoured by the sophists of the day. Similarly, Duane Litfin has argued that a core feature of Graeco-Roman oratory was to adapt one's message in order to create a reputation for oneself.[22] Paul's theology of proclamation, on the contrary, did not allow him to adapt the message of the crucified Christ in this way. This did not mean to Paul, however, that the gospel should not be presented in a persuasive and compelling fashion. Paul's speeches in Acts and his letters include carefully reasoned arguments and make persuasive appeals to their respective audiences. Neither of these, however, complies with the identifiable trademarks of the trained rhetoricians.[23]

In this regard, Paul rejects the use of rhetoric as defined as that ornamented style fostered by the sophistic orators of the period and used

---

21 Bullmore, *St Paul's Theology of Rhetorical Style*.

22 For the Corinthians' critique of Paul, cf. Litfin, *St Paul's Theology of Proclamation*, pp. 151–5.

23 Although H. D. Betz, *Galatians: A Commentary on Paul's Letter to the Churches in Galatia* (Hermeneia; Philadelphia: Fortress Press, 1979), and others, have argued that many of Paul's letters do reflect such a style, particularly with regard to the letter to the Galatians, it has been convincingly shown that that the rules of the rhetorical handbooks apply only to the genre of public speeches and declamations and not to the genre of the letter; accordingly, Paul does not employ the established art of rhetoric in his letters. With regard to Paul's letter to the Galatians, cf., Kern, *Rhetoric and Galatians;* J. Fairweather, 'The Epistle to the Galatians and Classical Rhetoric', *TynBull* 45 (1994), pp. 1–38; and J. Fairweather, 'The Epistle to the Galatians and Classical Rhetoric', *TynBull* 45 (1994), pp, 213–43.

exclusively in speeches, but he does not reject the skilled use of words when more broadly defined simply as the deliberate attempt to influence and persuade an audience, whether in speeches or letters. Accordingly, Paul announces that his goal is indeed to persuade (2 Cor. 5.11), and he sets about the systematic demolition of arguments that are opposed to the truth ('demolishing arguments and everything raised high against the knowledge of God', 2 Cor. 10.4-5). The goal of the trained orator was to entertain and impress; Paul's stated goal is to present the unchanging gospel and persuade his hearers and readers. If this view is correct, then we can consider that Luke's portrait of Paul's abilities as a public speaker may be helpful, that Paul's persuasive skills were consistent across both the written and spoken word, and that Paul's own apparent rejection of rhetoric is not an abandonment of all attempts to persuade people by means of words. It may have coincided with a lack of oratorical ability, but certainly it reflected an avoidance of that type of oratorical flourish that the Corinthians so favoured.[24]

b. *Paul and Verbal Persuasion*
If Paul rejected the rhetorical arts, we need next to consider the ways in which he sought to persuade his readers without using the grand style of the orators that was aimed to impress and win admiration. In communicating with his hearers and readers, Paul employs a number of verbal approaches to influence or persuade his readers. These vary depending on how intimately he knows his audience, and the extent to which he considers their beliefs or behaviour to be at variance with the gospel. Particularly important letters of persuasion include 1 and 2 Corinthians, Galatians and Philemon, in each of which the apostle is communicating with an audience whom he knows personally. In his letters, Paul uses a number of verbs of persuasion (most commonly in the first person singular and plural) that vary in their strength of coercion or pressure. The authority invested in Paul as an apostle of God permits him simply to command his readers; indeed, on occasion he does so. At other times, however, his preference is rather to make an appeal, and not uncommonly playing on the emotions of his readers.

At one end of the spectrum of persuasion, Paul adopts verbs of command, in the first person singular or plural. On seven occasions he employs the verb παραγγέλλω ('to order/command'). Writing to the Thessalonians, he gently urges them to live peaceable and diligent lives 'just as we instructed you (καθὼς ὑμῖν παρηγγείλαμεν)' (1 Thess. 4.11).

---

24 The absence of any detail regarding the comparisons made by the Corinthians between Apollos and Paul means that we have no clear evidence, however, as to whether or not Apollos was accomplished in that stylized oratory which the Corinthians applauded.

Similarly, in 2 Thess. 3.10, he reminds them of the instruction that he had previously given that only those who work should eat (τοῦτο παρηγγέλλομεν ὑμῖν).[25] He also uses this strong verb in giving instructions to Timothy, using a phrase that almost has the quality of an oath: 'I charge you in the presence of God (παραγγέλλω σοι ἐνώπιον τοῦ θεοῦ)' (1 Tim. 6.13). Furthermore, the Corinthians are reprimanded about their recognition of the Lord's Supper using this verb: 'In commanding you thus, I do not praise you (τοῦτο δὲ παραγγέλλων οὐκ ἐπαινῶ)' (1 Cor. 11.17). A similar verb conveying an order is διατάσσω, again used in the first person. On two occasions Paul uses this to draw attention to instructions that are applied in other churches (1 Cor. 7.17; 16.1); on another occasion he refers to further directives about the Lord's Supper that he will provide on a future occasion (1 Cor. 11.34). Additionally, he commands Titus to appoint elders in every town (Tit. 1.5). Similarly, the nouns ἐντολή[26] and παραγγελία[27] are used both in regard to congregations and individuals. Each of these instances where Paul exercises authority is presented as non-negotiable, and many are forceful. Paul also uses both of these verbs, however, in imperatival forms in regard to the leadership of Timothy and Titus. Like the apostle, these younger leaders are similarly to issue appropriate commands.[28] Indeed, Titus is urged to, 'say these things and exhort and reprove with all authority; allow no one to refuse to recognize your authority (ταῦτα λάλει καὶ παρακάλει καὶ ἔλεγχε μετὰ πάσης ἐπιταγῆς· μηδείς σου περιφρονείτω)' (Tit. 2.15). Notably, however, on three occasions, Paul expressly states that he is not issuing a command.[29]

Perhaps less forcefully, Paul uses three verbs of insistence or declaration (μαρτύρομαι, διαμαρτύρομαι, διαβεβαιόομαι). He declares to the Galatians that submitting to circumcision would require them to obey the whole law (μαρτύρομαι, Gal. 5.3); he insists that the Ephesians should no longer live as the Gentiles (μαρτύρομαι, Eph. 4.17); and he reminds the Thessalonians about his visit to them when he exhorted them and insisted (παρακαλοῦντες ὑμᾶς καὶ παραμυθούμενοι καὶ μαρτυρόμενοι, 1 Thess.

---

25 Indeed, Paul uses the verb παραγγέλλω four times in quick succession (2 Thess. 3.4, 6, 10, 12; cf. also 1 Tim. 6.13). In 2 Thess. 3.14, Paul gives the strong injunction: 'If any one does not obey the message of our letter, note that man, and have nothing to do with him, that he may be ashamed'; cf. also, 2 Cor. 10.6, 'we will be ready to punish every act of disobedience, once your obedience is complete'.

26 Col. 4.10; 1 Tim. 6.14.

27 1 Tim. 1.5. Cf. also its use in 1 Thess. 4.2; 1 Tim. 1.18 where Paul's instructions are identified as having divine authorization.

28 παραγγέλλω, 'to order/command' (1 Tim. 1.3; 4.11; 5.7; 6.17); ἐπιτιμάω, 'to rebuke' (2 Tim. 4.2).

29 ἐπιταγή, 'order/command' (1 Cor. 7.6; 2 Cor. 8.8); ἐπιτάσσω, 'to command/order' (Phlm. 8).

2.12) that they live lives worthy of God.[30] One particularly strong phrase
is used when Paul adjures the Thessalonians to read his letter to the other
brothers and sisters (ἐνορκίζω, 1 Thess. 5.27). As before, Timothy and
Titus are to persuade those in their congregations in like manner: Titus is
urged to insist on various matters in his congregation (διαβεβαιόομαι,
Tit. 3.8); and Timothy is to declare solemnly that people should not
quarrel about words (διαμαρτύρομαι, 2 Tim. 2.14).

Paul also uses a number of negative words of persuasion. The
Corinthians and Colossians are warned or admonished (νουθετέω,
1 Cor. 4.14; Col. 1.28). Similarly, the verb προλέγω is used to draw
attention to advice or instruction that had been given earlier.[31] More
frequently, however, Paul urges other leaders to rebuke, refute, expose,
warn or correct.[32] We have seen that the leaders in Thessalonica have a
duty to admonish, and are to be respected for this (νουθετέω, 1 Thess.
5.12).[33] Note, however, that Timothy is urged not to rebuke (ἐπιπλήσσω)
an older man (1 Tim. 5.1); he is urged to teach, particularly those who are
in error, with appropriate gentleness (2 Tim. 2.25), although also with an
appropriate measure of authority (Tit. 2.15); and similarly, masters are
not to threaten their slaves (ἀπειλή, Eph. 6.9).

In addition to these forceful words of commanding, instructing,
rebuking, warning and refuting, Paul uses a number of less urgent verbs
of persuasion.[34] His most frequent phrase in this regard is simply: 'I

---

30   Paul uses the stronger verb διαμαρτύρομαι 'solemnly charge', in regard to both the
Thessalonians and Timothy (1 Thess. 4.6; 1 Tim. 5.21; 2 Tim. 4.1).

31   2 Cor. 7.3; 13.2; Gal. 1.9; 5.21; 1 Thess. 3.4; 4.6.

32   ἐλέγχω, Eph. 5.11; 1 Tim. 5.20; 2 Tim. 4.2; Tit. 1.9, 13; 2.15.

33   Cf. also Rom. 15.14; Col. 3.16; 1 Thess. 5.14; 2 Thess. 3.15.

34   B. Wannenwetsch, '"Members of One another": *Charis,* Ministry and
Representation: A Politico-Ecclesial Reading of Romans 12', in C. G. Bartholomew, J.
Chaplin, R. Song and A. Wolters (eds.), *A Royal Priesthood?: The Use of the Bible Ethically
and Politically: A Dialogue with Oliver O'Donovan* (Carlisle: Paternoster Press, 2002), p. 200,
attempting a political reading of Romans 12, writes 'The difference between appeal and
command reflects not a downgraded authority but a different kind of authority, which does
not rely on the power to compel but on the freedom of the addressees to assent. For this
reason, it does not invoke the particular status of the one who exercises *paraklesis* ("as
apostle"), but rather invokes the status of the addressees ("brothers"). Or, more precisely, it
invokes the status which both, addressees and addresser, share'; cf. also, ibid., p. 202, '*[P]
araklesis* is a speech act that brings the apostle in a sense "down" to the same level as his
addressees. In this vein, Paul can introduce his paraklesis through the explicit reminder that
"we speak to you as your fellow-workers (*synergountes*), adding our exhortation (*paraklesis*)"
(2 Cor. 6.1) ... However, the picture is complicated by the observation that the apostle in
exercising *paraklesis* does also in a way represent God's voice and authority'; and, ibid., pp.
202–3, 'Let us ... note a perplexing duality: the language of *paraklesis* seems to be
characteristic of the kind of authority in the church as a political body; although juxtaposed
with the patriarchal language of command, it nevertheless aims at obedience'.

appeal to you (παρακαλῶ ὑμᾶς)'.[35] Titus is similarly expected to persuade his congregations by means of appeal and exhortation.[36] With an urgent tone, although far from commanding, Paul again uses the first person, imploring or beseeching the Galatians and the Corinthians.[37] In 2 Cor. 5.20, Paul maintains that his entreaty that the Corinthians be reconciled to God is an appeal, as it were, from God himself: 'We are as Christ's ambassadors, as though God were exhorting you through us (παρακαλοῦντος δι' ἡμῶν). We implore (δεόμεθα) you: be reconciled to God'. Although we have noted Paul's refusal to use the rhetorical flourish of 'persuasive words of wisdom (ἐν πειθοῖς σοφίας λόγοις)' (1 Cor. 2.4), he, nonetheless, uses the verb πείθω ('to persuade') both of his own actions, and those of his opponents.[38] Finally, at the gentler of the persuasive spectrum, Paul uses the simple verbs of request (ἐρωτάω, αἰτέω).[39]

This survey of vocabulary demonstrates that Paul used a wide range of approaches, of varying strength and forcefulness. These appeals concern issues of ethics, faith, the gospel, church order and practice. Although vocabulary of persuasion occurs in all his letters, it is by no means evenly distributed. In terms of the references identified, the frequency of such words is greatest in the individual letters of Titus, Philemon and 1 Timothy,[40] followed closely by 1 Thessalonians and 2 Thessalonians.[41] These words of persuasion occur significantly less frequently in 2 Corinthians, Galatians, 2 Timothy, Ephesians, Colossians, Philippians and 1 Corinthians.[42] The letter with the lowest frequency of words of persuasion is Romans.[43] Such a statistical survey is far from sophisti-

---

35   This particular form of the phrase is used in: Rom. 12.1; 15.30; 16.17; 1 Cor. 1.10; 4.16; 16.15; 2 Cor. 2.8; 10.1; 12.18; Eph. 4.1; Phil. 4.2; 1 Tim. 2.1; Phlm. 9–10. Cf. also Paul's use of the noun παράκλησις in 2 Cor. 8.4, 17; 1 Thess. 2.3. Cf. also, 1 Cor. 16.12, 15; 2 Cor. 5.20; 6.1; 8.6; 9.5; 13.11; 1 Thess. 2.12; 4.1, 10, 18; 5.11, 14; 2 Thess. 3.12; 1 Tim. 1.3; 5.1; 6.2; 2 Tim. 4.2; Tit. 1.9; 2.6, 15.

36   Tit. 2.15.

37   δέομαι, 2 Cor. 5.20; 10.2; Gal. 4.12.

38   2 Cor. 5.11; Gal. 1.10; 5.7-8; Phil. 1.14.

39   Phil. 4.3; 1 Thess. 4.1; 5.12; 2 Thess. 2.1; Eph. 3.13. In its negative form, cf., παραιτέομαι 'to refuse' (1 Tim. 4.7).

40   Approximately 9 times per 1,000 words.

41   Approximately 7–8 times per 1,000 words.

42   In descending order of frequency, from 3 to 2 times per 1,000 words.

43   Less than once per 1,000 words. R. Jewett, *Romans: A Commentary* (Hermeneia; Minneapolis: Fortress, 2007), p. 59, argues, 'In the case of Romans, we must exercise due care to respect the fact that the letter is not addressed to a congregation founded by Paul, and is not in the same genre as other Pauline letters that deal directly with congregational problems in an authoritative manner'; also, ibid., p. 70, Romans 'required an indirect and diplomatically nuanced address to the issues in a congregation that Paul had not founded'.

cated[44] and may serve only to suggest that Paul's use of these persuasive appeals tends to be more frequent when addressing individuals, and least frequent when addressing a city that he has not visited (although he knows a number of members in the Roman church by name and personally).[45] If so, his approach appears to vary in accordance with his familiarity with his audience, and does not rest simply on his status as an apostle to all Gentiles.[46] Consistent with this, Paul encourages other leaders, who are not apostles, to adopt similar approaches of persuasion in their congregations.

In addition to identifying particular occurrences of verbs of persuasion, we may also note a few instances where Paul is clearly appealing to the emotions of his correspondents. The manner in which Paul makes an appeal is said to be 'by the meekness and gentleness (διὰ τῆς πραΰτητος καὶ ἐπιεικείας) of Christ' (2 Cor. 10.1). A cursory study of the Gospels, however, reveals that some of Jesus' own appeals were not without their cutting edge.[47] Certainly for Paul, appeal or urging can turn to pleading when he senses that the very salvation of his readers is at stake (Gal. 4.12: 'Friends, I beg you (δέομαι), become as I am, for I also have become as you are'), or when the unity of the body is at risk (Rom. 16.17; 1 Cor. 1.10; 2 Cor. 2.8; Phil. 4.2). He also makes himself and his life vulnerable to the Corinthians, and implores them to be similarly open to him (2 Cor. 6.11-13; 7.2-3).

The context of Paul's letter to Philemon is traditionally reconstructed as one in which Paul, somewhat reluctantly, is returning the runaway slave, Onesimus, to his rightful owner – although the apostle's personal circumstances are such that he has a continuing need, while in chains,

---

44   I have based this survey on the following verses: Rom. 12.1; 15.14, 30; 1 Cor. 1.10; 2.4; 4.14, 16; 7.6, 17; 11.17, 34; 16.1, 12, 15; 16.17; 2 Cor. 2.8; 5.11, 20; 6.1; 7.3; 8.4, 6, 8, 17; 9.5; 10.1, 2; 12.18; 13.2, 11; Gal. 1.9-10; 4.12; 5.3, 7–8, 21; Eph. 3.13; 4.1, 17; 5.11; 6.9; Phil. 1.14; 4.2-3; Col. 1.28; 3.16; 4.10; 1 Thess. 2.3, 12; 3.4; 4.1-2, 6, 10, 11, 18; 5.11-12, 14, 27; 2 Thess. 2.1; 3.4, 6, 10, 12, 15; 1 Tim. 1.3, 5, 18; 2.1; 4.7, 11; 5.1, 7, 20–21; 6.2, 13–14, 17; 2 Tim. 2.14; 4.1-2; Tit. 1.5, 9, 13; 2.6, 15; 3.8; Phlm. 8–10; and I have identified the number of verses in which such words of persuasion occur, not the number of times these words occur; neither have I distinguished between those instances when Paul is the subject rather than another individual (e.g. Timothy or Titus); nor have I differentiated between grades of severity or the urgency of the presenting issues. However, an alternative analysis based instead on the number of imperatives in the Pauline letters reveals a similar pattern. The personal letters tend to include the most imperatives (2 Timothy, 1 Timothy, Titus, Philemon); a second group of letters have broadly similar frequencies of imperatives (Colossians, Philippians, Ephesians, 1 Thessalonians); approximately half this frequency is found in 2 Thessalonians, 1 Corinthians, Romans, Galatians and 2 Corinthians.

45   Cf. the list of names in Romans 16.

46   We noticed a similar distinction in regard to those people to whom Paul identified himself to be a fictive father.

47   Cf., for example, Mt. 23.2-39.

to keep the slave for his own support. At the heart of the letter there are a number of points at which his appeal is most especially emotive, including references to Paul's age, his chains and his personal needs. Paul's stated preference is to make a personal appeal, rather than lay down the law:

> Although having much boldness in Christ to command (ἐπιτάσσειν) you to do what is right, because of love I would rather appeal (παρακαλῶ) – and I, Paul, as an old man, and now also a prisoner of Christ Jesus. I am appealing (παρακαλῶ) to you for my child, Onesimus, whose father I became while in chains. Then he was useless to you, but now he is useful both to you and to me. I am sending him, that is, my heart, back to you. I wanted to keep him with me, so that he might be of service to me on your behalf during my imprisonment for the gospel; but I wanted to do nothing without your knowledge, in order that your good deed might be voluntary and not forced (Phlm. 8–14).

In this instance he is using the cultural code of reciprocity. Paul has been generous to Philemon, and is now calling in Philemon's debt, by urging that he follow Paul's appeal concerning Onesimus. Paul makes use of the principle of patronage, whereas with regard to the Corinthians he deliberately distanced himself from this. Philemon is recognized by Paul as a generous patron to the church that meets in his house, one who uses his faith and wealth to refresh the hearts of the saints.[48] Such a person would surely respond warmly to Paul's appeal, not least because that individual owes Paul his very salvation. Furthermore, such a person would perform this favour for his friend Paul who is now suffering both imprisonment and old age. The appeal is thus to Philemon's sense of honour, loyalty and debt.[49]

A similar emotional plea is presented in the matter of raising financial support for the famine-stricken believers in Judea. Paul says to the Corinthians 'I am not giving you a command (ἐπιταγή), but I am testing the genuineness of your love against the zeal of others' (2 Cor. 8.8). Here the appeal is combined with flattery: 'Now as you excel in everything – in faith, in utterance, in knowledge, in all earnestness, and in your love for us – see that you excel in this gracious work also' (2 Cor. 8.7). This use of flattery is preceded by a statement which is intended to arouse in this proud and highly competitive community in Corinth the desire to outdo the acts of generosity fulfilled by another community, namely the Thessalonians who are praised for having acted so generously notwithstanding their comparative poverty. Titus is then commissioned to elicit a response of no less generosity from the Corinthians (2 Cor. 8.1-6). Paul is thus using the example of the Macedonian Christians as a

---

48   Phlm. 2, 7.
49   Cf. in particular D. A. DeSilva, *Honor, Patronage, Kinship and Purity: Unlocking New Testament Culture* (Leicester: IVP, 2000), pp. 124–5.

means of goading the Corinthians into demonstrating generosity, but he is reciprocally using the example of the Corinthians to goad the Macedonians into generosity (2 Cor. 9.2). Paul reports that the Macedonians were neither forced nor cajoled into giving, but they pleaded to be able to contribute to the collection for the Jerusalem church. In so doing, they surprised even Paul. This portrait of the Macedonian churches provides the basis from which Paul can appeal to the Corinthians to be no less generous.

Clearly such an appeal was not uncommon in Graeco-Roman society where the institution of benefaction was highly competitive. Comparisons were widely made. No benefactor would like to be compared less favourably with another in terms of generosity. Note, however, that the goal of Paul's appeal is not to secure his own financial well-being, but to see that those in Jerusalem are adequately provided for in the face of famine and that there is comparative economic equality (2 Cor. 8.13-15) – Jerusalem being the city which had been, and would continue to be, repeatedly unwelcoming towards Paul (as Luke records in Acts). Thus, although patronage in ancient Mediterrranean society was largely self-serving, this is not a self-serving appeal; neither does Paul cite his own generosity, rather he highlights the example of the Macedonians, and more significantly Jesus himself (2 Cor. 8.9). Thus in this instance he uses appeal, flattery and advice rather than command (2 Cor. 8.8, 10, 17). All this is intended to appeal to the Corinthians' sense of personal honour and pride. Paul has expressed confidence that the Corinthians will be obliging and he does not want to be embarrassed at his description being found to be unworthy. He accordingly applies pressure (2 Cor. 9.4: 'if some Macedonians come with me and find that you are not ready, we would be humiliated – to say nothing of you – in this undertaking').

Paul also makes an emotional appeal to the Galatians. In particular, he reminds them of their loyalty to him when he first preached the gospel to them, indeed their personal care for him whilst he suffered from some medical ailment (Gal. 4.12-16). Their commitment to him as their apostle now appears to have been transferred to a group of infiltrators who do not have their best wishes at heart (Gal. 4.17). The appeal to the Galatians at this point is clearly intended to arouse sympathy and remind them of the honour of their devotion to him. This appeal to the Galatians' better nature is contrasted, however, with the rather more blunt appeal by Paul when he repeatedly shames them with somewhat vituperative language: 'I am so astonished that you are so quickly deserting him who called you in the grace of Christ and turning to a different gospel' (Gal. 1.6); 'O foolish Galatians! Who has bewitched you' (Gal. 3.1); 'I wish those who unsettle you would mutilate themselves!' (Gal. 5.12). Paul's message is unalterable, regardless of what suffering this entails for him. Those who are in the wrong can display this by altering their message so as to avoid persecution

(Gal. 6.12). Paul, however, is not seeking to gain approval from men (Gal. 1.10) – in contrast to some of the so-called apostles who have infiltrated the Corinthian church.

On another occasion Paul again appeals to the Corinthians' sense of honour, specifically by shaming them into more appropriate behaviour. In this regard Paul is at odds with the established practices of the trained orators of his day. To shame those whom you wanted to impress could hardly be considered an effective tool in a society where personal honour was so highly valued. It is true that shame was frequently employed in forensic speeches, but in those instances the goal was not to win over those who were being shamed, but rather to humiliate them as one's opponents, and to incite a jury against the shamed party. You would be advised not to shame those listeners whose support you sought to win. In contrast Paul adopts sarcasm in addressing the Corinthians, which is intended to highlight the ridiculous nature of the stance they are taking. With regard to those who seek to settle their civil litigation against a fellow brother in public, he poses the question as to whether this congregation, which so prides itself on the display of wisdom, really lacks anyone in the congregation who is 'wise' enough to adjudicate in such petty lawsuits (1 Cor. 6.5)? This is all the more pointed when it is noted that Paul considers even the least esteemed (according to their own standards, that is) in the church are actually appropriately qualified to judge angels, and therefore also to adjudicate in these minor matters of law (1 Cor. 6.2, 5). Accordingly, he specifically points out: 'I say this to your shame' (1 Cor. 6.5).

It should be noted that, on occasion, Paul is happy to disclose the agenda that lies behind his appeals. After a passage of great irony in 1 Cor. 4.8-13, Paul points out for the benefit of the Corinthians that his aim is not to shame them, but to warn them as a father warns his children (1 Cor. 4.14). To the Thessalonians he says that the nature of his appeals was not intended to flatter.[50] He points out in 2 Corinthians that his earlier letter had the intended goal of causing them sorrow that would lead ultimately to repentance (2 Cor. 7.8-13). In the process the Corinthians had indeed been sorrowful – but Paul's joy is in the outcome, namely forgiveness. Thus, Paul does not conceal his desire to persuade, indeed to suggest that he sought to manipulate by stealth is to ignore the number of times in which he makes plain to his audience both the goal and the method of his exhortations.[51]

Thus we can see that Paul regards his principal role is to persuade

---

50   1 Thess. 2.5.

51   Cf. the so-called covert allusion in 1 Corinthians 4; A. D. Clarke, *Secular and Christian Leadership in Corinth: A Socio-Historical and Exegetical Study of 1 Corinthians 1–6* (Paternoster Biblical Monographs; Milton Keynes: Paternoster, 2006), pp. 122–4; and B. Fiore, '"Covert Allusion" in 1 Corinthians 1–4', *CBQ* 47 (1985), pp. 85–102.

people (2 Cor. 5.11), and his goal is unashamedly to influence. His preference is to do this by means of appeal and encouragement, rather than laying down the law or condemnation (2 Cor. 8.8) or metaphorically using a whip (1 Cor. 4.21). The manner in which Paul makes his appeals is said rather to be 'by the meekness and gentleness of Christ' (2 Cor. 10.1). Accordingly, he can appeal to the Philippians, for example, to make his joy complete (Phil. 2.2). His confessed aim is certainly not to 'lord it over' the faith of his fellow believers (2 Cor. 1.24). It is this desire not to 'lord it over' the Corinthians in particular that leads Paul to restrain the strength of his response to them, and avoid a painful visit (2 Cor. 2.1-4) or to be harsh in the use of his authority, for authority should have the sole goal of building up and not destroying (2 Cor. 13.10).

Appeal can turn to more urgent pleading, however, when he senses that the very salvation of his readers is at stake (Gal. 4.12), or when the unity of the body is at risk (Rom. 16.17; 1 Cor. 1.10; 2 Cor. 2.8; Phil. 4.2). His forceful appeals are presented openly, avoiding the use of those rhetorical techniques that would cause his audience to be impressed by him as an individual, and so detract from his chief goal, namely that people respond appropriately to the gospel.

Paul's commitment to this goal drives him to be bold, not apologetic, in the presentation of his message. Flattery and praise alone could win many friends, but may not result in changed lives. Flowery rhetoric and display could impress many, but may not result in changed lives. Paul's goal was to win people for Christ rather than merely to win their friendship. Indeed, he recognizes that much of his message may indeed succeed in creating enemies. He can offer appeals from the heart, and then can say 'we will be ready to punish every act of disobedience, once your obedience is complete' (2 Cor. 10.6; cf. also 2 Cor. 13.2). To Philemon he appeals on the basis of love, but combines this with an emotive challenge (Phlm. 9–10). It is clear that Paul writes at different times and in different contexts with varying amounts of 'heat' or fervour. And he even highlights instances where he is not entirely happy with his tone (e.g. Gal. 4.20; 1 Cor. 4.21).

In addition, Paul notes in 2 Corinthians that his earlier letter had caused his readers sorrow. He has been made aware that his rhetoric was powerful in this regard, and after momentary regret he observes that the Corinthians' response ultimately led to godly repentance (2 Cor. 7.8-13). These examples serve to show that Paul is aware of the extent to which his words, both written and spoken, carried significant rhetorical force. In a society where the scientific analysis of rhetoric was highly developed, Paul makes plain that he is appealing on a variety of bases to his congregations. The grounds for the appeal are often in the moral sense of obligation that his audience should feel. It is their conformity to the gospel, rather than his reputation that is the driving force behind his rhetoric.

3. *Imitation*

To call others to imitate one is said to presume a privileged position over them, and to seek both to reinforce conformity and repress difference.[52] If the appeal is obeyed, then a measure of control has been exercised. If resisted, then conflict arises. This type of negotiation occurs in all societies and is a fundamental tool of leadership and social formation – indeed an essential tool of child development.[53] How the call to imitation is received is determined both by the dynamics of the particular relationship in question and the content of the imitation. The desire to effect change can be either self-seeking in motivation or benevolent. Similarly, in conforming to the model, the response can be made either willingly or under duress.

In the New Testament, a number of word-groups are used to convey the semantic domain of imitating a personal model. The one that has dominated scholarly discussion includes the noun 'imitator' (μιμητής), used some eleven times;[54] in addition, however, the word 'model' (τύπος) is also used some eleven times in this sense;[55] the word 'example' (δεῖγμα) is used some five times in this sense;[56] and the word 'pattern' (ὑπογραμμός) is used once.[57] All of these New Testament references to individuals as examples or models are to be found within the letters, with the one exception of Jn 13.15, where Jesus' action of washing his disciples' feet is presented as an example (ὑπόδειγμα) for the disciples to emulate. This concentration of imitation vocabulary within the letters, rather than the Gospels, is not surprising in that their purpose is more explicitly one of social formation than the narrative context of the Gospels and Acts. Sixteen of the references are found within the broader Pauline corpus, and the remaining nine in Hebrews, James, 1 and 2 Peter, 3 John and Jude. The motif is, thus, widely used by Paul, but, in proportion to the number of verses, it occurs more frequently in letters not attributed to him.[58]

---

52 E. A. Castelli, *Imitating Paul: A Discourse of Power* (Literary Currents in Biblical Interpretation; Louisville: Westminster John Knox Press, 1991), p. 22.

53 In addition to specific appeals to imitation, much development takes place through unprompted emulation.

54 Cf. 1 Cor. 4.16; 11.1; Eph. 5.1; 1 Thess. 1.6; 2.14; Heb. 6.12. Cf. also the noun 'fellow-imitator' (συμμιμητής) in Phil. 3.17, and the verb 'imitate' (μιμέομαι) in 2 Thess. 3.7, 9; Heb. 13.7; 3 Jn 11.

55 Used in this sense in Rom. 5.14; 1 Cor. 10.6; Phil. 3.17; 1 Thess. 1.7; 2 Thess. 3.9; 1 Tim. 4.12; Tit. 2.7; and 1 Pet. 5.3. Cf. also the noun 'model' (ὑποτύπωσις) in 1 Tim. 1.16 and 2 Tim 1.13; and the adverb, τυπικῶς, in 1 Cor. 10.11.

56 Cf. Jude 1.7. Cf. also ὑπόδειγμα, found in Jn 13.15, Jas 5.10, 2 Pet. 2.6, and possibly also Heb. 4.11.

57 Cf. 1 Pet. 2.21, where Jesus' suffering is held up as an example for Christian slaves to follow.

58 The ratio of occurrences per verse in the Pauline corpus in contrast to the non-Pauline letters is 2:3.

Paul, however, is the only New Testament writer explicitly to use this language in reference to imitation of himself as an ethical example. This motif of imitation is a central element of Paul's attempts to influence his readers,[59] which he uses on seven occasions and always in relation to those congregations that he has founded, namely, Thessalonica, Corinth, Galatia and Philippi. On the other occasions, the object of imitation is variously other individuals, Old Testament figures, Christ or God. It is important to note, however, that the motif of imitation is not restricted to those passages where Paul expressly uses this imitation vocabulary. A fuller assessment of the topic will take note also of those instances when Paul is highlighting examples to follow but makes no use of the standard imitation vocabulary.

We have seen that in her book, *Imitating Paul: A Discourse of Power*, Elizabeth Castelli argues that Paul's appeal to imitation of himself is power discourse, and is representative of his agenda for 'an economy of sameness' across his communities.[60] His attempts to coerce by repressing diversity are confirmed, it is argued, by the lack of specific content in his injunctions. Rather he urges his readers to a general emulation of him, which effectively privileges him as a person over his readers.[61] Paul is clearly not averse to drawing attention to his own example. Furthermore, 'by holding himself up as an example Paul seems to be contradicting his own command to self-humiliation'.[62] The charge of a self-seeking, manipulative control would, nonetheless, warrant revision if it could be demonstrated that Paul: offers specific content to his model; secondly, mitigates any privileged position he might hold; thirdly, does not present himself in an unassailable position of perfection; or fourthly, seeks to celebrate diversity.

a. *The Content of Paul's Model*

On a number of occasions Paul urges his readers to follow his example, but appears not to provide specific details as to what aspects of his life should be emulated. Thus, he twice urges the Corinthians 'be imitators of me (μιμηταί μου γίνεσθε)' (1 Cor. 4.16; 11.1), while to the Philippians he writes, 'join in imitating me (συμμιμηταί μου γίνεσθε), and observe those who live according to the example (τύπος) you have in us' (Phil. 3.17). An

---

59   V. A. Copan, *Saint Paul as Spiritual Director: An Analysis of the Imitation of Paul with Implications and Applications to the Practice of Spiritual Direction* (Paternoster Biblical Monographs; Milton Keynes: Paternoster, 2007), p. 220, 'In his person, Paul united all the roles in which imitation was normally found: (fictive) parent, teacher, and leader'.

60   Castelli, *Imitating Paul*, pp. 16–17.

61   Castelli, *Imitating Paul*, p. 31.

62   J. A. A. Brant, 'The Place of Mimesis in Paul's Thought', *Studies in Religion/Sciences Religieuses* 22 (1993), p. 285.

indeterminate call for others to imitate Paul goes beyond the mere task of social reform or ethical correction, but becomes more specifically a call to 'follow' him in all aspects. Such an injunction to 'follow' (ἀκολουθέω) is characteristic of Jesus in all four Gospels. While it is clear that Paul does not use this verb in his appeals to his readers, is it nonetheless the case that he effectively urges an unquestioning following of his lead?

1 Corinthians 4 draws to a close an extended appeal to the Corinthians that they avoid divisions in the church over different leading personalities. Paul is aware of reports that a number of apostolic figures are being played off against each other, and members of the community are variously siding with one or other of these elevated figureheads (1 Cor. 1.10-17; 3.1-4). The problem is identified as an inappropriate allegiance to specific leaders after the fashion of contemporary clients towards their patrons.[63] In the course of dealing with this situation, Paul first urges that the Corinthians resist 'following' specific leaders, including himself (1 Cor. 1.10-17); and he then employs considerable irony in drawing to the attention of the Corinthians the true nature of apostleship with specific reference to himself and Apollos, contrasting this reality of suffering apostles with the haughtiness and self-congratulation of the Corinthians (1 Cor. 4.8-13). He urges that both he and Apollos should be viewed rather as servants of God (1 Cor. 3.5; 4.1), who seek to carry out their task faithfully. It is this sober reflection that Paul has of his role and that of Apollos in relation to God and those whom they seek to serve, that the Corinthians ought to seek to imitate (1 Cor. 4.16). Accordingly, Paul's injunction, ostensibly to exclusive and general imitation of him, is in its wider context a clear criticism of the Corinthians, and it amounts to an injunction to adopt the kind of attitude and co-operation which characterize both Paul and Apollos, apostles who were instead being placed in competition with each other by the Corinthians.

The second occasion on which Paul urges the Corinthians to imitate him (1 Cor. 11.1) is widely recognized as the close of an extended section that spans 1 Corinthians 8–10. Here Paul is responding to questions raised by his correspondents, specifically about the rights that the believer has to eat meat that has been sacrificed to idols. The community appears to be divided between those who are confident in exercising what they perceive to be a right and those who are fearful of the connection with idols and demons. Paul's response is sustained across 1 Corinthians 8 and 10, and amounts to an insistence that in the context of the Christian community, one should lay aside what might be deemed a justifiable right if in so doing one would avoid offending the theological stance of a fellow believer. At the end of 1 Corinthians 8, Paul begins to frame his response with specific reference to himself and raises the hypothetical situation: 'therefore, if

---

63   See Clarke, *Secular and Christian Leadership in Corinth*, pp. 89–93.

food causes my brother to stumble, I will never eat meat again, in order that I may not cause my brother to stumble' (1 Cor. 8.13). He continues by citing some actual instances in which he has sacrificed personal privileges and rights in order not to cause detriment to the work of the gospel (1 Cor. 9.12, 15). Following this extended reference to his own actions, he urges the Corinthians to take note of the example from Israelite history in which many of the people of God were mixing eating and drinking with idolatry, and were severely judged (1 Cor. 10.6, 11, 18). The appeal to the Corinthians is, thus, both specific and detailed, and his second injunction that they imitate him is placed firmly as a conclusion to this appeal.[64]

A third instance in which Paul's appeal appears to be non-specific occurs in his letter to the Philippians. Philippians 3 opens with a vituperative outburst warning against those who would impose circumcision, and thus place confidence in the flesh (Phil. 3.2-4). In development, Paul then embarks upon a particularly detailed section of autobiography, highlighting his own determination to place confidence in Christ alone. In Phil. 3.12-14, this is presented as a specific goal that has not for him been fully achieved. It is in this context that Paul urges the Philippians to follow the example set by him and others, and in so doing he raises the contrasting example of those who are putting confidence in the flesh (Phil. 3.18-21).

In 2 Thess. 3.7 Paul urges his readers that they have an obligation to imitate him, 'you yourselves know how you ought to imitate us (πῶς δεῖ μιμεῖσθαι ἡμᾶς)'. The context of this injunction regards idleness in the Christian community, and Paul draws attention to those members of the community who were dependent on the support of their acquaintances, and did not earn their own bread. The Thessalonians are specifically reminded of the behaviour of Paul and his co-workers when last in Thessalonica; they had not been idle, and had so worked, night and day, as not to be a drain on their hospitality.

Paul writes to a fourth group of communities that he has founded and presents the enigmatic phrase, 'I beg you, become as I am, for I also have become as you are (γίνεσθε ὡς ἐγώ, ὅτι κἀγὼ ὡς ὑμεῖς)' (Gal. 4.12). The puzzle here is that, in addition to commending imitation of him, he also notes that in some sense he has already become like them. Here we do not find the standard imitation vocabulary, and should ask in what sense might Paul and the Galatians become like each other, or what is the

---

64 Copan, *Saint Paul as Spiritual Director*, p. 142, argues that in 1 Cor. 11.1, 'Paul is calling the Corinthian believers to imitate him in the way that he makes it his constant aim negatively not to cause anyone – believer or unbeliever – to falter in their relationship to God, and positively to intentionally seek the good of the many so that they may be ultimately saved'.

specific content of this imitation. The letter concerns the Galatian Gentiles' relationship to the law and the Abrahamic seed. In turning to Christ, the Galatians have found freedom, and should not return to a state of bondage – in this case, bondage to the law (Gal. 4.8-10). It is in this context that Paul urges his readers to become like him; presumably, therefore, as one who does not sit in bondage to the law, and more specifically, one who, in so doing, effectively became as a Gentile. He continues by decrying the zeal of those who are adversely influencing the Galatians towards submitting to the law, and thereby alienating them from him (Gal. 4.17-18). The zeal of these people is misplaced. Accordingly, in this instance, as with the instances in 1 Cor. 4.16 and 11.1, Phil. 3.17, and 2 Thess. 3.7, Paul's injunction to imitate is supported not simply by specific content from his own life and practice, but also in contrast to specifically detailed actions of others. The detailing of the content of the emulation means that Paul is not favouring himself over all others, so much as defending certain, specified actions (his own) over against contrary actions of some others that are inappropriate.

b. *The Privileging of Paul's Model*
In his use of the imitation motif, it has also been suggested that Paul is privileging his own model in relation to that of others, and thereby assuming an exclusive position of significant power by virtue of the uniqueness of his model. In the previous section it was noted that Paul repeatedly contrasts his own model with that of others. The question is then raised as to whether the Pauline model is being presented by him as an exclusive model that leaves no room for alternates or equivalents.

Following his injunction in 1 Cor. 4.16, 'I appeal to you, then, be imitators of me', Paul records that he is sending Timothy who will 'remind you of my ways in Christ Jesus, as I teach them everywhere in every church' (1 Cor. 4.17). In the absence of Paul, a close replica is to be sent, who will serve as a substitute, but nonetheless remind the Corinthians of the original. In one sense, Timothy is an alternative model, but he is expressly chosen because he is regarded by Paul to be a replica. The Pauline model is effectively privileged.

We have noted, however, that this instruction to the Corinthians was framed as part of a wider comparison between Paul and Apollos, both of whom characterized those qualities that the Corinthian Christians themselves lacked. It was argued that, whereas the Corinthians had been divided over Paul or Apollos, Paul himself was pressing that both he and his fellow apostle were united in their service of God, and were equally exemplary in their ministry. Although Timothy is the one who is to be sent, as Paul's child, to model Paul, the apostle has effectively presented Apollos, his equal rather than his junior, as an equally appropriate ethical model. Thus, it could be argued that Timothy and Apollos serve not because they model Paul, but because they model appropriate behaviour; indeed, precisely the humility that is characteristic of all apostles whom 'God has exhibited ... as last of all, as though sentenced to death ... a spectacle to the world, to angels and to mortals' (1 Cor. 4.9).

In the closing chapter of the letter, Paul urges the community to recognize the godly example set by three further individuals – Stephanas, Fortunatus and Achaicus – men who had exemplified themselves by virtue of their devotion, hard labour and service in refreshing the hearts of the saints (1 Cor. 16.15-18). These people have travelled to Paul and have been a source of information to him about their fellow Corinthians. Paul's commendation is not self-referential, indeed he notes his own indebtedness to them 'for they refreshed my spirit as well as yours' (1 Cor. 16.18). I have elsewhere noted the significance of the likelihood that these people comprise a comparatively wealthy householder, Stephanas, together with two of his slaves or freedmen.[65] They are appropriate models to the Corinthians, not because they all share the relevant social credentials, but because they exemplify appropriate behaviour. This raises the probability that Paul's underlying concern is not the privileging of his own model, but the reinforcement of appropriate ethical standards, regardless of who is the model.[66] A similar reaction may be seen in Paul's contention with the Philippians that he is less concerned with who preaches the gospel, and with what motives, so long as the gospel continues to be preached, even if it be at a cost to his own reputation (Phil. 1.15-18). Again, Paul's concern is not the privileging of his own position, but the spread of the gospel, reinforced by congregations whose behaviour is consistent with that gospel. It is the content of the gospel that is to be privileged (Gal. 1.6-9), and not the individuals who present it.

In writing to the Thessalonians, Paul reminds his readers of the actions, not just of himself, but also of his co-writers, Silvanus and Timothy, when they had first visited the community in Thessalonica (1 Thess. 1.5-7). In 2 Thessalonians, again Paul draws attention to the example that was jointly set by him and his missionary team (2 Thess. 3.6-7). Furthermore, Paul even, indeed repeatedly, commends the example set by the Thessalonians

---

65 Cf. A. D. Clarke, '"Refresh the Hearts of the Saints": A Unique Pauline Context?', *TynBull* 47 (1996), pp. 277–300.

66 Copan, *Saint Paul as Spiritual Director*, pp. 124, understands the injunction to imitate in 1 Cor. 4.14-16, thus: 'Imitation has a specific as well as a general referent: specifically it refers to living a life of humble, sacrificial service to others because of implications of the message of the cross of Christ, which should lead to the rejection of what the world considers to be wisdom, strength, and honor; generally it refers holistically to everything in Paul's life (actions, virtues, emotions, and lifestyle) that flows out of his relationship to and service of Christ'.

themselves (1 Thess. 1.3; 3.6; 4.10), which commendably resulted in others from Macedonia and more distant Achaia emulating the Thessalonians (1 Thess. 1.7). In these instances, Paul is noting their emulation, rather than urging them so to do. Furthermore, the Thessalonians, in their suffering, had also successfully copied the example of the Judean churches (1 Thess. 2.14), although it should be noted that this might simply have meant that the Thessalonians had endured a similar experience to the Judeans, and may not have set out deliberately to emulate them.[67] While the Thessalonians are here commended for having set an example for others in the wider region of Macedonia and Achaia, we have already noted that the Macedonians were further being promoted as an example to those in the Achaian city of Corinth, specifically in terms of their liberality, notwithstanding great poverty (2 Cor. 8.1-7).

These instances that demonstrate Paul's pointing both to other leaders and Christian communities who set an equivalent example would suggest that he is not consistently seeking to carve out a unique role for himself, nor indeed to attract exclusive allegiance to himself. This is reinforced in the Corinthian correspondence when Paul expressly urges that individuals do not divisively elevate him on a pedestal, and reminds them that he baptised only Crispus, Gaius and the household of Stephanas (1 Cor. 1.14-16). However, it may be argued that Paul's highlighting of both his own example and that of others, is presented as entirely secondary, however, to the supreme imitation of God, in Christ, which is a goal for Paul and presented as being a goal for his readers ('Be imitators of me, *as I am of Christ'*, 1 Cor. 11.1). It is widely recognized that Paul's letters reveal few direct references to the life of Christ, indeed this has suggested to some that Paul rather regards himself as the founder of Christianity. The number and context of those references to the example of Christ is, nonetheless, significant, not least because they lack specificity, and consequently are privileged over the examples of others, and amount to a call to follow. In a similar vein, although in 1 and 2 Thessalonians, Paul repeatedly reminds his readers of his own example, and commends them for their example, there is also an underlying message of the imitation of God, to the glory of Christ, in the text (1 Thess. 2.12; 2 Thess. 1.5, 11–12; 2.14). Most significantly, on a number of occasions in his letters this primary model is promoted without reference to himself (Phil. 2.5-11; Rom. 15.2-3; 2 Cor. 8.9).

We have noted that in Philippians, Paul presents his own life as a model for his readers (Phil. 3.17; 4.9). The lynch-pin of the letter, however, is

---

67   W. Michaelis, 'μιμέομαι', in G. Kittel (ed.), *TDNT* (vol. 4; Grand Rapids; London: Eerdmans, 1968), p. 667, writes, 'there can be no question of taking their fate (no their conduct) as an example. What is meant is that (through nothing that you have done) the same fate has overtaken you; you have to suffer the same things as they did before'.

rather the model of Christ which is presented in the Philippian hymn. His readers are challenged with regard to their unity and humility (Phil. 2.1-4), and are then directed to the supreme example ('Let the same mind be in you that was in Christ Jesus', Phil. 2.5). Indeed, Christ is expressly presented as the one who did not privilege his own position 'but emptied himself' (Phil. 2.6). This passage has generated extensive debate, particularly over whether a hymn in which the equality of Christ with God, and his eventual exaltation, can be realistic material for imitation. The Philippians here are criticized, however, for their artful political manoeuvring;[68] the exaltation of Christ is not then presented as an aspirational, self-seeking goal, but divine confirmation that the path of humility and self-sacrifice is what is ultimately commended.

Paul's letter to the Romans is not characterized by the presence of imitation language, and this has widely been considered a consequence of the reality that the apostle has not had the opportunity to visit Rome, and therefore his lifestyle is not personally know to them – although, we should note that Romans 16 presupposes that he is remembered by a number in the city. In this letter, however, there is explicit reference to the example of Christ (Rom. 15.3, 7). As with the Philippian hymn, Paul does not here refer directly to isolated actions in the life of Christ that his readers could emulate. Instead, Christ is offered more generally as one who 'did not please himself' and who accepts others. The surrounding context is that of encouraging the strong to bear with the weak. A third occasion on which Paul highlights the supreme example of Christ is in the statement 'For you know the generous act of our Lord Jesus Christ, that though he was rich, yet for your sakes he became poor, so that by his poverty you might become rich' (2 Cor. 8.9). In addition to the generosity of Christ, the Corinthians are also reminded of his love (2 Cor. 5.14), meekness and gentleness (2 Cor. 10.1).[69]

In sum, Paul's example is on a number of occasions drawn to the attention of his readers. The fact that his example is not exclusively used would suggest that he does not see himself as an exclusive and normative figure for his readers to follow. More significantly, Paul draws attention to the model of Christ that he is following, and privileges this over his own, and urges others so to follow Christ.

c. *The Perfection of Paul's Model*

A third way in which Paul could be interpreted as using the motif of imitation as a self-serving tool of social control would be if he were to

68   Cf. Phil. 2.3-4.

69   L. L. Belleville, ' "Imitate Me, just as I Imitate Christ": Discipleship in the Corinthian Correspondence', in R. N. Longenecker (ed.), *Patterns of Discipleship in the New Testament* (Grand Rapids: Eerdmans, 1996), p. 127.

promote his own model as in some way perfected – an ultimate goal to which others should aspire.[70] Castelli holds that, inherent in the mimetic relationship is the perspective that, 'The distance between the model and the copy is never completely erased ... the copy is a derivation from the perfection of the model'.[71] Critical in our investigation of this is the construction of the letter to the Philippians. We have noted that at a number of points in the letter Paul makes reference to himself and his example. In ch 1 we are aware of his situation in chains and his reaction to those who have been maligning him. Following the autobiographical section in ch 3, Paul refers to the pattern of his life again (Phil. 3.17), and in closing the letter he urges 'Keep on doing the things that you have learned and received and heard and seen in me' (Phil. 4.9). This modelling of himself, however, is set against the overriding example of Christ in the Philippian hymn. Most critically, Paul presents his own search to know Christ (Phil. 3.8-10) in terms of an ongoing journey – a goal that he is striving towards (Phil. 3.13-14).

In the course of describing this upward journey, Paul twice reinforces his own sense that he has not reached perfection – 'Not that I have already obtained this or have already reached the goal ... I do not consider that I have made it my own' (Phil. 3.12-13). Consequently, at heart, his readers are being urged to emulate his search for perfection – a perfection that is resolved only in Christ. In so saying, we note the ironical implication of his following statement that, in effect, all who are 'mature' should recognize their need for yet greater maturity: (Phil. 3.15) 'Let us live up to what we have already attained.'

d. *The Celebration of Diversity*

Castelli claims that, 'The mimetic relationship replicates the harmonious quality of the cosmos; sameness and the desire to achieve it are tied to the cosmic order. By inference, difference is relegated to the realm of discord and chaos'.[72] It is clear that Paul uses the motif of imitation as a tool to tackle dissension within the congregations. Significantly, however, his goal is not to replace dissension with conformity, but with unity. Victor Copan notes that a key element of Paul's response in this regard is his application of the motif of the body, which preserves and reinforces diversity; thus, 'all the members [of the body] do not have the *same* function' (Rom. 12.3), but are incorporated within a unity focused around 'the *same* Spirit ... the *same* Lord ... the *same* God' (1 Cor. 12.4-6).[73] Indeed, an essential element of Paul's use of the metaphor of the body is to ensure that the

---

70   Castelli, *Imitating Paul*, p. 86.
71   Castelli, *Imitating Paul*, p. 80.
72   Castelli, *Imitating Paul*, p. 81.
73   Copan, *Saint Paul as Spiritual Director*, p. 207.

different elements of the body do indeed receive appropriate honour, and that none is relegated to obscurity.[74]

Paul's recognition of diversity is also seen in two key passages where the strong are urged to adapt in order to accommodate the weak, rather than force conformity to their own preferences, or indeed to Paul's stance. The Roman congregations clearly reflected diversity of practice in regard to diet. Paul's response was to protect such diversity (Rom. 14.1-4, 6). The one group should not despise the other, nor should they, in turn, be judged. Similarly, different groups treated certain days as special, and sought to celebrate them as such. Paul's response was not to determine which group was right, but to give each the freedom to do as they felt appropriate (Rom. 14.5-6). Although Paul is thoroughly convinced about his freedom to eat all foods (Rom. 14.14), neither group should offend the other, rather they should all pursue peace and what serves to build up the body (οἰκοδομή, Rom. 14.19). It is in this context that Paul offers the example of Christ who welcomes all (Rom. 15.3, 7).

A second passage in which Paul protects diversity is in regard to the issue of meat sacrificed to idols. Paul shared the view of some of the Corinthians who were 'liberated' and understood that such food could not defile them (1 Cor. 8.4-6). He was aware, however, of those who did not possess such knowledge (1 Cor. 8.7). On this issue, knowledge was shown to puff up, where love instead had the capacity to build up (οἰκοδομέω, 1 Cor. 8.1). For Paul, he would rather not eat meat again than allow his own actions to offend his fellow believer (1 Cor. 8.13). It is again at the end of this section in which diversity is protected that Paul uses the motif of imitation, both positively and negatively (1 Cor. 10.6; 11.1).

These passages, however, must be placed alongside instances where Paul does clearly reinforce sameness. We have seen that Paul used the motif of imitation at a number of points in writing to the Philippians. He urges his readers to have the same mind (τὸ αὐτὸ φρονῆτε), the same love and the same accord (Phil. 2.2); indeed, they should have the same mind (τοῦτο φρονεῖτε) as that of Christ Jesus (Phil. 2.5). Later in the letter, he encourages: 'Let those of us then who are mature be of the same mind (τοῦτο φρονῶμεν); and if you have a different mind (ἑτέρως φρονεῖτε) about anything, this too God will reveal to you' (Phil. 3.15). We have already identified, however, that in the first of these passages Paul is urging conformity to Christ, and in the last he is urging conformity to Paul's own ongoing striving after knowing Christ. The issues on which Paul seeks conformity focus on Christ and his gospel; on other issues, Paul identifies difference and protects diversity.

---

74 Cf. the core argument in S. M. Pogoloff, *Logos and Sophia: The Rhetorical Situation of 1 Corinthians* (Atlanta: Scholars Press, 1992).

4. *Conclusion*

We have here identified two key tools to Pauline leadership, both of which are practised by Paul and encouraged in other leaders. The first is to seek to persuade verbally. Although Paul distanced himself from the self-promoting rhetoric of the orators, he placed great store by verbal persuasion, evidenced both in his injunctions to his readers, but also in his stress that other leaders ought also to persuade. The range of force in this persuasion is wide, including gentle encouragement and forthright rebuke; and it varies both in regard to Paul's familiarity with his audience, and the urgency and issues concerned. This stress on verbal persuasion reflects Paul's emphasis on teaching as a core task of the leader that was identified in the previous chapter.

The second key tool of the Pauline leader focuses on life, rather than speech, and is reflected in Paul's emphasis on the character of the leader, not merely as an essential pre-requisite, but as an ongoing context of the leader's life. This focus on the life of the leader is exemplified by Paul's encouragement of mimetic relationships, reflecting his imitation of Christ as well as the ways in which other appropriate leaders modelled an appropriate lifestyle.

These two tools are recognized to be widespread mechanisms of social formation both in Paul's world as well as our contemporary contexts. At the same time, however, it is recognized that Paul's social context differs significantly from our own. Accordingly, these tools are now increasingly criticised as unwelcome and unjustified mechanisms of manipulation, and tend to be used in fewer social and political contexts than previously. In this regard, Paul has been the object of much censure both for his promotion of the mimetic relationship and for his focus on verbal persuasion. Today these two tools of influence are predominantly reserved for the domestic setting of the family and extended household. For Paul, however, we have noted not only that the similarities between the domestic and the ecclesial contexts were far greater than is generally found to be the case today, but also that he did not use these two tools of leadership indiscriminately, but focused their application in regard to those people with whom he had developed an especially close, even paternal, relationship.

Chapter Eight

Conclusion

The aim of this study has been to construct a Pauline theology of leadership while reflecting on contemporary methodological and hermeneutical challenges. I have employed historical critical tools, but have criticized the narrowly ideas-based, historical critical approach that has categorized much research into New Testament ecclesiology since the nineteenth century. I have valued the innovative perspective of the social historians and social theorists who have demonstrated that the Pauline texts do not present a theology that can be accessed apart from the social contexts that gave rise to the apostle's responses. I firmly defend the perspective that research into Paul's views about church order and leadership is more reliable if based on careful study both of the particular situations that prompted his letters and the wider cultural contexts in which those communities and individuals lived. Accordingly, my own previous research into the nature of leadership in the different Pauline communities and in their contemporary Graeco-Roman society has been foundational.

However, I have also reflected on the ways in which interpretations of such texts and contexts are subtly and inescapably influenced by the interpreter. Texts that have a normative status for the life and order of contemporary Christian communities are especially prone to the influences of individual interpreters and their faith communities; and, in large measure, this explains the extraordinarily diverse range of perspectives about Paul, his leadership, and his communities. It is clear that the historical and cultural divides that separate us from Paul leave many gaps in our understanding. Careful historical critical study together with exploration of the social dynamics of the Pauline contexts seek to bridge some of this divide; nonetheless, the process of research continues to be influenced, and the remaining lacunae in knowledge are resolved, by the leanings, desires and expectations of the interpreter. I have sought to identify something of this diversity, and reflect upon the necessity that interpretation be pursued ethically, responsibly and in dialogue.

Among the conclusions reached during the course of this study, a number may be regarded as more significant. In particular, I have argued that the household is the fundamental context to the Pauline communities, and provides an essential framework for understanding Paul's assumptions and injunctions about church, and especially his conception of the nature and scope of the authority of its leaders. This is not, of course, to say that Paul was necessarily opposed to a larger setting for the congregation; but rather, that throughout the timeframe of the Pauline epistles multiple domestic contexts in a town remained the normal unit of church meetings. Consequently, Paul's comments and instructions about church life, order and practice are directed towards and presuppose such situations, and must be interpreted accordingly.

It is this setting that explains Paul's portrait of church communities with its leadership structure that, although comparatively simple, was nonetheless hierarchical. The overseer has been the most neglected of the offices in Pauline studies, and yet it emerges that this is the essential post of leadership in all communities. I have argued that the leader of a house-church was the head of the household, and came to be known as the overseer. The core duties of the overseer were leadership and care of the house-church, and teaching. In this regard, the essential requirement that an overseer is able to 'manage his household' is precisely because this is a fundamental element of the job description – and not merely evidence of the potential overseer's character. This pattern is reflected in the latest of the Pauline letters and, I argue, is effectively what was the case in the earliest of the Pauline communities.

Elders only existed in local situations where there were a reasonable number of house-churches, and therefore sufficient overseers to warrant a council of elders. I have argued that such a body would have included all overseers; and in some situations may also have included other respected individuals who were not overseers, did not lead a house-church and did not, therefore, need to demonstrate the ability to teach. The council of elders did not have jurisdiction over a house-church or house-churches – this was the responsibility of the head of the household, that is its overseer. Rather, an elder's duties were within the eldership or council of elders. Accordingly, where a community had an eldership, all overseers would have been elders, but not all elders were necessarily overseers. The office of overseer required greater qualifications, whereas membership of the council of elders reflected status within the community, rather than specific responsibility.

The term deacon is the most problematic because it is used in such diverse ways, and only rarely as a title. Where it was a local church office, as opposed to service in some wider or more general capacity (for example, service of the gospel or of Christ), the responsibilities were again in regard to a house-church, but did not necessarily include teaching. Some churches may not have had deacons in addition to overseers;

consequently, these posts may simply have occurred where an overseer required additional help.

The status of all leaders was unequivocally located within a hierarchical structure in which leaders should lead, instruct and command. An egalitarian church structure is not presupposed in the Pauline corpus, and there is no clear evidence or Pauline defence for one. Paul's lack of a focus on organizational structures in some letters, his promotion of the weak, his collaboration with fellow workers, and his use of 'brother' language may all be confused for evidence of egalitarianism. There is more evidence, however, for the status inconsistency associated with a leader seeking to serve. If διάκονος is not taken as necessarily and always reflecting servility, then the number of occasions in which a servile metaphor is used to describe or promote the actions of a leader towards others (as opposed to in relation to God) is comparatively small. This reflects also the important, but few, occasions in which this language is used by Jesus in the Gospels. In both the Pauline and the dominical contexts, such service does not replace hierarchy, but qualifies the ways in which authority is exercised. Thus, Jesus can wash the feet of his disciples while saying both that 'no slave is greater than his master' (Jn 13.16), and also that he is their 'master and teacher' (Jn 13.13-14).

There has been significant interest in Pauline discourse as 'power discourse'. While it is clear that much discourse is indeed power discourse, the nature and location of power in the Pauline mission is much more complicated than is often presented. Paul was exercising authority within contexts in which his authority was being challenged, and at times when his life's work, indeed his life, were at risk. Power in the Pauline mission was not, therefore, held unilaterally. Our greatest difficulty in this area, however, is our ability, on the basis of the extant evidence, to identify such power plays and evaluate their extent and impact. There is a consequent tendency to make assumptions about how Paul's power gambits are likely to have originally been received on the basis of their reception today; in other words, the assumption that these power gambits are universal, rather than directed at particular contexts.

The task of Pauline leaders is integral to the context of the church. Two metaphors are helpful in this regard. The metaphor of the body is discussed by Paul alongside references to local church leadership, and presupposes a hierarchy. A task of local leaders is consequently seen to be the building up of the body. This includes ensuring that due honour and recognition are given to the weak, vulnerable and marginalized, and that all members of the body are fulfilling their God-appointed task and contribution to the body of Christ. A second key metaphor of the church is associated with the context and setting of the church, namely the household. Familial metaphors are used widely, but not in an exclusive way, by Paul, and reflect a number of aspects of the task of leaders. The task of the leader that is most frequently and specifically referenced, however, is that of teaching. Paul's major contribution is clearly one of teaching, but he encourages others to teach and requires that overseers fulfil this task as of paramount importance. This teaching takes place within the small group context of the house-church, where the leader and the members of the house-church share significant familiarity.

Accordingly, teaching is one of two essentials tools of leadership. The number and range of instances in which Paul records or promotes persuasion through verbal means are great. Significantly, however, this does not occur evenly across the Pauline corpus, but is concentrated around those contexts in which Paul has a particularly close relationship with his correspondents. Where Paul was more remote from a community, the tone of his teaching and commands is noticeably less forceful. This applies also to a second tool of leadership, namely modelling the imitation of Christ. There is evidence that Paul tailored both his use of rhetoric and his appeal to imitation to those situations where he had the closest relationship. Both of these tools of the leader are not only exercised by Paul but are widely commended in and to other leaders. It is interesting to note that they also reflect the extended passages in 1 Timothy 3, 5 and Titus 1 concerning the qualities and qualifications of the overseer. Both the character of the overseer and his ability to teach are essential pre-requisites for this key office within the Pauline communities. The small, house-church setting, with its associated familiarity, means that personal example and insistent teaching may have been regarded as acceptable tools of persuasion.

I defended in the opening chapter the reasons for considering leadership across the extended Pauline corpus, specifically including the Pastoral Epistles, because they are so informative in regard to church order, as well as the other so-called deutero-Pauline letters. No study of New Testament ecclesiology is complete without interacting with these core texts. However, I have simply adopted their Pauline authorship as a convenience, rather than as an argued and defended stance.

As I have explored issues about the nature, dynamics, goals and structures of Pauline leadership it has emerged that there are elements that are consistently presented across this wider corpus. Key among these are the household context and the basic structure of hierarchical leadership with a head of household with responsibilities of teaching and household management. Other features, however, are less uniformly distributed across this wider corpus. The pattern of distribution, however, does not clearly reflect a distinction between Pauline and deutero-Pauline texts, or early and later texts, or primitive and institutionalized order. Such distinctives more commonly reflect the differences between personal letters (the Pastoral Epistles and Philemon) as opposed to congregational letters; or letters to contexts well known to Paul as opposed to those from which he was more distant. Too much weight has been given to Paul's silence about titles in some letters; and, similarly, the earlier, and therefore anomalous, references to overseers and deacons have had to be marginalized. I do not see clear evidence for significant straight-line development between the Pauline and the deutero-Pauline letters. Features such as hierarchy, leadership within house-churches, the importance of teaching, imitation and the body of Christ – the core elements of Paul's theology of leadership – are distributed widely, although not uniformly, across the wider corpus; and they do not show clear evidence of significant and consistent development over time.

One significant question for many who reflect on Pauline ecclesiology is the extent to which such a theology can or should be normative. Clearly, the task and tools of Pauline leaders, as I have outlined them, are being applied by Paul to Pauline communities, and specifically for their size, setting, inherent intimacy, fictive familial relationships and core mission. I have argued that the domestic setting circumscribed the kind of hierarchy and authority structures within the Pauline communities, and gave rise to a unique set of problems addressed by Paul. The task of transposing these features of Pauline leadership to an alternative church setting is not straightforward. A structure where the primary leadership is centralized and the principal context for meeting is as a single congregation differs substantively from a situation where the core leaders are a number of overseers, each with their own group for whom they individually provide teaching and pastoral care, and over whom they are effectively a head of a household.

The picture of a single, combined meeting, where a key focus and investment of resources are on led worship and formal teaching, reflects a dominant model throughout the subsequent history of the church, in large measure facilitated by, or dictated by, the use of buildings designed for worship and formal teaching, rather than eating and pastoral care. This is notably different from the Pauline conception. In a singular and centralised congregation the leaders are necessarily more remote, physically and relationally, from the congregation by virtue of greater numbers in the congregation and architecture. This significantly alters the nature and frequency of their personal interaction, and by extension it necessarily affects the type of hierarchy that exists, and how that hierarchy is perceived – from above and below. Such a conception of church also affects the scope and tone of teaching, the nature of pastoral care, the modelling of lifestyle and the ability to involve all members in the ministry of the church. We have seen that the Pauline leaders' responsibilities were to model a particular lifestyle, and to challenge and confront directly in the context of a familial relationship. Accordingly, aspects such as a leader's tone in pastoral exhortation, the ability to draw attention to personal example, and the ways in which different parts of the body are to become less marginalized would all need to be modified in contexts where the size of a congregation, or its context for meeting, or the length of a time that a leader has been with a congregation means that a leader does not or cannot have a familial relationship with the members.

This work is framed as a *Pauline* theology of leadership. I have argued that Paul consistently presents it across the Pauline corpus. Whether or how it can be transposed to different contexts is undeniably complex.

Bibliography

Adam, A. K. M., *What is Postmodern Biblical Criticism?* (Guides to Biblical Scholarship New Testament Series; Minneapolis: Fortress, 1995).

Aichele, G., *The Postmodern Bible* (New Haven; London: Yale University Press, 1995).

Barclay, J. M. G., 'Thessalonica and Corinth: Social Contrasts in Pauline Christianity', in E. Adams and D. G. Horrell (eds.), *Christianity at Corinth: The Quest for the Pauline Church* (Louisville; London: Westminster John Knox Press, 2004), pp. 183–96.

Bash, A., *Ambassadors for Christ: An Exploration of Ambassadorial Language in the New Testament* (WUNT; Tübingen: J. C. B. Mohr, 1997).

Belleville, L. L., ' "Imitate Me, just as I Imitate Christ": Discipleship in the Corinthian Correspondence', in R. N. Longenecker (ed.), *Patterns of Discipleship in the New Testament* (Grand Rapids: Eerdmans, 1996), pp. 120–42.

Best, E. E., *Paul and His Converts: The Sprunt Lectures 1985* (Edinburgh: T. & T. Clark, 1988).

——*A Critical and Exegetical Commentary on Ephesians* (International Critical Commentary; Edinburgh: T. & T. Clark, 1998).

Betz, H. D., *Galatians: A Commentary on Paul's Letter to the Churches in Galatia* (Hermeneia; Philadelphia: Fortress Press, 1979).

Beyer, H. W., 'διακονέω, διακονία, διάκονος', in G. Kittel (ed.), *Theological Dictionary of the New Testament* (vol. 2 [D–E]; Grand Rapids; London: Eerdmans, 1964), pp. 81–93.

Bockmuehl, M., *A Commentary on the Epistle to the Philippians* (Black's New Testament Commentaries; London: A. & C. Black, 4th edn, 1997).

Boers, H., *What is New Testament Theology?: The Rise of Criticism and the Problem of a Theology of the New Testament* (Guides to Biblical Scholarship New Testament Series; Philadelphia: Fortress, 1979).

Brandt, W., *Dienst und Dienen im Neuen Testament* (Gütersloh: C. Bertelsmann, 1931).

Brant, J. A. A., 'The Place of Mimesis in Paul's Thought', *Studies in Religion/Sciences Religieuses* 22 (1993), pp. 285–300.

Briggs Kittredge, C., *Community and Authority: The Rhetoric of Obedience in the Pauline Tradition* (Harvard Theological Studies; Harrisburg: Trinity Press International, 1998).

Bruce, F. F., *1 and 2 Thessalonians* (Word Biblical Commentary; Waco: Word Books, 1982).

Bullmore, M. A., *St Paul's Theology of Rhetorical Style: An Examination of 1 Corinthians 2. 1-5 in Light of First Century Graeco-Roman Rhetorical Culture* (San Francisco: International Scholars, 1995).

Burke, T. J. and J. K. Elliott, eds., *Paul and the Corinthians: Studies on a Community in Conflict: Essays in Honour of Margaret Thrall* (*Novum Testamentum* Supplements, 109; Leiden: Brill, 2003).

Byron, J., *Slavery Metaphors in Early Judaism and Pauline Christianity: A Traditio-Historical and Exegetical Examination* (WUNT; Tübingen: Mohr Siebeck, 2003).

Campbell, R. A., *The Elders: Seniority within Earliest Christianity* (Studies of the New Testament and its World; Edinburgh: T. & T. Clark, 1994).

Carroll, R. P., 'Poststructuralist Approaches: New Historicism and Postmodernism', in J. Barton (ed.), *The Cambridge Companion to Biblical Interpretation* (Cambridge Companions to Religion; Cambridge: Cambridge University Press, 1998), pp. 50–66.

Castelli, E. A., *Imitating Paul: A Discourse of Power* (Literary Currents in Biblical Interpretation; Louisville: Westminster John Knox Press, 1991).

Clarke, A. D., '"Refresh the Hearts of the Saints": A Unique Pauline Context?', *Tyndale Bulletin* 47 (1996), pp. 277–300.

——'"Be Imitators of Me": Paul's Model of Leadership', *Tyndale Bulletin* 49 (1998), pp. 329–60.

——*Serve the Community of the Church: Christians as Leaders and Ministers* (First-Century Christians in the Graeco-Roman World; Grand Rapids; Cambridge: Eerdmans, 2000).

——'Jew and Greek, Slave and Free, Male and Female: Paul's Theology of Ethnic, Social and Gender Inclusiveness in Romans 16', in P. Oakes (ed.), *Rome in the Bible and the Early Church* (Carlisle; Grand Rapids: Paternoster; Baker, 2002), pp. 103–25.

——'Equality Or Mutuality?: Paul's Use of "Brother" Language', in P. J. Williams, A. D. Clarke, P. M. Head and D. Instone-Brewer (eds.), *The New Testament in its First-Century Setting: Essays on Context and Background in Honour of B. W. Winter on his 65th Birthday* (Grand Rapids; Cambridge: Eerdmans, 2004), pp. 151–64.

——*Secular and Christian Leadership in Corinth: A Socio-Historical and*

Exegetical Study of 1 Corinthians 1–6 (Paternoster Biblical Monographs; Milton Keynes: Paternoster, 2nd edn, 2006).

Collins, J. N., 'Once More on Ministry: Forcing a Turnover in the Linguistic Field', *One in Christ* 27 (1991), pp. 234–45.

Collins, J. N., *Diakonia: Re-Interpreting the Ancient Sources* (New York; Oxford: Oxford University Press, 1990).

Copan, V. A., *Saint Paul as Spiritual Director: An Analysis of the Imitation of Paul with Implications and Applications to the Practice of Spiritual Direction* (Paternoster Biblical Monographs; Milton Keynes: Paternoster, 2007).

Coutsoumpos, P., *Community, Conflict, and the Eucharist in Roman Corinth: The Social Setting of Paul's Letter* (Lanham: University Press of America, 2006).

Crafton, J. A., *The Agency of the Apostle: A Dramatic Analysis of Paul's Responses to Conflict in 2 Corinthians* (Journal for the Study of the New Testament Supplement Series; Sheffield: JSOT Press, 1991).

Cranfield, C. E. B., *A Critical and Exegetical Commentary on the Epistle to the Romans* (International Critical Commentary; 2 vols.; Edinburgh: T. & T. Clark, 1979).

Crossan, J. D., *The Birth of Christianity: Discovering what Happened in the Years Immediately After the Execution of Jesus* (Edinburgh: T. & T. Clark, 1998).

Dahl, R., 'The Concept of Power', *Behavioral Science* 2 (1957), pp. 201–15.

De Vos, C. S., *Church and Community Conflicts: The Relationships of the Thessalonian, Corinthian, and Philippian Churches with their Wider Civic Communities* (SBL Dissertation Series; Atlanta: Scholars Press; Flinders University of South Australia, 1999).

DeSilva, D. A., *Honor, Patronage, Kinship and Purity: Unlocking New Testament Culture* (Leicester: InterVarsity Press, 2000).

Dodd, B. J., *Paul's Paradigmatic "I": Personal Example as Literary Strategy* (Journal for the Study of the New Testament Supplement Series; Sheffield: Sheffield Academic Press, 1999).

Dowding, K. M., *Power* (Concepts in the Social Sciences; Buckingham: Open University Press, 1996).

Dunn, J. D. G., *Unity and Diversity in the New Testament: An Inquiry into the Character of Earliest Christianity* (London: SCM Press, 1977).

——*New Testament Theology in Dialogue* (Biblical Foundations in Theology; London: SPCK, 1987).

——*Romans 9–16* (Word Biblical Commentary; Dallas: Word Books, 1988).

——*Unity and Diversity in the New Testament: An Inquiry into the Character of Earliest Christianity* (London: SCM, 2nd edn, 1990).

——*The Theology of Paul's Letter to the Galatians* (New Testament Theology; Cambridge: Cambridge University Press, 1993).

——*The Epistles to the Colossians and to Philemon: A Commentary on the Greek Text* (New International Greek Testament Commentary; Grand Rapids; Carlisle: Eerdmans; Paternoster, 1996).

——*The Theology of Paul the Apostle* (Grand Rapids: Eerdmans, 1998).

Dutch, R. S., *The Educated Elite in 1 Corinthians: Education and Community Conflict in Graeco-Roman Context* (Journal for the Study of the New Testament Supplement Series; New York; London: T. & T. Clark, 2005).

Ehrman, B. D., *et al.*, *The Text of the New Testament in Contemporary Research: Essays on the Status Quaestionis* (Eugene: Wipf and Stock, 2001).

Ellingworth, P., 'Translating the Language of Leadership', *Bible Translator* 49 (1998), pp. 126–38.

Elliott, J. H., 'Jesus was Not an Egalitarian: A Critique of an Anachronistic and Idealist Theory', *Biblical Theology Bulletin* 32 (2002), pp. 75–91.

——'The Jesus Movement was Not Egalitarian but Family-Oriented', *Biblical Interpretation* 11 (2003), pp. 173–210.

Esler, P. F., 'Family Imagery and Christian Identity in Galatians 5. 13 to 6. 10', in H. Moxnes (ed.), *Constructing Early Christian Families: Family as Social Reality and Metaphor* (London: Routledge, 1997), pp. 121–49.

——*Conflict and Identity in Romans: The Social Setting of Paul's Letter* (Minneapolis: Fortress, 2003).

——*New Testament Theology: Communion and Community* (Minneapolis: Fortress, 2005).

Evans, R. J., *In Defence of History* (London: Granta, 1997).

Fairweather, J., 'The Epistle to the Galatians and Classical Rhetoric', *Tyndale Bulletin* 45 (1994), pp. 1–38.

——'The Epistle to the Galatians and Classical Rhetoric', *Tyndale Bulletin* 45 (1994), pp. 213–43.

Fee, G. D., *The First Epistle to the Corinthians* (New International Commentary on the New Testament; Grand Rapids: Eerdmans, 1987).

Fewell, D. N., 'Reading the Bible Ideologically: Feminist Criticism', in S. L. McKenzie and S. R. Haynes (eds.), *To Each its Own Meaning: An Introduction to Biblical Criticisms and Their Applications* (Louisville: Westminster John Knox Press, rev. and expanded edn, 1999), pp. 268–82.

Fiore, B., '"Covert Allusion" in 1 Corinthians 1–4', *Catholic Biblical Quarterly* 47 (1985), pp. 85–102.

Follett, M. P., *et al.*, *Dynamic Administration: The Collected Papers of Mary Parker Follett* (London: Pitman, 1941).

Foucault, M., *Discipline and Punish: The Birth of the Prison* (London: Allen Lane, 1977).

Furnish, V. P., 'Fellow Workers in God's Service', *Journal of Biblical Literature* 80 (1961), pp. 364–70.

Gehring, R. W., *House Church and Mission: The Importance of Household Structures in Early Christianity* (Peabody: Hendrickson, 2004).

Georgi, D., *The Opponents of Paul in Second Corinthians* (Studies in the New Testament and its World; Edinburgh: T. & T. Clark, 1987).

Gill, D. W. G., 'The Importance of Roman Portraiture for Head-Coverings in 1 Corinthians 11.2-16', *Tyndale Bulletin* 41 (1990), pp. 245–60.

Gini, A., 'Moral Leadership: An Overview', *Journal of Business Ethics* 16 (1997), pp. 323–30.

Gooder, P., '*Diakonia* in the New Testament: A Dialogue with John N. Collins', *Ecclesiology* 3 (2006), pp. 33–56.

Gorringe, T., 'Political Readings of Scripture', in J. Barton (ed.), *The Cambridge Companion to Biblical Interpretation* (Cambridge Companions to Religion; Cambridge: Cambridge University Press, 1998), pp. 67–80.

Grant, R. M., *Paul in the Roman World: The Conflict at Corinth* (Louisville; London: Westminster John Knox Press, 2001).

Greenleaf, R. K., *Servant Leadership: A Journey into the Nature of Legitimate Power and Greatness* (New York: Paulist Press, 1977).

Hack Polaski, S., *Paul and the Discourse of Power* (Gender, Culture, Theory; Sheffield: Sheffield Academic Press, 1999).

Haney, E. H., *The Great Commandment: A Theology of Resistance and Transformation* (Cleveland: Pilgrim Press, 1998).

Harrill, J. A., *Slaves in the New Testament: Literary, Social, and Moral Dimensions* (Minneapolis: Fortress, 2006).

Harris, M. J., *Slave of Christ: A New Testament Metaphor for Total Devotion to Christ* (New Studies in Biblical Theology, 8; Leicester: Apollos, 1999).

Hawthorne, G. F., *Philippians* (Word Biblical Commentary; Waco: Word Books, 1983).

Hennessey, L. R., '*Diakonia* and *Diakonoi* in the Pre-Nicene Church', in J. P. Williman and T. Halton (eds.), *Diakonia: Studies in Honor of Robert T. Meyer* (Washington: Catholic University of America Press, 1986), pp. 60–86.

Hoehner, H. W., *Ephesians: An Exegetical Commentary* (Grand Rapids: Baker, 2002).

Holmberg, B., *Paul and Power: The Structure of Authority in the Primitive*

Church as Reflected in the Pauline Epistles (Coniectanea biblica, New Testament, 11; Lund: Gleerup, 1978).

Horrell, D. G., *The Social Ethos of the Corinthian Correspondence: Interests and Ideology from 1 Corinthians to 1 Clement* (Studies of the New Testament and its World; Edinburgh: T. & T. Clark, 1996).

——'Leadership Patterns and the Development of Ideology in Early Christianity', *Sociology of Religion* 58 (1997), pp. 323–41.

——'From ἀδελφοί to οἶκος θεοῦ: Social Transformation in Pauline Christianity', *Journal of Biblical Literature* 120 (2001), pp. 293–311.

Jewett, R., *Christian Tolerance: Paul's Message to the Modern Church* (Biblical Perspectives on Current Issues; Philadelphia: Westminster Press, 1982).

——*Romans: A Commentary* (Hermeneia; Minneapolis: Fortress, 2007).

Kern, P. H., *Rhetoric and Galatians: Assessing an Approach to Paul's Epistle* (Society for New Testament Studies Monograph Series; Cambridge: Cambridge University Press, 1998).

Kloppenborg, J. S., 'Collegia and *"thiasoi"*: Issues in Function, Taxonomy, and Membership', in J. S. Kloppenborg and S. G. Wilson (eds.), *Voluntary Associations in the Graeco-Roman World* (London ; New York: Routledge, 1996), pp. 16–30.

Knight, G. W., *The Pastoral Epistles: A Commentary on the Greek Text* (New International Greek Testament Commentary; Carlisle; Grand Rapids: Paternoster; Eerdmans, 1992).

Kowalski, W., 'The Reward, Discipline, and Installation of Church Leaders: An Examination of 1 Timothy 5.17-22' (unpublished PhD dissertation, University of Gloucestershire, 2005).

Kreisberg, S., *Transforming Power: Domination, Empowerment, and Education* (SUNY Series, Teacher Empowerment and School Reform; Albany: State University of New York Press, 1992).

Kuck, D. W., *Judgement and Community Conflict: Paul's Use of Apocalyptic Judgement Language in 1 Corinthians 3.5-4.5* (Supplements to Novum Testamentum; Leiden; New York: E. J. Brill, 1992).

Lassen, E. M., 'The Use of the Father Image in Imperial Propaganda and 1 Corinthians 4.14-21', *Tyndale Bulletin* 42 (1991), pp. 127–36.

Levine, L. I., 'Synagogue Officials: The Evidence from Caesarea and its Implications for Palestine and the Diaspora', in K. G. Holum and A. Raban (eds.), *Caesarea Maritima: A Retrospective After Two Millennia* (Documenta et Monumenta Orientis Antiqui; Leiden: Brill, 1996), 392–400.

Lincoln, A. T., *Ephesians* (Word Biblical Commentary; Dallas: Word Books, 1990).

Litfin, A. D., *St Paul's Theology of Proclamation: 1 Corinthians 1–4 and Greco-Roman Rhetoric* (Society for New Testament Studies

Monograph Series; Cambridge; New York: Cambridge University Press, 1994).

Lukes, S., *Power: A Radical View* (Basingstoke: Palgrave Macmillan, 2nd edn, 2005).

Lundin, R., *et al.*, *The Responsibility of Hermeneutics* (Exeter; Grand Rapids: Paternoster; Eerdmans, 1985).

MacDonald, M. Y., *The Pauline Churches: A Socio-Historical Study of Institutionalization in the Pauline and Deutero-Pauline Writings* (Society for New Testament Studies Monograph Series, 60; Cambridge: Cambridge University Press, 1988).

——'The Shifting Centre: Ideology and the Interpretation of 1 Corinthians', in E. Adams and D. G. Horrell (eds.), *Christianity at Corinth: The Quest for the Pauline Church* (Louisville; London: Westminster John Knox Press, 2004), pp. 273–94.

Marshall, I. H., *The Pastoral Epistles* (International Critical Commentary; Edinburgh: T. & T. Clark, 1999).

Martin, D. B., 'Social-Scientific Criticism', in S. L. McKenzie and S. R. Haynes (eds.), *To Each its Own Meaning: An Introduction to Biblical Criticisms and their Applications* (Louisville: Westminster John Knox Press, rev. and expanded edn, 1999), pp. 125–41.

Meeks, W. A., *The First Urban Christians: The Social World of the Apostle Paul* (New Haven; London: Yale University Press, 2nd edn, 2003).

Michaelis, W., 'μιμέομαι', in G. Kittel (ed.), *Theological Dictionary of the New Testament* (vol. 4; Grand Rapids; London: Eerdmans, 1968), pp. 659–74.

Moore, S. D., *Poststructural-Ism and the New Testament: Derrida and Foucault at the Foot of the Cross* (Minneapolis: Fortress, 1994).

Morriss, P., *Power: A Philosophical Analysis* (Manchester: Manchester University Press, 2nd edn, 2002).

Moxnes, H., 'What is Family?: Problems Constructing Early Christian Families', in H. Moxnes (ed.), *Constructing Early Christian Families: Family as Social Reality and Metaphor* (London: Routledge, 1997), pp. 13–41.

Murphy-O'Connor, J., 'Co-Authorship in the Corinthian Correspondence', *Revue biblique* 100 (1993), pp. 562–79.

——*Paul the Letter-Writer: His World, His Options, His Skills* (Good News Studies, 41; Collegeville: Liturgical Press, 1995).

O'Brien, P. T., *The Epistle to the Philippians: A Commentary on the Greek Text* (New International Greek Testament Commentary; Carlisle; Grand Rapids: Paternoster; Eerdmans, 1991).

Oxford English Dictionary Online (Oxford: Oxford University Press, 2000).

Parsons, T., 'On the Concept of Political Power', *Proceedings of the American Philosophical Society* 107 (1963), pp. 232–62.

Petersen, N. R., *Rediscovering Paul: Philemon and the Sociology of Paul's Narrative World* (Philadelphia: Fortress, 1985).

Pinnock, J., 'The History of the Diaconate', in C. Hall (ed.), *The Deacon's Ministry* (Leominster: Gracewing, 1991), pp. 9–24.

Richards, E. R., *Paul and First-Century Letter Writing: Secretaries, Composition and Collection* (Downers Grove: InterVarsity Press, 2004).

Romaniuk, K., 'Was Phoebe in Romans 16,1 a Deaconess?', *Zeitschrift für die neutestamentliche Wissenschaft* 81 (1990), pp. 132–4.

Rosenau, P. M., *Post-Modernism and the Social Sciences: Insights, Inroads, and Intrusions* (Princeton: Princeton University Press, 1991).

Schenk, W., *Die Philipperbriefe des Paulus: Kommentar* (Stuttgart: W. Kohlhammer, 1984).

Schmithals, W., *Die Gnosis in Korinth: Eine Untersuchung zu den Korintherbriefen* (Forschungen zur Religion und Literatur des Alten und Neuen Testaments; Göttingen: Vandenhoeck & Ruprecht, 2nd edn, 1965).

Schüssler Fiorenza, E., *In Memory of Her: A Feminist Theological Reconstruction of Christian Origins* (London: SCM Press, 1983).

——'Rhetorical Situation and Historical Reconstruction in 1 Corinthians', *New Testament Studies* 33 (1987), pp. 386–403.

——' "Waiting at Table": A Critical Feminist Theological Reflection', in N. Greinacher and N. Mette (eds.), *Diakonia: Church for Others* (Concilium; Edinburgh: T. & T. Clark, 1988), pp. 84–94.

——'The Ethics of Biblical Interpretation: Decentering Biblical Scholarship', *Journal of Biblical Literature* 107 (1988), pp. 3–17.

——*Bread Not Stone: The Challenge of Feminist Biblical Interpretation* (Edinburgh: T. & T. Clark, 1990).

——*Discipleship of Equals: A Critical Feminist Ekklesia-Logy of Liberation* (London: SCM Press, 1993).

——*Rhetoric and Ethic: The Politics of Biblical Studies* (Minneapolis: Fortress, 1999).

——'Rhetorical Situation and Historical Reconstruction in 1 Corinthians', in E. Adams and D. G. Horrell (eds.), *Christianity at Corinth: The Quest for the Pauline Church* (Louisville; London: Westminster John Knox Press, 2004), pp. 145–60.

——'Umasking Ideologies in Biblical Interpretation', in W. Yarchin (ed.), *History of Biblical Interpretation: a Reader* (Peabody: Hendrickson, 2004), pp. 383–97.

Schweizer, E. R., *Church Order in the New Testament* (Studies in Biblical Theology; London: SCM Press, 1961).

Seidman, S., *The Postmodern Turn: New Perspectives on Social Theory* (Cambridge; New York: Cambridge University Press, 1994).

——*Contested Knowledge: Social Theory in the Postmodern Era* (Malden; Oxford: Blackwell, 2nd edn, 1998).

Slee, M., *The Church in Antioch in the First Century CE: Communion and Conflict* (Journal for the Study of the New Testament Supplement Series; Sheffield: Sheffield Academic Press, 2003).

Steinmetz, D. C., 'The Superiority of Pre-Critical Exegesis', in S. E. Fowl (ed.), *The Theological Interpretation of Scripture: Classic and Contemporary Readings* (Cambridge, Mass.; Oxford: Blackwell, 1997), pp. 26–38.

Still, T. D., *Conflict at Thessalonica: A Pauline Church and its Neighbours* (Journal for the Study of the New Testament Supplement Series; Sheffield: Sheffield Academic, 1999).

Tannehill, R. C., 'Paul as Liberator and Oppressor: How should we Evaluate Diverse Views of First Corinthians?', in C. H. Cosgrove (ed.), *The Meanings we Choose: Hermeneutical Ethics, Indeterminacy and the Conflict of Interpretations* (Journal for the Study of the Old Testament Supplement Series, 411; London: T. & T. Clark, 2004), pp. 122–37.

Theissen, G., *The Social Setting of Pauline Christianity: Essays on Corinth* (Studies in the New Testament and its World; Edinburgh: T. & T. Clark, 1982).

Thiselton, A. C., *Interpreting God and the Postmodern Self: On Meaning, Manipulation and Promise* (Scottish Journal of Theology. Current Issues in Theology; Edinburgh: T. & T. Clark, 1995).

——*The First Epistle to the Corinthians: A Commentary on the Greek Text* (New International Greek Testament Commentary; Carlisle; Grand Rapids: Paternoster; Eerdmans, 2000).

Tobin, T. H., *Paul's Rhetoric in its Contexts: The Argument of Romans* (Peabody: Hendrickson, 2004).

Vanhoozer, K. J., *Is there a Meaning in this Text?: The Bible, the Reader, and the Morality of Literary Knowledge* (Grand Rapids; Leicester: Zondervan; Apollos, 1998).

Verner, D. C., *The Household of God: The Social World of the Pastoral Epistles* (SBL Dissertation Series, 71; Chico: Scholars Press, 1983).

Walker, D. D., *Paul's Offer of Leniency (2 Cor 10.1): Populist Ideology and Rhetoric in a Pauline Letter Fragment* (WUNT; Tübingen: Mohr Siebeck, 2002).

Walker-Ramisch, S., 'Graeco-Roman Voluntary Associations and the Damascus Document: A Sociological Analysis', in J. S. Kloppenborg and S. G. Wilson (eds.), *Voluntary Associations in the Graeco-Roman World* (London; New York: Routledge, 1996), pp. 128–45.

Walton, S., *Leadership and Lifestyle: The Portrait of Paul in the Miletus Speech and 1 Thessalonians* (Society for New Testament Studies

Monograph Series, 108; Cambridge: Cambridge University Press, 2000).

Wanamaker, C. A., *The Epistles to the Thessalonians: A Commentary on the Greek Text* (New International Greek Testament Commentary; Grand Rapids; Exeter: Eerdmans; Paternoster Press, 1990).

Wannenwetsch, B., ' "Members of One another": *Charis*, Ministry and Representation: A Politico-Ecclesial Reading of Romans 12', in C. G. Bartholomew, J. Chaplin, R. Song and A. Wolters (eds.), *A Royal Priesthood?: The Use of the Bible Ethically and Politically: a Dialogue with Oliver O'Donovan* (Scripture and Hermeneutics Series, 13; Carlisle: Paternoster Press, 2002), pp. 196–220.

Weima, J. A. D., ' "But we Became Infants among You": The Case for νήπιοι in 1 Thess 2. 7', *New Testament Studies* 46 (2000), pp. 547–64.

Whelan, C. F., '*Amica Pauli:* The Role of Phoebe in the Early Church', *Journal for the Study of the New Testament* 15 (1993), pp. 67–85.

Williams, D. K., *Enemies of the Cross of Christ: The Terminology of the Cross and Conflict in Philippians* (Journal for the Study of the New Testament Supplement Series; London: Sheffield Academic Press, 2002).

Winter, B. W., 'The Importance of the *Captatio Benevolentiae* in the Speeches of Tertullus and Paul in Acts 24.1-21', *Journal of Theological Studies* 42 (1991), pp. 505–31.

——'On Introducing Gods to Athens: An Alternative Reading of Acts 17.18-20', *Tyndale Bulletin* 47 (1996), pp. 71–90.

——*Philo and Paul among the Sophists: Athenian and Corinthian Responses to a Julio-Claudian Movement* (Grand Rapids; Cambridge: Eerdmans, 2nd edn, 2002).

Yarchin, W., ed., *History of Biblical Interpretation: A Reader* (Peabody: Hendrickson, 2004).

INDEX OF ANCIENT SOURCES

Index of Authors and Subjects